The Evolution of
INTERNATIONAL ORGANIZATIONS

STUDIES IN INTERNATIONAL ORDER
General Editor: Evan Luard

The Evolution of
INTERNATIONAL
ORGANIZATIONS

Edited by
David EVAN Trent LUARD

FREDERICK A. PRAEGER, *Publishers*
New York · Washington

BOOKS THAT MATTER

Published in the United States of America in 1966
by Frederick A. Praeger, Inc., Publishers
111 Fourth Avenue, New York 3, N.Y.

Library of Congress Catalog Card Number: 66–18908

Printed in Great Britain by
The Camelot Press Ltd, London and Southampton

CONTENTS

Mr Martin Hill and Mr Ralph Townley are serving members of the United Nations Secretariat. The views they express in this volume are their own and not necessarily those of the United Nations Organization.

FOREWORD

This book is not intended as a general history of international organizations. Such histories are available, in much greater detail than could here be attempted, already in abundance. It is intended rather as a series of case-studies, undertaken by acknowledged experts in each field, designed to consider the changes that have taken place in the structure of some of the most important international organizations so far in existence; and to assess, on the basis of this history, what are the factors that have mainly influenced or inhibited change during their evolution.

Changes may take place in international organizations for a number of causes and by a number of procedures. They may take place, for example, through mainly internal developments, or as a result of external events; through explicit constitutional amendments, or through a series of imperceptible shifts in the direction of activity; through the actions of national governments or that of international officials; through changes in the attitudes of public opinion or alterations in the needs to be confronted. Changes may be deliberate or unintended; highly publicized, or semi-secret and almost unnoticed; universally accepted, or disputed and controversial. Even when the need for change is accepted, the different procedures for bringing this about may vary in their efficacy. The studies in this book may help to make clear which are the factors, and the procedures, that have been most influential in bringing about change, and which are the

7

obstacles that have most often prevented effective adaptation to new needs.

The book is therefore not intended so much as a contribution to historical literature (though it may help to provide a convenient introduction for the general public to the development of international organizations), but rather as a contribution to political science. It might perhaps be regarded as a preliminary essay in the neglected sociology of international institutions: a study of the mechanics of change within international organizations.

EVAN LUARD

St Antony's College
Oxford

A full list of abbreviations used in the text will be found on page 333.

1 THE PROCESS OF CHANGE IN INTERNATIONAL ORGANIZATIONS

Evan Luard

The most vital political problems today are perhaps those that relate to institutional evolution. Prescribed constitutional procedures alone cannot always ensure the successful adaptation of existing institutions to needs and circumstances. Even revolution, the most violent and radical type of political change, fails in its effect unless it subsequently finds the means to transform the institutional structure which it finds already established. But with the complexity of modern administrative methods, large-scale institutions often acquire a scale, power and rigidity which makes effective adaptation increasingly necessary but more and more difficult. Such bodies often acquire a life of their own, largely independent of the political institutions which nominally control a nation's affairs.

Very large numbers of individuals may participate in these institutions. They thus share a vested interest in resisting drastic change. While in former days the number who had an active interest in the perpetuation of the existing system was often relatively small, today that interest is shared by a large proportion of the population, from political leaders to bureaucracies, from the managers of state enterprises to local officials, from the satisfied to the apathetic, in every field of activity. With rising standards of living and improved welfare systems, even those who share no strong interest in the *status quo*, may not be sufficiently dissatisfied to demand radical alterations. The existing

9

institutional structure itself moulds expectations increasingly powerfully, so that any deviation from that norm is regarded as an aberration and a threat to cherished expectations. The machinery of mass communications available and the uniformity of its effect throughout society serves to condition the general public to the existing institutional framework far more effectively than the more primitive educational and communications facilities of earlier days. At the same time, the effect of modern opinion-testing techniques on the democratic system is that political parties increasingly converge in reflecting the dead-centre of public opinion, which is conservative, rather than compete in representing radical opinion at the wings. The political system itself thus inhibits drastic change. Revolutionary doctrines become as discredited as revolutionary parties.

Even within national states the difficulty makes itself felt acutely enough. Many institutions within the nation, the civil service, large corporations and nationalized industries, local government and welfare agencies, acquire an independence and authority that makes them in practice partly immune from legislative decisions. The internal activities and decisions of such institutions may be more important to the lives of citizens than is the legislature itself. Changes in the structure of trades unions or the composition of boards of directors may matter more to the man in the street than parliamentary majorities. And within each such organization the resistances to change are powerful. Thus instead of the institutional structure being moulded by legislatures and their electorates, very often the reverse is the case.

Within international organizations, the difficulties in securing change are even greater. They are also perhaps more serious in effect. Many of the most vital political problems of the day are those that concern international organizations and their relation to national authorities. Though seen in their most acute form in the problems of international security, they occur equally in many other fields of activity. Because of the shrinking of distance in the modern world, an increasing range of functions once performed primarily at national level or below, can now only be adequately conducted, or at least controlled, on an international scale. Yet the resistances to changes that involve a transfer of authority from the national state to a higher level are perhaps more intense than those that occur at any other level.

National institutions have acquired, through their history, a power and authority that cannot easily be modified. This has served to accumulate round them a cluster of loyalties that buttresses them against outside encroachments. Because they have acquired, equally, ultimate authority over the instruments of military power, this resistance cannot easily be overcome by armed force. A preponderance of power at the highest level cannot therefore, even if desired, be imposed by compulsion, as the preponderance of power at the national level was itself established. Any effective modification in the structure of power must here be largely voluntary. But the precedents for important abdications of authority by voluntary processes are not encouraging.

The processes of political change within states have been intensively studied by political scientists over many years. The processes of change within international organizations, that may be even more crucial to human welfare, have been far less examined. Effective study of the factors encouraging or inhibiting changes of this sort must be primarily an empirical one. It must therefore study the way in which change has mainly taken place in international organizations so far. It must study the types of change that may take place; the factors encouraging change; the procedures by which change is instituted; and the resistances to change that are encountered. The bulk of the chapters which follow are designed to examine these points in relation to individual organizations. But it may be useful, as a preliminary, to consider briefly in general terms the main forms which institutional change may take, and the special problems to be encountered in accomplishing this at the international level.

The way in which institutional change takes place depends, in the first place, on the initial structure of the institutions concerned; on the way the change-making functions are distributed between organizations and within society as a whole.

The most important distributions of this kind are four. There is the *centralized* authority where all important decisions are made at the highest level; a *hierarchical* authority, with considerable delegated power at lower levels, though ultimate power still remains at the centre; a *federal* system, with a strict division of powers between centre and regions, and no superior power for the centre enabling it to alter that division on its own authority alone; and, finally, a *functional* division of powers, by which power is accorded according to the type of function to be performed rather than by the geographical region to be administered. Within many states there is a mixture of several of these systems.

The relation of international organizations to national authorities shares something of the last two of these relationships. In some ways it resembles a federal system, with only very weak power at the centre compared to the regions. In other respects there is a functional division between national and international bodies, as well as between international organizations themselves. National ministries of health and education and international bodies may share some functions in the health and educational field, while WHO and UNESCO may perform a smaller number peculiar to themselves in each sphere. But there is no direct subordination of authority, as under both the first two systems, by which decisions in international organizations can exert an automatic effect on national states or ministries. Even in their own fields the authority of international organizations is mainly only advisory. To a large extent, therefore, the processes of change take place independently in international and national organizations.

What, next, are the main *procedures* of change within these various types of institutional structures? The simplest and perhaps most common instrument of change is that of *direct decision-making*. In some cases political institutions, in national states and international organizations alike, possess functions directly related to the process of change. In national states, there are often separate bodies whose main function is to propose change (cabinet and government); to influence it (press, public opinion and pressure groups); to discuss (and in theory to amend) it (parliament); to execute it (the bureaucracy); and to apply it (the law-courts). These are usually the main instruments of change, where change takes place as a result of direct decision-making.

A somewhat similar division of function exists within international organizations. Most of these today have separate organs or functionaries for discussion (Assemblies), execution (international officials) and application of decisions (the International Court of Justice, other legal bodies, and the inspection or reporting procedures of some of the specialized agencies). Influence on change, similar to that exerted in national states is wielded by the international press, public opinion and sometimes by international or other pressure groups as well, but here normally exerts a far weaker power. The main difference is that the key propository role, that of presenting proposals for approval by the legislative body, as performed by the cabinet and government within states, must here take a far more tentative form. Because there exists no institution whose main function this is, proposals usually have to be made (as once in many national states) through an individual proposal by a member of the legislature or Assembly. In many cases the Secretariat may play an important part (just as the bureaucracy within states often did) in initiating or influencing proposals. But in either case their advocacy possesses nothing like the authority that the advocacy of a national cabinet will have over national legislation. The only exception, among the organizations discussed here, is the EEC, which has a body

13

(the Commision) specifically designed for proposition; and consequently far more often gets things done as well as discussed.

Direct decision-making in international organizations may nevertheless sometimes occur. The procedure by which the amendments to the Charter, enlarging the Security Council and ECOSOC, were recently brought about, and the decisions of the IMF to increase currency quotas, represent changes brought about by this means. But, as the succeeding chapters show, this is perhaps the least common of all the instruments of change in international organizations. The reasons for this are clear. The type of change we are here concerned with may occur either as an organizational change within the international institution concerned; or as a change affecting the relations between the organization and a national state. Changes of both kinds can be far less easily effected than corresponding changes within national states through the direct decision-making procedures.

This is not only because there exists no body for making proposals. A second difficulty is that ultimate authority at the centre (for deciding as well as proposing) rests in an amorphous body – the Assembly in question – representing many radically opposed views. Securing a change through direct decision-making means here inducing a large number of governments of very different views to give their explicit agreement to the proposed change. This will not often happen. Because there exists no developed party system, there is no comparable assurance of securing the assent of the Assembly as a whole when proposals are introduced. The position is thus more comparable to that in the early eighteenth century in England before the development of the party system (when proposals might be introduced with little assurance except a hazy calculation of known opinions that they would prove acceptable to the membership as a whole) than to the developed two-party systems known in the contemporary Anglo-Saxon world. The political difficulties of securing change are therefore such that they will rarely be even attempted by this means. Only when the consensus of opinion is overwhelming (as over the recent increase in membership of the Security and Economic and Social Councils) are such measures initiated. It is noteworthy that, though the UN is able to carry through individual amendments of the Charter at any time without a review conference, and though there is widespread agreement that many parts of the Charter require amendment, no amendments other than these have even been attempted, let alone carried through.

A third difference is that there is no simple hierarchy of authority such as exists usually within states. Even if agreement can be reached, the ultimate sanctions available to each organization for enforcing decisions are weak or non-existent. A federal government, even if the area of its power is limited, has the means of enforcing its authority in the area of its own competence against all lower authorities. And in the ultimate resort, as in the United States at Little Rock, all are conscious that this ultimate power is available in case of necessity. International organizations, though they may possess some sanctions – the withdrawal of UN aid, the withholding of financial support by the IMF or other institutions, exclusion from the facilities provided, for example by ICAO or other institutions, the inconveniences and isolation of banishment from organizations whose membership is almost universal – possess nothing like equivalent means of ensuring that their decisions are carried out, and are therefore reluctant to attempt to carry through important changes by direct decisions which may be defied with impunity.

Finally, a fourth difference in the procedure of direct decision-making in international organizations is that the process of *influence* occurs here in a far weaker form. For the most part press and public opinion are insufficiently aware of the proposals for change contained in particular resolutions, or are insufficiently concerned about them, to express themselves in emphatic form, as they will over proposals for national legislation. The process of consultation takes place, over a relatively short period of two or three weeks only, largely in the secrecy of the corridors. Decisions of each state are made (equally secretly) within individual governments, deciding to support or oppose individual resolutions often largely unconscious of views held elsewhere. And because home opinion is so badly informed and so indifferent, this usually has little influence on the decision.

As a result of these difficulties, other processes of change are normally necessary. The second main instrument of change is that of *bureaucratic decision-making*. Change may often come about without any act of legislation or decision in any representative body, but through the decision of departments or individual civil servants. Ministries may issue regulations, bureaucracies may apply previous legislation in new ways, agencies may adopt new practices, and may affect the everyday life of the citizen as directly by this means as by any formal act of parliament.

This is a process that occurs all the time within international organizations. Decisions by the UN Secretariat, for example to set up a committee to study a particular subject (as on compensatory finance for fluctuations in commodity trade), to issue a statement on a particular topic (as on Vietnam), to appoint a personal adviser in a particular part of the world (as in Laos in 1959) or on a particular subject (such as the UN military adviser in New York), may eventually exert significant influence on the organization's structure and capacities, without any decision by a representative organ of the organization. In addition members of the Secretariat may exert a powerful influence on initiatives or resolutions of national states.[1] Just as civil servants in national ministries may exert the ultimate influence on the form of legislation proposed within states, so the influence of international civil servants may be crucial in determining the nature of resolutions and other proposals put forward in international bodies. The effect of bureaucratic decision-making, in national and international organizations alike, is often to by-pass the processes of discussion, influence and approval that take place in direct decisions. While less democratic, therefore, it may make possible more controversial changes than would be possible through direct decision-making. It has been perhaps even more significant as an instrument of change in the specialized agencies than in the UN itself.

A third instrument of change in the structure and powers of institutions is of *indirect decision-making*, that is, as the end-result of a series of decisions and actions to confront individual situations. Added together, the effect of these may be to establish a wholly new pattern of activity and power for the organization.

This too has been a frequent instrument of change in international organizations. Particular crises may call for action that in time brings about a permanent adjustment of the organization's role (such as the various crises leading to the establishment of UN peace-keeping forces). The gradual emergence of important new needs may bring about a gradual shift in the total balance of an organization's functions (such as the series of decisions enlarging the aid-administering and other economic agencies of the UN). Decisions taken in isolation may create precedents that permanently influence future actions (such as the decision to accept UN competence to discuss the Indonesia dispute in 1947, permanently influencing UN readiness to discuss subsequent colonial problems). A succession of different decisions, that are of little significance in themselves, taken together may lead to a substantial modification of the organization's practice (such as the effect of decisions to discuss apartheid in the General Assembly and the Security Council on the general interpretation of Article 2(7)). A new agency may be set up, that gradually by its activity acquires an authority and influence never originally foreseen (such as the Committee on Information from Non-Self-governing Territories). Committees of experts may be set up to study a problem, whose reports mobilize support for action that might never otherwise have been undertaken (such as the committee set

17

up to consider alterations in the structure and purpose of GATT).

Finally, change may come about, without any formal decision being taken at all, whether general or particular, but through the gradual growth in the *influence* a particular organization is able to exert in relation to others. Within states, the civil service or technical experts of a particular kind, may gradually increase their influence over that of politicians in the formulation of policy; the press may acquire greater influence than parliaments in the criticism of acts of government. In the international field the General Assembly may gain an influence over the Security Council or vice versa. Or changes in influence may come about through changes in governments themselves. New parties, more sympathetic to the role of international organizations may come to power. There may be a change in policy by existing governments. Public opinion in a certain country may become more or less favourable to co-operation with international organizations.

Sometimes, however, this type of change may come through internal changes in the organization concerned. This may adopt policies more likely to secure co-operation among governments. It may acquire more effective means of publicizing, and winning goodwill for, its initiatives. It may acquire better means of communication with individual governments. Or finally it may acquire more effective sanctions for enforcing its will on governments in extreme cases. Perhaps most commonly changes of this sort come about through a gradual shift in the climate of international opinion as a whole. The increase in conformity by some nations may encourage it in others; a greater general awareness of the services the organization may procure may come about; improvements in communications, and therefore in interdependence, may make the benefits of international co-operation more readily apparent.

Changes that have come about through a gradual increase of influence may be more fundamental in importance than almost any other factor, because it is the condition of effective change by other means. Changes brought about by the passage of resolutions or regulations may fail in effect if they are not accompanied by changes in the real influence of international organizations on opinion as a whole. Without the latter they may appear imposed from without and more easily evoke the opposition of national states. The establishment of widely known and respected norms of economic conduct, as obtained through regular confrontation in OEEC or comparable organizations may be more effective in securing co-operative action than occasional explicit prohibitions or resolutions as used by GATT; it may be easier to secure monetary discipline through friendly but persistent persuasion by IMF officials, than through the threat of severe sanctions in the granting of exchange credits by the organization. Like other kinds of political change, the changes effected in international organizations, are unlikely to take permanent effect unless they come to appear acceptable to those mainly affected by them.

Finally, it may be worth considering the principal kinds of *obstacles* to institutional change that may arise.

Clearly the most common of all obstacles of this kind are the resistances that are set up by the institutions that already exist. These resistances may derive from the interests of particular individuals in the existing structure of power. Within national states, individual leaders, bureaucrats or local councillors may resist any change in government structure likely to lead to a loss of influence or authority for themselves. Entire organizations, such as County Councils or local police forces, threatened with a loss of authority, may unite to prevent any loss of their power to other authorities. This process may occur equally within international organizations, when proposals for change are made. The refusal of Mr Hammarskjöld to accept most of the proposals of the expert committee set up to examine the UN's information activities, or the resistance of ECOSOC to repeated proposals to reduce and rationalize its activities are another (though ECOSOC itself encounters similar resistance on the part of the ACC when it proposes reorganization).[2]

Equally important are the resistances that occur, not in order to preserve individual power, but because of the structure of loyalties surrounding existing institutions. Resistance to proposals for local government reform within states may occur as much for reasons of local loyalty as because of the fear of loss of personal or collective authority. In international organizations this is an even more powerful factor, perhaps the most important single inhibition to change that occurs there. Here the loyalties that have accumulated around national states during the centuries in which it has possessed a preponderance of power are such that proposals for change in international organizations are often regarded largely in this light. The emotive language and powerful symbols that have grown up around the nation condition individuals to support national autonomy against the encroachments of international authority. International organizations themselves, on the other hand, have not yet managed to gather to themselves loyalties of sufficient strength (nor the myths and symbols that support them) to act as a counterweight.

Thirdly, resistances from existing organizations may result from simple inertia. There may, that is, be resistance to change in itself, as well as to the undesirable results of change. The existing system may be so firmly established that any alternative appears as undesirable; or as a burdensome inconvenience. New organs may not be able to wrest from pre-existing authorities the financial independence essential to their growth. These factors also operate in obstructing change in international organizations. On the one hand, national governments are reluctant to make the changes in established practices necessary for the more rational distribution of powers at a higher level. National parliaments, that long ago gained the power of the purse for themselves, are reluctant now to surrender it to other and higher authorities;

for example to concede to international organizations the right of direct taxation powers on their own citizens. This is seen in the resistance of many aid-giving countries to the establishment of SUNFED, even when they recognize the advantages of multilateral aid over national programmes. On the other hand, the procedures of international bureaucracies may themselves become so firmly institutionalized that proposals for change come to be resisted there too. The resistance of the specialized agencies to attempts to integrate their activity locally through the Technical Assistance resident representatives, and the reluctance of the ILO to transfer its attention from the problems that had preoccupied it between the wars to those of the developing countries today, are examples of this kind of institutional inertia.[3]

Another kind of obstacle to change comes, not through the tenacity of existing organizations to the *status quo*, but through the political difficulties in introducing controversial changes. Within states this may be seen in the political friction and controversy surrounding particular proposals. But there the traditions of majority rule and democratic procedures usually ensure that minorities will in the final resort submit, except in the most controversial matters, to the will of the majority. In the international field, because the tradition of majority rule is not yet firmly established, and the doctrine of sovereignty so powerful in its effect, this submissiveness is usually lacking. The refusal of the richer countries to accept proposals for SUNFED or a similar fund, the refusal of some powers to accept the majority opinion of the International Court of Justice on the financing of peace-keeping operations, even when it was endorsed by an overwhelming majority of the General Assembly, are examples of recalcitrance of this kind. Traditional defences of national sovereignty (as in Article 2(7)) on other matters are another. The *legitimacy* of international decisions on questions of this kind is not yet established. The most that occurs is that the pressure of opinions within the UN and other organizations may make countries less willing to express views or cast votes in ways different from the majority: the increasing unanimity of votes on colonialism and apartheid are examples of convergence of this type. But because of the lack of ultimate power to enforce majority opinions, political change in international organizations requires a degree of consensus not necessary for political change within states.

Resistances of this kind are not merely constitutional. Objections to peace-keeping forces or SUNFED, for example, are not fundamentally on constitutional grounds, even where they are expressed in this form. They relate to differing conceptions of the function and purpose of international organizations. The extent to which resistances are based on genuine interests or convictions of this type will vary from case to case. Sometimes (as over the proposals for peace-keeping forces) the resistances raised reflect a genuine interest and conviction that must be taken into account as the condition of change. In other cases differences, such as those that occur over proposals for tariff reductions or liquidity reform, may result from a faulty conception of national interests: the inability to apprehend the long-term, collective interest (in greater volumes of trade, or currency stability) against apparent short-term or sectional interests (in industrial protection or monetary independence). While the former kind of conflict may be impossible or very difficult to resolve, the second may be resolved by the development of more adequate conceptions of national interest, a synoptic conception of collective as well as partial interests. International organizations themselves sometimes contribute to developing this.

Finally, the particular structure of an organization may make it unadaptable and resistant to change. Within states, a written constitution, or an over-powerful bureaucracy, may act as obstacles to change of this kind. The existence of a multi-party system that requires every important decision to be acceptable to a broad range of parties and interests may have the same effect. There are a number of factors of this kind that may restrict the capacity of international organizations for change. The procedures for formal constitutional amendments are sometimes such as to make their passage difficult or virtually impossible. The fact that every amendment to the UN Charter must have the assent of every permanent member and two-thirds of all members means that change by this means will not be easily secured. Perhaps even more important is the tradition that all formal meetings must take place in public. This has the effect that meetings tend to be devoted almost entirely to the statement of prepared and public positions of individual member states, rather than for the discussion and decision of substantive proposals by the collective body as a whole. As Professor Claude shows in relation to the Security Council below, one effect is that there exists very little corporate spirit within most of these organizations.[4] They are regarded far more as battle-grounds for fighting out disputes between members, than as independent entities possessing an identity, and power of decision, of their own. Only a few of the functional organizations, that normally meet with little publicity, and perform services that are largely uncontroversial, begin to develop a collective spirit of this sort. They thus begin to appear to the outside world rather as executive bodies than, as the political organizations do, mainly as debating-chambers; as instruments for doing rather than talking. Because the cabinets which primarily reach decisions within national states, reach decisions in private, the representatives of different groups or political parties or ministries within them find it easier to sink their differences to present a common front than they would if their discussions had to be reached in public. Facilities for private meetings in international organizations will not reduce the genuine conflicts of interest that exist; but they might reduce the need to persist in previously adopted attitudes which at present often frustrate change in international organizations. At least appropriate facilities for exploring and discussing change would be provided which at present are largely lacking.

These then would appear to be the principal procedures for instituting change in international organizations that exist; and the main obstacles which occur to prevent it. From the studies of individual organizations contained in the following chapters, it may be possible to judge more clearly which of each of these occur most commonly in international organizations; and what are the factors that are most favourable in securing effective evolution to meet new needs.

TEXT REFERENCES

1. See J. G. Hadwen and J. Kaufman, *How UN Decisions Are Made*, Leyden, 1961, p. 21.

2. See Chapter 6, pp. 122-6.

3. For a discussion of both these types of resistance, see A. Shonfield, *The Attack on World Poverty*, London, 1960, pp. 187, 217.

4. See Chapter 4, pp. 88-9.

BIBLIOGRAPHY

Claude, I. L., *Swords into Ploughshares* (3rd edition), New York, 1964.

Deutsch, K. W., *Political Community at the International Level*, New York, 1954.

Goodspeed, S. S., *The Nature and Function of International Organizations*, Oxford, 1958.

Hadwen, J. G. and Kaufmann, J., *How UN Decisions are Made*, Leyden, 1961.

Loveday, A., *Reflections on International Administration*, Oxford, 1956.

Mangone, G. J., *A Short History of International Organizations*, New York, 1954.

Nicholas, H. G., *The United Nations as a Political Institution*, London, 1959.

Plischke, E., ed., *Systems of Integrating the International Community*, Princeton, 1964.

Potter, P. B., *Introduction to the Study of International Organizations*, New York, 1948.

Wilcox, F. O. and Marcy, C. M., *Proposals for Change in the United Nations*, Washington, 1955.

2 THE LEAGUE OF NATIONS

F. P. Walters

An attempt to contribute a chapter on the League of Nations to a study of the evolution of international organizations is faced with special difficulties. The League is now a matter of history; after twenty years of a difficult existence, it succumbed to an unprecedented outbreak of nationalism which for a time bid fair to destroy not only the international institution itself but the moral and political foundations on which it was built. Its evolution is a story whose end is known in advance, and cannot therefore be considered in the same spirit as that of living institutions with, one hopes, a long future before them.

Secondly, the development of the League was a highly complex affair. Conceived originally as a political system for keeping the peace, it became from the first the unique and universal centre for every activity in which international[1] co-operation was needed. Its image must include, not only its central directing organs – the Council, the Assembly, the Permanent Court, and the Secretariat – but the many subsidiary bodies which it created and which were an organic part of it. Though its membership was never all-inclusive,[2] the fact remains that, so long as it lived, all officially constituted forms of international organization were of necessity centred around it, and no new growth not so centred could claim the name of international in the full sense.

A further complexity arises from the strong and fluctuating currents of public opinion which ebbed and flowed around the League. The devotion of countless supporters, the hostility of less numerous but often more influential opponents, were based as much on passion and prejudice as on a reasoned appreciation of political reality. On each side 'the League' was thought and spoken of as something with a will of its own, not merely as an instrument to be used by its Members for their own purposes and policies. And it must be taken as a fact of history – even if it be a fact that defies attempts to define or analyze it – that it was in one sense a living entity transcending the sum of its individual Members. At the same time, its activities were governed, both in theory and in practice, by strict constitutional forms. All the decisions, developments or abandonments which make up the history of the League were the official acts of its Member States, taken by virtue of the powers and obligations laid down in the Covenant or in other treaties or agreements. Public opinion, friendly or hostile, could have no influence on the common action until it was formulated in the appropriate place as the policy of a member government.

The coming into existence of the League of Nations at the end of the First World War was something entirely new in the political development of the world. It sprang from a combination of violent pressures which need not be here described. No precedent existed. No plan, even, had existed five years earlier; and such plans as were elaborated in the later stages of the war were known to few; they had in themselves no impact whatever on the world in general, and were looked on with dislike and apprehension by the diplomatic profession. However, world opinion pressed massively upon the Peace Conference of Paris; and some, at least, among its leaders were nobly inspired by the unprecedented occasion. Thus it was that the Covenant, as it emerged from the Conference, was on the whole much more complete and far-reaching than the plans prepared in official circles before the Conference began.[3] Accordingly, the league appeared to the diplomatic world, even at its first beginnings, as being already at full stretch and requiring to be restrained rather than expanded. This sentiment was reinforced when a minority in the Senate was able to prevent the United States from taking up membership.

For this and other reasons the central organs of the League – the Council, Assembly and Secretariat – were in its earliest years comparatively little occupied with their essential function of dealing with disputes liable to endanger peace. Nevertheless, they displayed, each in its own way, a vitality which neither supporters nor critics of the new system had foreseen. The Covenant laid down that the Council must meet at least once a year: it held ten sessions in its first year, and thereafter an average of five per year, each lasting about a week. In 1923 it decided to hold regular sessions (four a year, later reduced to three) at fixed dates. This apparently formal act was of very great practical importance, since it made it easy for the Foreign Ministers of Council Members to attend all regular sessions, and enabled the many other governments which needed to take part, or the various committees which had reports to present, to make their own arrangements in good time. It is much to be regretted that the Security Council has not followed this example (with necessary adjustments to fit its more limited role), and combined one or more fixed annual sessions with the fulfilment, at long last, of the clear intention of Article 28 (2) of the Charter, of which it has hitherto been in permanent breach.[4]

From 1926 onwards the Council's membership was increased to 14 (later to 15), so as to provide a place for each of the various groups which considered that they had a right to be represented. This increase did away with electioneering rivalries in the Assembly, and did not, in practice, delay or hamper the Council's work.

The Assembly was, in 1919, expected to meet every third or fourth year; and if the Covenant provided that it should meet 'at stated intervals', this was a precaution against its not meeting often enough to maintain itself as an essential part of the system. All such ideas were blown away like smoke when it met, for the first time, in November 1920. In four weeks it developed a strong corporate feeling, based not precisely on opposition to the Council, but certainly on the sentiment that the greater powers claimed for themselves, there and elsewhere, an unjustified preponderance in the direction of affairs; and that in future every member, small or great, must have the right and the opportunity to take its own part, express its own views, criticize if need be the action of the Council, share in the control of the budget and in the establishment or development of the auxiliary organizations. From this it was an obvious step to decide that the Assembly should meet thenceforward at a fixed date every year.

The Secretariat, also, represented a complete break with previously accepted ideas. It quickly proved that an international service could function with an efficiency and an *esprit de corps* equal to those of any national body. Its full growth, however, was soon checked, not by any direct opposition, but by the unrelenting compression imposed from first to last upon the budget of the League.

In other ways also the League grew with unexpected rapidity. By 1922 the makers of the Covenant would perhaps have hardly recognized the institution which they had launched only three years earlier. They had had no clear intention of adopting the principle that, side by side with its primary functions, the League must also be centre 'for harmonizing the actions of nations in the attainment of their common ends' – a vision foreshadowed in Smuts's 'Practical Suggestion', and given full expression in the Preamble and in Article 1 of the UN Charter. But, almost as an afterthought, they had included, in Article 23, provisions which in effect gave Covenant authority for the creation of secondary organizations to deal with the international aspect of social, economic and humanitarian progress. Since the Members of the League attributed decisive value to the words of the Covenant, the authority thus given was of great importance. The new organizations[5] were set up without delay, and for the most part were able to get promptly into full working order. They filled, as the phrase goes, a long-felt want.

Unknown to the general public, and disregarded by professional diplomacy, there existed in the more advanced countries a strong demand for a new approach to the problems of social and technical progress, and for new methods to overcome the difficulties arising from conventional traditions of national sovereignty. Experts and technicians, many of whom had worked together in wartime inter-allied organizations, saw in the modest provisions of Article 23 the opportunity to combine and extend their action. It was thus by serving purposes and needs already recognized by many authorities in each subject, that the technical and functional organs of the League began their lives with unexpected energy and fulness.

This was especially true – to take a single example – of the Organization for Communications and Transit, which in its first four years created for itself a constitution enabling non-Member States to participate in its work; held two world-wide conferences and established, by four important treaties, a generally accepted international régime for problems of transit, for waterways, for maritime ports, and for railways. However, the Transit Organization, though at first the most active and successful of them all, was never again able to produce results of comparable importance. The non-co-operative attitude of the US and the USSR in particular was enough to prevent effective progress in the international regulation of the problems of air travel and of broadcasting. Such regulation was desirable, indeed essential, in the general interest; but these truths, however obvious, had not then acquired sufficient driving power to overcome the various obstacles interposed by nationalism, by vested interests, or perhaps by sheer inertia.

Other auxiliary organs of the League were less quick off the mark, but displayed a more durable vitality. Their subject-matter was of more evident public interest; and their efforts in the fields of commerce, of finance, and especially of public health, were as a rule warmly supported by government departments and by unofficial experts. Their constitutional forms ranged from the elaborate tri-partite system of the ILO, or the strictly governmental membership of the Transit Committee, through various mixtures of official and non-official participation to the Permanent Mandates Committee, which alone formally excluded any government servant from being eligible for membership. In theory, at least – and this was certainly more true in practice then than it is today – the special knowledge and influence possessed by official members was balanced by the freedom of speech or suggestion which unofficial experts could exercise. How far each permutation might be the most efficient formula varied with the problem to be solved and with the circumstances of the time: when, for example, it was required to float a large public loan as part of the plan to rescue the crumbling economy of Austria, this clearly called for the co-operation of private bankers and treasury officials. All that can here be said is that some degree of elasticity in this respect was then, and probably is still, a necessary condition of the optimum working of international economic, social, and humanitarian institutions.

All these developments were essentially the result of the natural human wish for a steady improvement in the material conditions of life, coupled with a new understanding of the fact that such progress depended on the maintenance of peace and on international co-operation. Their growth, therefore, was normal and healthy so far as it went. But it could be achieved only through the constitutional machinery of the League – no other basis was possible; and the League itself was based, not only on aspirations shared in one way or another by the world as a whole, but also on the specific texts of the Treaty of Versailles. That the Covenant should be a part of the Peace treaties, and that many provisions of the treaties should be placed under the supervision of the Council, was a plan deliberately chosen by Woodrow Wilson and accepted by the Peace conference. It would be irrelevant here to discuss the reasons for and against it, but it is certain that Wilson himself looked forward to a time when, under the leadership of the US, and through the machinery of the Council, the inequalities imposed by the treaties should die a natural death – the reparations account closed, disarmament generalized, frontier changes corrected or peacefully accepted. Instead of this, the Council began to appear as an instrument for the execution of the Peace treaties – a role disliked by many Members and strenuously resisted by a few.

This double aspect of the League – on the one hand the centre for world-wide co-operation in purposes which all could support, on the other a political agency closely bound up with a treaty which was far from being universally approved – was a weakness which slowed up and limited its expansion. And recovery, though not impossible, was doubly difficult so long as the United States remained outside, depriving the world organization of the material contribution of its wealth and power, and the moral contribution of its impartiality in the traditional quarrels of Europe.

Even without American help, there remained the possibility of reconciliation between victors and vanquished. In respect of Germany's allies, indeed, this was, by and large, a manageable problem; and even in respect of Germany the task was made difficult less by the actual terms of the treaty than by the nationalist forces on either side. For a few years beginning in 1924, with the Locarno treaties and Germany's admission to the League as a starting-point, a good deal of progress was made. But it was made at heavy cost, in that during those few years of relative peace and prosperity, when conditions seemed more favourable than ever before for a world-wide development of the activities of the League, its efforts were far too much concerned with a special aspect of European affairs. The fact that Brazil resigned from membership when, in 1926, Germany was made a permanent Member of the Council and her own demand was rejected, was perhaps unjustified by the immediate circumstances, but it was the symbol of an important political reality.

The excessive economy forced upon the League,[6] mainly by its richest Members, was frustrating and exasperating: it created artificial and unnecessary difficulties where there were already plenty of natural and unavoidable ones. It was certainly not the main reason why expansion slowed up after the first few years. But it contributed to the preponderance of Europe in League affairs. For economy's sake it was difficult to hold meetings away from Geneva. The cost of bringing committee members or advisers from distant countries often led to the appointment of Europeans in their place. Thus non-European countries were deprived of part, at least, of what seemed to many of them the main benefit to be derived from membership; and the League was hampered in its duty of building up an adequate network of world-wide connections.

What might have been a natural line of expansion was indicated by the inauguration, in the autumn of 1929, of a new plan, worked out by the Secretariat and by the Chinese government in Nanking, the purpose of which was to help the latter to cope with its overwhelming problems in the fields of public health, communications, flood control, agriculture, education. A number of Member States had already called on one or another League organization for its advice on some question in its special field; and these requests had naturally been met by sending one or more experts to study the question on the spot. The help thus given was expert, inexpensive, and disinterested: further, it involved no loss of *amour-propre*, since it was something any Member could claim as a natural right of membership. The traditional relation of inequality between China and the European powers made these advantages specially important. The plan set on foot in 1929 was a development of previous practice, in that the experts were sent, not to pay a visit and make a report, but to reside in China and work directly with the government. The cost was met from China's accumulated deficit on past budgets of the League.

This initiative never reached anything like its intended development, for reasons which need not detain us here. Still in spite of every catastrophe, the link between Geneva and Nanking remained unbroken until 1940. It may be considered as the forerunner of similar, but far more extensive and effective, action by the United Nations.

For many years Geneva was the scene of long and laborious efforts to give effect to what many considered as the heart of the Covenant: 'the reduction of national armaments to the lowest point consistent with national safety and the enforcement by common action of international obligations'. Meeting followed meeting; extensive and complicated commissions were set up; plans were elaborated to strengthen the peace-keeping provisions of the Covenant and so facilitate a general reduction. No more need here be said, since the difficulties and disagreements which proved insurmountable then are no less evident today.

Nevertheless, in spite of political and administrative limitations, the years from 1924 to 1929 were on the whole a time of progress; and the Tenth Assembly was the occasion of much self-congratulation on past results and much optimism in regard to future plans. Since its last meeting, the Briand–Kellogg pact had come into force, an agreed settlement of the reparations problem had been reached, Briand's proposals for European Union were announced. But within a few weeks many hard-won agreements were abandoned, and all prospect of future progress was darkened by the sudden and catastrophic incidence of the great economic depression.

In 1931 the League entered upon the third period of its history.

Five years of swift and natural growth had been followed by six years of relative stability and prosperity, in which growth could still continue, but had to be worked for; now, under the influence of the economic depression and its train of unemployment, poverty and hunger, the world had to face a disastrous revival of national bitterness and military aggression.

The period of conflict opened when, in September 1931, the Japanese army seized and annexed Manchuria under the pretext of establishing a new and independent state. After full enquiry on the spot, the Assembly formally declared that Japan was violating the Covenant and that no League Member would recognize the puppet state of Manchukuo. No attempt was made, however, to enforce this verdict by the application of sanctions; and though the circumstances of the case gave good reasons for this, the natural result was to weaken the authority of the League and to strengthen the hands of those who declared that collective security was an illusion and that each country must trust to its own arms and its own alliances.

Meanwhile, the World Disarmament Conference, towards which so much of the League's efforts had been directed, had met at last (February 1932). Its task was complicated and difficult enough, and the conflict with Japan added an unforeseen obstacle. During the first year of the conference, it seemed more than once that a general Disarmament Treaty might yet be achieved. But such hopes received their death blow when Hitler became the master of Germany, and soon found pretexts for withdrawing from the conference and from the League itself (October 1933).

However, the central framework of the League, battered and injured, remained in being. The open breach with Japan and Germany did not prevent the few countries which had hitherto remained outside, with the exception of the United States, from requesting admission; it was indeed the direct reason for the entry of the USSR, which, having done its best to weaken and frustrate the League from its earliest days, now hoped to find in it some reinforcement against the threat of aggression in Europe and in Asia. Meetings of the Council and the Assembly were as regular, and as well attended, as in the past; and states other than great powers continued to bring their disputes and difficulties to Geneva. It was during this period that, for the first time, an International Force was formed under Council authority and stationed in the Saar Territory to ensure public order during the plebiscite of 1935.

When, therefore, in October 1935, Mussolini decided in his turn to attack Ethiopia in open and unquestionable violation of the Covenant, the Council and Assembly were still capable of mobilizing world opinion against the aggressor, and for the first and last time the League as a whole decided to employ the economic weapon of Article 16 on behalf of the victim. The sanctions applied were far from complete; but the Italian economy was highly vulnerable, and the pressure was already beginning to be severely felt when the unity of League action was broken by a sudden *volte-face* on the part of the British and French governments. Though they were forced by public opinion to withdraw their proposals and to continue the existing sanctions, no additional pressure could thereafter be organized and the conquest and annexation of Ethiopia were duly consummated.

It might well be expected that while the new and frail structure of collective security was undergoing such disastrous trials, the economic organizations of the League would have been amongst the earliest victims. And in truth, so long as they tried to continue working along the conventional lines of official action, they were more and more ineffective. Each country found the best of reasons for strengthening the defences of its own economy, even if such action might weaken those of others. The climax of this unhappy conjuncture was the World Economic Conference held in London in June 1933, which ended in almost total failure within five weeks of its opening. The auxiliary institutions of the

League were thus compelled to seek for new methods of work. And having found them, they underwent an unexpected renaissance.

Abandoning the fruitless effort to bring about formal agreements, they began to concern themselves less with the action or inaction of governments than with the cares and interests of the individual citizen. Scientific advance had made it possible, under favourable conditions, to bring about a great and general improvement in the standard of living. But the standard was, in fact, not rising but falling – the result of unemployment in the rich countries, poverty in the rest, ignorance in all. They concluded, therefore, that if political conditions prevented any hope of reform through international contract, the elaborate structure of economic and social organizations built up by the League could still perform services which no single country could attempt, through the encouragement of mutual help and the exchange of knowledge and experience.

At the same time, the organizations were of their own accord beginning to combine their own activities much more completely than in earlier days. There had been of course many instances of collaboration in the past – usually on the initiative of the Council, when it needed expert advice to help in the settlement of some political dispute. But their new approach was creating a realization of the need for continuous co-operation amongst themselves and also with the International Labour Organization, now strengthened by the adhesion of the United States. The Health Committee had already established its competence to take initiatives of its own – a competence possessed from the first by the ILO; and their spirit of enterprise infected the rest. New joint organizations – a Nutrition Committee and a Housing Committee being the most important – began to work with great energy. National committees were established in numerous countries to support their efforts. In contrast to former habits, they now sought publicity instead of avoiding it: and since food, housing, health are subjects of interest to everybody, their reports did in fact reach a wide audience.

All this development brought with it a demand for institutional changes. From the beginning, the economic and social agencies of the League had been formally dependent on the Council. It was the Council which nominated their members, whether states or individuals; their reports on work done, their proposals for future programmes, were submitted to the Council for consideration. And yet the Council, consisting of Foreign Ministers or their substitutes, could not claim to possess any real competence in regard to their activities. Nor indeed did it pretend to do so; its usual action on each report was merely to order it to be circulated to all Members and be placed on the agenda of the Assembly.

Dependence upon a body which could impose delay or limitation, but could never give any effective impetus or help, had been made tolerable by the fact that the reports and proposals of the various agencies were fully debated by the Assembly before it voted their budget for the coming year. Most delegations included experts or officials capable of appreciating their problems, and the four or five weeks of Assembly session gave time for adequate consideration. Even so, discussion by civil servants in an Assembly committee might be technically competent, but was much more likely to dampen enthusiasm than to generate it and if this system had been tolerable while the work of the agencies was centred mainly on promoting formal agreements between governments, it was totally inadequate to their new forms of action. They needed a directing body consisting of responsible ministers in their various fields, corresponding in authority to a Council of Foreign Ministers, and meeting, like it, regularly and frequently. This view was powerfully reinforced when in February 1939 the United States government formally assured the Secretary-General of its warm support for the social and economic organizations of the League and its readiness to continue and extend the share it was already taking in their work.

Thus was born the plan for a new central organ which should take over for the future the responsibilities both of the Council and the Assembly for all economic and social affairs. It was to consist of Ministers of Finance, Commerce, Transport, or Health, and while remaining an integral part of the League was to be open to non-Members who might choose to participate on equal terms with the rest.

The whole plan was completed in August 1939, and set forth in a report to the Assembly, usually known as the Bruce Report in recognition of the decisive contribution made to it at every stage by the Australian statesman. A few days later the outbreak of the Second World War brought to a stop all the essential activities of the League, and no further steps could be taken to carry out the proposed reform. However, the lessons of twenty years experience were not finally wasted, and the principles of the Bruce Report were effectively embodied in the Economic and Social Council of the United Nations.

After the League had been forced to abandon its efforts to save Ethiopia, it became evident that it could no longer be counted on to preserve the peace. Member states began to look upon the Covenant not as an element of protection but as involving them in enormous and avoidable dangers. At the Assembly of 1938, three-quarters of the Members declared that, while they desired to keep the League in being, and still believed in its basic principles, nevertheless in the circumstances of the time they could no longer consider themselves as bound to carry out the obligations of Article 16, nor as entitled to call on their fellow-Members to do so. In face of the mounting aggression of the Axis powers, the Council was unable to offer any real help to their victims, and had no part to play in the last vain struggles of the democracies to avert the impending disaster.

The life of the League of Nations took place, from first to last, in the public eye. No secrets remain to be disclosed in regard to the proceedings of its constitutional organs great or small. Nor is it probable that any important revelation on the subject can be expected from eventual publication of the archives of its Member States, since their policies on League affairs were in most cases debated in their own press and parliament, and in any case could have no effect until they had been openly declared in the appropriate organ of the institution itself. The record is available to the seeker: and his task will be one, not of discovery, but of synthesis if he has the skill, and of judgement if he has the courage.

In the perspective of history, the twenty-year evolution of the League will surely be seen, both in its political and its constitutional aspects, as a period of experiment. The experiment continues; but the immense changes of recent years present us with a scene which differs so widely from that of say forty years ago, and the operations of the international organizations are on a scale so much greater than was then possible, that special prudence is called for in any attempt to offer valid analogies or useful lessons based on League history, in connection with the United Nations and its various component institutions. However, these institutions, modified and magnified as they may be, are in practically every case the direct and recognizable offspring of those of the League. And it is well to remember that much of what is now taken for granted as the accepted and permanent background of international activities is, historically speaking, the consequence of changes introduced by the provisions of the Covenant and by the practice of the Council and the Assembly.

TEXT REFERENCES

1. In this chapter, the word 'international' is intended to mean 'concerning (or open to) all states'.

2. With the single exception of the United States, all recognized states were Members of the League during all or part of its existence; but never all at the same time.

3. It fell short, in most respects, of General Smuts' great work, *The League of Nations, a Practical Suggestion,* which was published just before the Conference. But Smuts was then writing in a personal capacity.

4. Under Article 28 (2) of the Charter the Security Council is to 'hold periodic meetings at which each of its members may, if it so desires, be represented by a member of the government or by some other specially designated representative'.

5. It may be useful here to mention the principal subsidiary organizations of the League:

Political and Legal Organizations
The Permanent Court of International Justice.
The Permanent Advisory Commission on Military, Naval and Air Questions.
The Commission for the Reduction of Armaments (replaced in 1925 by the Preparatory Commission for the Disarmament Conference).
The Permanent Mandates Commission.

Economic and Social Organizations
The Economic and Financial Organization.
The Communications and Transit Organization.
The Health Organization.
The Committee on Traffic in Opium and other Dangerous Drugs.
The Committees on Traffic in Women and on Child Welfare.
The Committee on Intellectual Co-operation.
The Organization for Refugees.
(For the International Labour Organization see Chapter 8.)

6. The average annual budget, covering all expenses (including capital expenditure) of the League, the ILO, and the Permanent Court, was about $5,400,000.

BIBLIOGRAPHY

Azcarate y Florez, P. de, *League of Nations and National Minorities*, New York, 1945; London, 1946.

Cecil, Viscount, *A Great Experiment*, London, New York, 1941.

Claude, I. L., *Swords into Ploughshares* (3rd edition), New York, 1964.

Conwell-Evans, T. P., *The League Council in Action*, London, New York, 1929.

Davis, H. E., ed., *Pioneers in World Order*, New York, 1944; London, 1945.

Duncan Hall, H., *Mandates, Dependencies and Trusteeship*, London, Washington, D.C., 1948.

Greaves, H. R. G., *The League Committees and World Order*, London, New York, 1931.

Hill, W. M., *Economic and Financial Organization of the League of Nations*, Washington, D.C., 1946; London, 1947.

Loveday, A., *Reflections on International Administration*, Oxford, 1956.

Hunter Miller, D., *The Drafting of the Covenant*, New York, London, 1928.

Morley, F., *The Society of Nations*, Washington, D.C., London, 1932.

Myers, D. P., *Handbook of the League of Nations*, Geneva, Boston, 1935.

Ranshofen-Wertheimer, E. F., *The International Secretariat*, Washington, D.C., London, 1954.

Zimmern, A. E., *The League of Nations and the Rule of Law, 1918-1935*, 2 vols., 2nd rev. ed., London, New York, 1939.

Walters, F. P., *History of the League of Nations*, London, New York, 1952.

Webster, C. K. and Herbert, S., *The League of Nations in Theory and Practice*, London, Boston, 1933.

3 THE GENERAL ASSEMBLY OF THE UNITED NATIONS

Geoffrey Goodwin

The General Assembly of the United Nations is the only body in that organization on which all the members of the United Nations are represented. That membership has increased from the 51 present at San Francisco in 1945 to the 114 members of 1965. In the process of this rapid expansion the political complexion and also the role of the General Assembly has changed so much that it would be as well to examine it from five different though related aspects.

The first concerns the powers of the General Assembly and in particular the relations between the General Assembly and the Security Council in regard to the maintenance of international peace and security. The second relates to a basic duality in the nature of the Assembly: in many respects it is little more than a diplomatic conference in the traditional vein; yet it also embodies the embryo of that 'organized international community' to which Dag Hammarskjöld and many others have aspired. The third and related aspect is connected with the status of General Assembly resolutions; how far may they be said to reflect 'the moral judgements of the conscience of the world' and how far are they to be seen primarily as registers of diplomatic attitudes to which states may occasionally defer not out of any sense of moral compulsion but rather on grounds of expediency? The fourth aspect of the Assembly concerns its role as a mirror of the diplomatic world. Does it accurately reflect the facts of diplomatic life? Or is it something of a distorting mirror in so far as it does not include all the states of the world and its proceedings are based on a principle of 'one state, one vote' which may so obscure the facts of power as to lend an air of unreality to its proceedings? The fifth and final aspect of the General Assembly to be examined is its use as an instrument of what might be called 'pressure politics'. How far, for instance, has the General Assembly acted as an effective catalyst of Afro-Asian pressures on colonial issues or in the realm of economic development?

In considering the relations between the General Assembly and the Security Council it must be remembered that the basic conception of the original Dumbarton Oaks proposals (which were agreed upon by the United States, the Soviet Union, the United Kingdom and China in October 1944) was that of an 'Armed Concert' of the victorious powers in whom would reside the main responsibility for the maintenance of peace, the main threats to which, it was supposed, would come from the then undefeated enemy states – Germany and Japan. In other words, there was no question of the Security Council and the General Assembly having parallel competence in the maintenance of international peace and security as was the case with the Council and the Assembly in the League of Nations. Nevertheless, although the Security Council was intended to be the effective guardian of international peace, unlike the League Council it was not made competent to discuss any matter within the sphere of action of the whole organization. All matters other than those dealing with security were to be the prerogative of the General Assembly and of the functional bodies (e.g. the Economic and Social Council) operating under its authority.

The membership of the San Francisco Conference (April to June 1945) was much wider than that at Dumbarton Oaks and it was understandable that the great mass of middle and small powers should seek to extend the authority of the General

Assembly as a means of offsetting the privileged position of the Great Powers on the Security Council. Moreover, at this stage the United States itself was responsive to this pressure, Senator Vandenberg seeing the General Assembly as the 'town meeting of tomorrow's world'.[1] Consequently, in the Charter agreed upon at San Francisco the General Assembly was given the right to *consider* 'the general principles of co-operation in the maintenance of international peace and security, including the principles governing disarmament and the regulation of armaments' (Article 11 (1)). It was also given the right to *discuss* 'any questions or any matters within the scope of the present Charter' (Article 10) or 'any questions relating to the maintenance of international peace and security' (Article 11 (2)). The Assembly's further right to *make recommendations* on these matters, including the right to 'recommend measures for the peaceful adjustment of any situation, regardless of origin, which it deems likely to impair the general welfare or friendly relations among nations' (Article 14)[2] was subject to the proviso that they were not already being dealt with by the Security Council (Article 12). Yet this extension of the Assembly's competence was a far cry from the original conception of an 'Armed Concert' of the Great Powers maintaining the peace, and misgivings that the General Assembly's new role might undermine the authority of the Security Council were not entirely stilled by the explicit affirmation of the Security Council's primary responsibility for the maintenance of international peace and security in Article 24.

It may be helpful at this stage to give a brief résumé of the powers of the General Assembly as set out in the Charter. As has been seen, its powers in the field of international peace and security are in principle *secondary to* those of the Security Council. In certain other fields the General Assembly's powers are *co-ordinate* with those of the Security Council. For instance, in the case of membership (Article 4) the admission of a state to membership in the United Nations is to be effected by a decision of the

General Assembly, but the Assembly can only act upon the recommendation of the Security Council. Again, the General Assembly's power to suspend a member from the exercise of the rights and privileges of membership (Article 5)[3] or to expel a member from the organization (Article 6) is dependent upon a recommendation of the Security Council. The appointment of a Secretary-General under Article 97 is by the General Assembly, but again 'upon the recommendation of the Security Council'. Moreover, these are matters upon which any permanent member of the Security Council is entitled to exercise its veto rights to prevent the Council from reaching a recommendation. So in a number of important realms although the powers of the General Assembly are, formally speaking, co-ordinate with those of the Security Council, in practice their exercise is dependent upon the existence of unanimity between the permanent members of the Security Council. This is, in effect, to make the Assembly subordinate to, not co-ordinate with, the Security Council. Moreover, although amendments to the Charter can be 'adopted' by a vote of two-thirds of the members of the General Assembly, they cannot come into force until they have been ratified by two-thirds of the members of the United Nations and this two-thirds must include *all* the permanent members of the Security Council (Article 108).

However, the General Assembly has certain *supervisory* responsibilities of a more exclusive nature. Article 60 accords responsibility for the discharge of the functions of the Organization in the field of international economic and social co-operation to the Assembly, placing the Economic and Social Council 'under the authority of the General Assembly' even though the latter is listed, with the General Assembly, as a 'principal organ' of the United Nations (Article 7). Similarly, the General Assembly has responsibility for ensuring the effective operation of the international trusteeship system under Chapters XII and XIII; in particular, under Article 16 it must approve the trusteeship agreements for areas not designated as strategic, and Article 87 indicates that the Trusteeship Council is to operate 'under its authority'.

There are a number of matters on which the General Assembly may be held to have the right to reach *decisions*. It is true that the term 'decision' is apt to give rise to some misunderstanding. For instance, Article 18 stipulates that decisions of the General Assembly on important questions shall be made by a two-thirds majority of the members present and voting and on other questions by a simple majority. But here the term 'decision' is used to cover both a recommendation to member governments and what can more properly be termed a decision in that the resolution agreed upon is executory not *through* members of the Organization but *by* the Organization itself, as in the case of elections, the adoption of the Assembly's own rules of procedure, etc. In other instances, e.g. questions relating to the operation of the trusteeship system or the approval of the budget of the Organization and the apportionment of budgetary contributions, the Assembly in a sense takes decisions, but the ultimate responsibility for the implementation of these decisions rests upon member governments.

It can, however, be argued that occasionally the General Assembly has exercised powers which go a good deal further than those outlined above and which might be held to approach something like *quasi-legislative* powers. In addition to approving the terms of trusteeship agreements (other than those for strategic areas) the Assembly has taken the initiative in drafting such conventions as the Genocide Convention and has in this sense acted as a quasi-legislative body, even though the draft conventions approved by the General Assembly have, of course, to be ratified by the stipulated number of member states before they can come into force. The General Assembly was also accorded quasi-legislative powers of a rather different kind when the United Kingdom referred the issue of Palestine to the General Assembly in 1947, and when the Council of Foreign Ministers referred the question of the future of the Italian colonies to the General Assembly in 1948. In the case of Palestine the Assembly's partition proposals might be held to have given a measure of legitimacy to the new state established by Israeli military successes; in the case of the former Italian colonies (where British co-operation was forthcoming as it had not been in the case of Palestine) the General Assembly's resolutions did, in a real sense, decide the future of Libya, of Eritrea and of Somalia.

This analysis of the Assembly's powers, brief though it has necessarily been, may serve as a backcloth to a more detailed examination of the evolution in the relations between a General Assembly in which every member of the United Nations has a voice – regardless of size – and a Security Council of only fifteen members[4] on which the five permanent members occupy a dominant position.

For the most part this relationship between the General Assembly and the Security Council has been a function of two interacting variables; the one the state of tension between the permanent members of the Council, the other the size and complexion of the General Assembly (which is, of course, the same as that of the United Nations as a whole). Up to about the end of 1946, despite the often virulent diatribes between the Soviet and British delegates, the permanent members still seemed intent on preserving the Council as a medium of co-operation. During this time the Security Council held the centre of the stage. Thereafter as tension grew between the permanent members, and particularly between the Soviet Union and the United States, the General Assembly, mainly because of the absence of the veto, its wider membership, and its greater potentialities as a propaganda platform, came to overshadow the Security Council even in matters of international peace and security. The trend was reflected in the setting up in November 1947 on American initiative of the Interim Committee of the General Assembly, a kind of 'reserve team' Assembly which, like the Security Council, would be in continuous session (i.e. immediately available) and competent to step in whenever the Security Council was paralyzed by disagreement between the permanent members. The advent of the Korean War accelerated the trend[5] and the Uniting for Peace resolution of 3 November 1950 was intended to allow the General Assembly to consider a threat to, or breach of, international peace and security whenever the Security Council was prevented from doing so. The resolution provided for emergency sessions of the General Assembly; for the establishment of a Peace Observation Commission; for the earmarking of national contingents for service with the United Nations; and for the establishment of a Collective Measures Committee. At the time of the Suez crisis in October 1956 the Assembly acted under the procedures set out in this resolution to set up the United Nations Emergency Force.

The Soviet Union have strenuously denied the legality of the Uniting for Peace Resolution and even the International Court of Justice has described it as based upon a 'courageous' interpretation of the Charter. Yet the resolution did in fact do little more than spell out a role for the Assembly which, if not obviously implicit in, is at least not excluded by, the terms of the Charter. Britain and France did not seriously question its legality, but they did have reservations about its expediency, both out of fear that as colonial powers they might find themselves in a minority in the Assembly and because one of the main impulses behind the resolution was an American disposition to exploit their voting majorities in the Assembly to turn the UN into an anti-communist front.[6]

With the advent of something like a 'nuclear stalemate' and a fairly stable balance of power between the nuclear powers, American attitudes have recently shifted slightly in favour of using the Organization to explore the possibilities of Great Power agreement. This has logically directed attention to the Security

Council rather than to the General Assembly. Another factor in bringing about this shift was the rapid growth in the membership of the United Nations – and so of the General Assembly. Much of this increased membership came, especially in the 1960s, from Asia and Africa. For instance, in 1945 there were 51 members of whom only 13 were Afro-Asian members; in 1960 there were 82 members of whom 29 were Afro-Asian members; in 1964 there were 114 members of whom 59 – i.e. rather over half – were Afro-Asian members. This growth of membership has had a number of consequences. The first has been to make the United States, as well as Britain and France, rather more cautious about relying on the General Assembly, since many new members pursue 'non-aligned' policies and the United States can therefore no longer count upon mobilizing the necessary two-thirds majority in the General Assembly to endorse United States initiatives. The advent of the many Afro-Asian members into the United Nations has also strengthened the anti-colonialist pressures in the Assembly where the system of majority voting allows massive majorities to be mobilized behind resolutions exhorting the colonial powers to mend their ways and threatening sanctions against those (e.g. Portugal) who do not. Albeit for rather differing reasons the United States has veered in the direction of the view fairly consistently held by Britain, France and in more extreme fashion the Soviet Union, that the authority of the Security Council should not be drained away by the Assembly. In the United Nations peace-keeping activities between 1960 and 1964 the authorizing resolutions have usually emanated from the Security Council and not from the General Assembly. Thus the three main resolutions of 14 and 22 July and 9 August 1960 setting up and defining the powers of the United Nations force in the Congo, as also the resolutions of February 1961 and November 1961 dealing with Katanga, were resolutions of the Security Council not of the General Assembly. Where disagreement between the permanent members has become so acute as to frustrate the Council then the natural reaction has been to convene the General Assembly under the Uniting for Peace procedures (as, for instance, in September 1960). And there are such exceptions as the case of West Irian where it was the General Assembly which on 21 September 1962 authorized the setting up of the United Nations Temporary Executive Authority. Nevertheless, by and large the Security Council has resumed its primary responsibility for keeping the peace. Thus, in the case of the Yemen the United Nations Observation Group was set up by a Security Council resolution of 10 June 1963 and the United Nations force in Cyprus was constituted by the Security Council resolution of 4 March 1964 and its mandate has subsequently been renewed by Security Council resolutions.

A further reason for this shift back to the Security Council has been that the sheer size of the General Assembly has made it an extraordinarily cumbersome and unpredictable body and so aggravated the already substantial difficulties of securing agreement on resolutions which are precise enough to afford a basis for action. Moreover, the appallingly disruptive impact on the Eighteenth Session of the General Assembly of the differences between the Great Powers over the financing of peace-keeping operations has led several of the not-so-great Powers (e.g. the Netherlands) to the view that the Uniting for Peace Resolution no longer serves a useful purpose and that the General Assembly should not attempt to encroach upon the Security Council's ground.

For these and other reasons the General Assembly has come to be somewhat eclipsed by the Security Council in the last year or two in the field of international peace and security, and there has been something of a reversion[7] to the original intention of the drafters of the Charter, namely that the Security Council should have 'primary' responsibility in this field.[8] What now divides the permanent members (other, of course, than 'China') is whether this 'primary' responsibility is to be regarded as, in effect, an 'exclusive' responsibility (as the Soviet Union and, it would appear, France contend), or whether the General Assembly should retain a residual responsibility in the event of the Council being unable to act (as the United States and Britain contend).[9] With the enlargement of the Security Council, and the widespread desire for a narrowing of the differences between the present permanent members, it should not be impossible to arrive at some, possibly tacit, understanding of the respective roles of the two bodies – and of the Secretary-General – once the financial problems of peace-keeping have been resolved.

In turning to consider the nature of the General Assembly it is as well to recall that, as part of the United Nations, it is an inter-governmental assembly based on 'the principle of the sovereign equality' of all its members; that its resolutions are agreed upon through a process of majority voting; and in so far as these resolutions are addressed to Member States they take the form of recommendations only, which states are under no legal obliga-tion to comply with.[10] Further analysis reveals, however, two not easily reconcilable views about the Assembly. To some it is little more than a 'static diplomatic conference' in the traditional vein. To others it embodies most strikingly the conception of the United Nations as a dynamic instrument of an emerging world community – to use Dag Hammarskjöld's words – in which resides an authority which transcends the authority of its indivi-dual members; it is, in effect – to use William Clark's phrase – the 'Sixth Great Power'.

The notion of the General Assembly as a 'static diplomatic conference' was said by Dag Hammarskjöld – in an intentionally disparaging way? – to belong to the 'traditions of the national policies of the past'.[11] Certainly, to the traditionalist the Assembly is essentially a diplomatic contrivance, not an organ of govern-ment. Consequently, it is what states do and not the precise institutional pattern which is of first significance. In other words, to use Brierley's phrase, the General Assembly, like the United

Nations itself, is a 'they', not an 'it'. The structure of the Assembly and the six or more committees, the procedures which have been developed, and the practices which have been adopted, may make a certain difference to the manner in which Member States behave. But to the traditionalist the fundamental premise of all the Assembly's major activities is that its recommendations depend for their implementation upon the active co-operation of the member states to whom they are addressed. These states, being sovereign, cannot be dragooned into compliance, they must be persuaded. This calls for negotiation; and it presupposes that in the process of negotiation – which may involve some very tough bargaining – there must be some element of give and take, some willingness on the part of the majority to take account of the wishes and interests of the minority.

At first sight the 'open diplomacy' of the General Assembly does not provide a particularly congenial setting for the traditional tasks of diplomacy which need to be conducted in private. The General Assembly debates may serve as a useful 'barometer' of the diplomatic climate of opinion, but they all too easily degenerate into exercises in forensic propaganda. There is the well-known tale of one delegate's speech which was annotated in the margin: 'Weak point. Shout!' But this is not the whole story. The Assembly serves also as a valuable setting for 'personal contacts, private meetings, casual discussions, exchanges of view, exploratory soundings. . . .'[12] Assembly resolutions are usually the end-product of a long process of negotiation which has taken place in the delegates' lounges, offices, etc., under cover of the formal meetings; they do indeed usually represent: 'Open agreements, privately agreed upon.' Nor is the process of almost continuous negotiation and consultation necessarily limited only to United Nations affairs. Old-style diplomats may be taken aback by the antics of their fellow diplomats in the General Assembly – the atmosphere of the Assembly has been described as that of a 'den of thieves' as compared with the 'church-like' atmosphere of the

Assembly of the League of Nations. Nevertheless, however irritating the 'diplomacy by loudspeaker' and the 'diplomacy by insult' of the formal debates, this should not conceal the fact that the Assembly provides a diplomatic meeting-place with a range of diplomatic representation quite unparalleled by any other body in the world and an excellent cover for private negotiation in the traditional diplomatic style.

This rather sober – and narrow? – view of the Assembly is not good enough for those who see it as one of the main instruments for achieving that 'organized international community' in the direction of which, Mr Hammarskjöld contended, the Charter took a first step. For them the 'conference concept' is no more than a starting-point which will be gradually overshadowed by 'the concept, clearly implied in the Charter, of an international community for which the Organization (and by implication the General Assembly) is an instrument and an expression and in which anarchic tendencies in international life are to be curbed by the introduction of a system of equal political rights, equal economic opportunities and the rule of law.'[13] This is the import of the Purposes and Principles of the Charter and it is argued that the General Assembly is not just a piece of 'conference machinery' intent solely on the reconciliation of conflicting national policies regardless of how far they conform with the Charter. Rather its task has been, and must be, to encourage member states to adhere ever more closely to the Charter's requirements. Its task, in other words, is to work 'for the translation into practical realities in international life of the democratic principles which are basic to the Charter'; it must translate 'the principles into action intended to establish through self-determination a free and independent life as sovereign states for people who have expressed in democratic forms their wish for such a status',[14] it must make its full contribution to securing equal economic opportunities especially for newly independent states; and it must, as the most representative body in the Organization, serve as the natural protector of the rights of countries which lack the might to ensure respect of them of their own accord. There is in this conception of the General Assembly's role a sense of direction and of purpose, the ultimate end of which is 'to save succeeding generations from the scourge of war'.

Linked with this community approach is the view that the Assembly's procedures (as indeed those of other collective organs of the United Nations) show aspects of a parliamentary or quasi-parliamentary character. In Dean Rusk's phrase they constitute a form of 'parliamentary diplomacy'. This is exemplified in particular in the system of majority voting and in the formation of voting caucuses, and in the actual procedural rules.

The community concept is an attractive one. Yet does it not presuppose an underlying consensus as to the principles applied and the direction to be taken which in practice is at best fitful and feeble and at worst almost wholly non-existent? If so, are not analogies drawn from the domestic life of states misleading and possibly even dangerous if the 'majority' will comes to be enshrined as the repository of all wisdom? If a divided and nuclear-charged world is to survive, if co-existence is to be peaceful though competitive, and if the new and potent forces of change are to be absorbed into, without destroying, the existing international system, is not the Assembly's prime task, as indeed that of the United Nations as a whole, to serve as a 'centre for harmonizing the actions of states'?

The status to be accorded to General Assembly resolutions is intimately linked with the views just described of what kind of body the Assembly is. Three rather different views of their status can be discerned. In the first case those resolutions which purport to give precision to existing provisions are often held to have acquired sufficient legal force to make them more than mere recommendations. In so far as they may be held to express a majority consensus and to involve the application of the binding principles of the Charter they may be expected 'to come more and more close to being recognized as decisions having a binding effect on those concerned'.[15] Thus the Declaration of 14 December 1960 on the Granting of Independence to Colonial Countries and Peoples (Resolution 1514) is held to have lent precision to Article 1, paragraph 4 of the Charter which enjoins observance of the principle of national self-determination and therefore to possess a certain legal as well as moral status. It is not argued that these resolutions impose binding legal obligations upon member states, but rather that they are indicative of a newly emerging body of customary law to which states should, and will, increasingly defer.[16] It is further argued that the General Assembly can, by resolution, legitimize the actions of states, whether acting individually or collectively, by declaring them to be in conformity with the Charter. The above Declaration (1514) and the General Assembly resolution of 28 November 1961, setting out the claims to national sovereignty of indigenous peoples, have, strictly speaking, no legal status. But they have been cited as giving a basis of legitimacy to collective action, even the use of physical force, against recalcitrant colonial powers or European minorities; in other words, since these resolutions purport merely to elaborate what is already one of the Purposes of the Charter, the use of force in furtherance of their objectives does not fall within the prohibitions of Article 2, paragraph 4, on the 'threat or use of force'. The implications of this line of argument are, to say the least, disturbing. To legitimize the use of force to remedy injustice is rather an odd way of encouraging the 'peaceful adjustment of any situation ... [which may] impair the general welfare or friendly relations among nations' (Article 14).

Another view of these resolutions is that they reflect, as Mr Dulles asserted in October 1947, the 'moral judgements of the conscience of the world'. This is a bold claim indeed which one suspects came more easily from the delegate of a country that at that time could pretty confidently count upon being on the side of the majority. It is not to be confused with the contention that a member state, in terms of its obligations under the Charter, is *politically* obliged to pay careful heed to, or at least not persistently to disregard, Assembly resolutions. Nor is it to be equated with the observation that these resolutions may have moral consequences, in the sense that public opinion within member states, though to a strikingly different degree, may portray a certain moral sensitivity to the 'good opinion' of the United Nations. To argue that Assembly resolutions impose 'moral' obligations presupposes, for instance, that there exists a community of mankind to whose moral judgement the Assembly is responsive and that consequently 'the collective opinion of the Assembly is superior to the individual opinion of any of its Members'.[17] To find flaws in this argument is not necessarily to share Sir Winston Churchill's view that Assembly decisions are taken 'on grounds of enmity, opportunism or merely jealousy and petulance' or simply to have reservations about how representative the Assembly is of 'the world'. Rather it is to doubt the validity of the analogy usually drawn by those who share Mr Dulles' conviction, between majority rule within a parliamentary democracy and majority rule in an international institution, on the grounds that the broad moral consensus as to ends and means – the sense of community – on which domestic parliamentary procedures are predicted rarely, if ever, exists at the international level.

The third view of the status of General Assembly resolutions is that as they emanate from what is, in effect, a standing diplomatic conference they merely register what might best be called a diplomatic consensus, that is, the degree of agreement that obtains on the issue concerned between the diplomatic representatives[18] in the Assembly at the time. Consequently in assessing a resolution's significance delegates look more closely at the composition of a vote – the diplomatic alignments behind the voting figures – than at the actual size of the majority. And a member state's decision how far to comply with an Assembly resolution will be determined more by considerations of the possibly adverse diplomatic and domestic repercussions of non-compliance than by any belief in the legal or moral authority of the majority, however large it may have been.

To some, especially those whose states are habitually in the minority, General Assembly resolutions may represent little more than fulminations of an irresponsible body of humbugs, the vapourings of a 'machin' – a 'what-not' – the hypocritical utterances of a capitalist-dominated arithmetical majority, to be shrugged off as of little or of no consequence. To others, especially those whose states are habitually in the majority, or those in whom some spark of idealism is still alive, they may represent the findings of an embryo world authority, a world arbitral tribunal, a world public opinion forum with real moral and sometimes legal force. So far as states are concerned, there is bound to be a lot of picking and choosing between the mass of resolutions adopted by the Assembly each year. Those in today's majority on one issue may be in tomorrow's minority on another issue. States that have successfully sponsored a resolution are liable to inflate its status; those whose protestations have been overridden to insist upon its defects, especially if it provides useful grist to an opposition mill. Governments may treat these resolutions primarily as indicative of diplomatic attitudes, but if their electorate – or a significant proportion of it – tend to ascribe moral or legal force to them, this is a political factor most governments cannot afford to ignore. Of fundamental importance is the place accorded to the United Nations in the general context of a state's foreign policy. And, in so far as governments generally have become increasingly inclined to give precedence to their alliance obligations and regional loyalties over their commitments to the United Nations, one might well expect General Assembly resolutions to carry rather less weight today than they did say ten or fifteen years ago. Yet to deny altogether some moral or legal force to many such resolutions would be to take too narrow a view; to some extent they crystallize and express the norms of political behaviour of an emerging diplomatic community held together by a sense of common peril, and even indeed of common need. States may challenge these norms when they appear to conflict with what they deem to be their national interest; but the reluctance of most States to do so too frequently suggests that conformity is generally seen as a diplomatic asset not to be lightly frittered away.

Whether the General Assembly is reflective of an emerging world community or of the world of diplomacy it should be as representative as possible. Yet the principle of universality is hedged around with difficulties. In an organization in which majority voting is the rule there is bound to be no great enthusiasm for admitting a state that is likely to vote in the opposite camp. Although the Soviet Union and Britain have generally favoured universality, in the early 1950s when the tensions of the Korean War were at their height admission was apt to be treated by the United States almost as an award for meritorious conduct in the 'cold war', on the grounds it would seem, that only anti-communist states could satisfy the criteria of Article 4.[19] However, in the last decade the 'package deal' of 1955 and the almost automatic admission of African states which have achieved independence indicate a swing in favour of the principle of universality as well, one suspects, as a diminishing concern about voting strengths. Nevertheless, despite the rapid growth in its membership the United Nations, and so the General Assembly itself, is still not an altogether accurate 'mirror' of diplomatic life. And this for two reasons. The first is that representation still falls a good deal short of the ideal of universality. The Chinese seat is not occupied by Communist China; the unhappily divided countries of West and East Germany, North and South Korea, and North and South Vietnam are debarred from membership; and Indonesia has recently withdrawn from the Organization.

The United Nations and its General Assembly is still a 'would-be' world institution. States commanding nearly one-third of the world's population have no voice in the Assembly. Their absence is bound to lend a certain air of unreality to the proceedings of the General Assembly and its committees, especially those that deal with the problems of arms control and disarmament or the issues of peace and war in Southeast Asia. The presence of Communist China and the neighbouring régimes in North Korea and North Vietnam would greatly reinforce the more militant Afro-Asian representatives in their advocacy of the use of force to root out the last vestiges of European colonialism in Africa; but their absence does lend a grain of plausibility to denunciations of the United Nations as an unrepresentative body dominated by 'imperialist capitalist powers'. And there is some danger that those 'blackballed' from the club may set up a rival one.

Another distorting factor has been that the system of majority voting[20] has led to the growth of a system of what might be called 'voting power' politics, the aim of which is to muster the number of votes (either a two-thirds or simple majority) required to secure the passage of a resolution. If the prescribed majority can be secured, the minority can be voted down. But a voting system in which each state has one vote, irrespective of its size or power, often results in a striking discrepancy between voting weight and diplomatic weight. This has led to pleas for a sytem of weighted voting, akin to that in the International Monetary Fund or the World Bank. With a system of weighted voting General Assembly resolutions might acquire rather greater authority, on the grounds, for instance, that they would more accurately reflect 'world public opinion' (if this can be said to exist) or a genuine diplomatic consensus. And it is naturally irritating that those with power – and the responsibilities that go with it – should frequently find themselves outvoted by those who have little of either. To a substantial extent, however, the absurdities of the present system are offset by the attention member states pay to the actual diplomatic weight a resolution carries. By the practice, in other words, of 'mental weighting' of the voting. Moreover, not only does majority voting prevent the Assembly being hamstrung, as was its predecessor, by the 'veto' of a single state, but the difficulties of hitting upon an acceptable system of weighting would be formidable indeed. What criteria should be employed in computing voting strength? Population? United Nations budgetary contributions? *Per capita* income? Would not each state insist on criteria which would inflate its own weighting? If several factors were to be taken into account how much weight should be attached to each? And should not the weighting vary with each issue on which a vote is to be taken so as to take account of the relevant responsibilities of states? In face of such intimidating difficulties the present system of 'mental weighting' is not at all a poor substitute for a more formal weighting system.

Two other facets of the Assembly's proceedings which call into question the authenticity of Assembly resolutions as registers of a diplomatic consensus deserve brief mention. The first is that they are said to result from a process of 'horse-trading' between voting caucuses,[21] often irrespective of the 'intrinsic merits' of a question. Certainly there is a good deal of 'If we vote for you on this, will you vote for us on that?' so that the issue in question is often lost sight of in a swarm of extraneous calculations. Yet the voting caucuses represent a real if inchoate identity of interests and provide an element of stability and predictability in voting patterns; there is a sizeable 'floating vote' to be won over by argument as well as by bribes and 'arm-twisting'; and the important resolutions by and large register not a mere passing coincidence of ill-considered attitudes but the end result of a long process of informal discussions and formal negotiations in which it is nearly always the greater powers that take the lead.

The second criticism is that Assembly resolutions give a distorted picture because of the 'double standards' applied by most

African and Asian states on colonial and other issues. A colonial power that uses force to preserve order in an overseas dependency has contravened the Charter; an ex-colonial power that uses force to 'liberate' an adjoining territory has acted in conformity with the Charter to remedy an injustice. The outright condemnation of 'Western' imperialism – in whatever guise – has on occasions been matched by a more equivocal attitude towards Soviet expansion. Negotiating formulae have sometimes been sought which in assuming that parliamentary democracies are more willing to compromise – to show a 'decent respect for the opinions of mankind' – than authoritarian or totalitarian states tend to favour the latter. Yet most, if not all, delegates will be disposed to apply one standard – given to lofty moral generalities – when their interests are not immediately engaged and another – a thoroughly realistic one – when they are. States are bound to give the benefit of doubt to allies and to suspect the motives of their former rulers. And a close examination of General Assembly resolutions suggests that it is not only the Afro-Asian powers who practise double standards. All do, in some degree. By doing this they are merely practising in the Assembly their customary behaviour in diplomatic life generally.

Perhaps a more accurate term than 'voting power' politics for describing what goes on in the General Assembly is: 'pressure politics'. The Assembly – and the United Nations itself – is merely one instrument among many in the diplomatic arsenal which states can use to bring pressure on each other in furtherance of their own particular national objectives. Nor is it a substitute for other means of pressure: usually it can best reinforce and supplement rather than initiate. And its efficacy as an instrument of pressure will vary with the nature of the issues at stake and the vulnerability to pressure of the powers concerned. It has, of course, been used by the most powerful – the nuclear giants – to bring pressure on each other, on their allies, and, above all, on the uncommitted, non-aligned, neutralist countries of the Afro-Asian world. But the pressure has been by no means one-sided. Even the greatest Powers are not immune from, or altogether invulnerable to, pressure, especially when it is exerted by allies (as in the case of Commonwealth pressure on the United States in favour of armistice negotiations during the Korean War) or by the non-aligned (as in the case of African pressure on both the United States and the Soviet Union during different stages of the Congo operations). Indeed, a General Assembly in which, unlike in the Security Council, power brings no special voting rights, is the main – or at least the most readily available – channel through which the powerless can first 'internationalize' an issue and can then, both individually and collectively, exert pressure on the powerful. The developing countries have not succeeded in persuading the industrialized countries to establish a United Nations Capital Development Fund, but their efforts to this end played no small part in injecting a welcome element of flexibility into the World Bank complex. By providing the anti-colonial, developing, Afro-Asian states with a convenient forum and pressure point the General Assembly has come to function not as a protector of the *status quo* but as a 'revolutionary' society dominated by the 'struggle for freedom' of colonial peoples. The Assembly does not, of course, create these pressures; but it does often enable them to be wielded more effectively. Nationalist leaders no longer have to bargain on their own with the colonial authorities; they can now turn to the Assembly for support in their 'struggle' for independence and, as in the case of Aden, Assembly recommendations can be held to set out the terms on which independence negotiations should be conducted.

Yet there is a real danger that this kind of pressure will prove double-edged. Assembly strictures on South Africa have had the effect of closing the ranks of both Afrikaans and English-speaking South Africans behind Dr Verwoerd's apartheid policies. Assembly – and Security Council – pressure probably served to

exacerbate the situation in Southern Rhodesia through contributing to the overthrow of the more moderate government of
Sir Edgar Whitehead (by rallying support behind Rhodesian
Front leaders intent on maintaining white supremacy at least for
many years to come). Over the years the hypocritical exhorta-
tions and ill-considered condemnations with which otherwise not
unsensible Assembly resolutions have often been flavoured –
frequently at the instance of delegates from the most backward
countries – has deprived them of any moral force in the eyes of
those to whom they are addressed and has merely excited irrita-
tion and resentment. In this respect at least the Assembly has
served more as a school for political demagogues than as a
'kindergarten for peace'. But, by and large, these are the exceptions rather than the rule.

What are the factors that have most influenced the evolution of
the General Assembly during its twenty years' life?

The General Assembly is but one of the principal organs of the
United Nations. Its impact on the policies of member states is
therefore very largely a function of the place accorded to the
United Nations by those states in the context of their general
foreign policy objectives. This, in turn, is broadly a function of
the extent to which the United Nations – and the General
Assembly – is seen as a useful, or potentially useful, collective
instrument for the furtherance of particular national objectives.
Moreover, although the Assembly can focus attention on a
problem, can evoke a marginally greater contribution from its
members, and can often help to bring those contributions to bear
more effectively, basically it can make no greater contribution to
world peace and prosperity than its members themselves are prepared to make at any one time.

Nor is there any evidence to indicate that during its life the
General Assembly has diminished member states' assertion of
their sovereignty. Indeed, not only is the United Nations itself

intended to preserve the 'sovereign equality' of states, but it is arguable that the General Assembly has often tended to encourage, not discourage, national particularism and individualism by, for instance, encouraging an often naïve deference to the principle of national self-determination, a divorce of responsibility from power through the internationalization of issues more susceptible to private negotiation by the countries directly interested, and a persistence in the incongruity of the principle of 'one state, one vote' in subsidiary bodies (e.g. the Trade and Development Board) where some form of weighted voting would be far more appropriate.

On the other hand, the Assembly has sometimes helped to check the disruptive consequences of sovereignty by inducing sovereign states to pursue their interests with a slightly greater regard for the interests of their fellows. It has offered, and still offers, a means whereby middle powers (e.g. Canada, India, Mexico, Netherlands, Nigeria, Sweden, Tunisia) can initiate, and maybe execute, collective measures (e.g. UNEF or the Special Fund) which are to the 'general interest' of all, or nearly all, including the Great Powers. And by encouraging personal diplomacy between foreign ministers (and their immediate advisers) the Assembly may set some brake on the suspicion and mistrust to which doubts about each other's real intentions so easily give rise. It has probably given the great powers' representatives a closer understanding of – in some cases even a closer sympathy with – new forces at work in the world. Many delegates from newly independent countries have learnt better to appreciate the realities of diplomatic life, particularly that policies cannot be determined by votes.

There have been no constitutional developments within the General Assembly necessitating formal amendment of the Charter as has the expansion of the membership of the Security Council and the Economic and Social Council. But it is possible that the expanded membership of these two Councils, by making each more representative of the expanded membership of the United Nations as a whole, will make it less easy for member states to degrade their competence in favour of that of an Assembly, now swollen to such elephantine proportions as to threaten to become little more than a 'talking-shop'. For this and other reasons such quasi-constitutional developments as those portended in the Uniting for Peace Resolution are now less likely to prove constitutional growing points within the Organization.

Finally, it must be admitted that the General Assembly, as part of the United Nations, was in part the product of the fleeting, effervescent, and often illusory hopes engendered by the ravages of war. As memories grow dim, hopes evaporate and disillusion sets in, so the cement of collective action threatens to crumble. Politically (i.e. in terms of the repercussions of political events in other parts of the world) and technologically the world continues to shrink. Diplomatically (i.e. in the sense of the number of diplomatic entities) it continues to grow – and the embers of nationalism glow as brightly as ever.

Yet in many ways it was precisely to deal with the tensions engendered by these contradictory trends that the United Nations and its General Assembly were created. Both have shown a remarkable resilience under pressure and a capacity for adaptation to changing circumstances which may yet confound the gloomier prognostications. Of all the United Nations bodies the General Assembly above all stands for a conception of the world as a true 'comity of nations' rather than a mere conglomeration of regional blocs or hegemonical spheres. It is a not ignoble one.

TEXT REFERENCES

1. A. H. Vandenberg, Jr., ed., *The Private Papers of Senator Vandenberg*, Boston, 1952, p. 190.

2. The International Court of Justice found that the setting up of UNEF by the Assembly was legal as it was covered by Article 14.

3. This is not the same as depriving a member of the right to vote in the General Assembly under Article 19, which is a matter for the Assembly alone.

4. The membership of the Security Council has recently been expanded to 15, that of the Economic and Social Council to 27.

5. After the return of the Soviet delegate to the Security Council, shortly after the outbreak of the war, deadlock again ensued in the Council (see Chapter 4).

6. For a further discussion of the Uniting for Peace proposals see G. L. Goodwin, *Britain and the United Nations*, London, 1957, pp. 245-55.

7. This is not, of course, to overlook the very far-reaching powers exercised by the Assembly in other fields, particularly in the field of trusteeship, of economic and social affairs, and in matters which concern the general running and financing of the organization.

8. The practice of considering abstention by a permanent member as not invalidating a resolution which has otherwise secured the necessary majority on the Council has greatly contributed to the better working of the Council by making it possible for it to act without the positive concurrence of *all* the permanent members (see Chapter 4).

9. The USA and Britain appear to concede that the General Assembly can have no 'peace-enforcement' role (which implies some element of compulsion), but only a 'peace-keeping' role (based on the consent of the countries concerned) (see Chapter 6); see R. Higgins, 'United Nations Peace-Keeping – Political and Financial Problems', in *World Today*, August 1965.

10. This is still so even when the Assembly has, quite improperly, adopted resolutions 'calling upon' member states to adopt certain policies.

11. D. Hammarskjöld, *Introduction to the Annual Report of the Secretary-General on the work of the Organization, 16 June 1960 – 15 June 1961*, General Assembly Official Records: Sixteenth Session, Supplement No. 1A (A/4800/Add. 1), p. 1.

12. S. D. Bailey, *The General Assembly of the United Nations*, London, 1960, p. 74.

13. D. Hammarskjöld, op. cit., p. 2.

14. Ibid., p. 2.

15. Ibid., p. 3.

16. See, for instance, an excellent study: R. Higgins, *The Development of International Law through the Political Organs of the United Nations*, London, 1963.

17. F. S. Northedge, 'The Authority of the United Nations General Assembly', in *International Relations*, October 1957, p. 357.

18. A fair proportion of whom (especially those from newly independent states) will probably not have received instructions from their government.

19. I.e. are 'peace-loving' states which accept the obligations contained in the Charter and are able and willing to carry them out.

20. Voting in the Assembly of the League of Nations, at least on major issues, was based upon the principle of unanimity.

21. For an examination of the different caucus arrangements see: G. Goodwin, 'The Expanding United Nations: I – 'Voting Patterns', in *International Affairs*, April 1960.

BIBLIOGRAPHY

Bailey, S. D., *The General Assembly of the United Nations: A Study of Procedure and Practice*, rev. ed., New York, 1964.

Ball, M. M., 'Bloc Voting in the Assembly', *International Organization*, February 1951.

Goodwin, G. L., 'The Expanding United Nations: I – Voting Patterns; II – Diplomatic Pressures and Techniques', *International Affairs*, April 1960 and April 1961.

Haviland, H. F., *The Political Role of the General Assembly*, New York, 1951.

Johnson, D. H. N., 'The effect of resolutions of the General Assembly of the United Nations', *The British Yearbook of International Law*, 1955-56.

Northedge, F. S., 'The Authority of the United Nations General Assembly', *International Relations*, October 1957.

Rusett, A. de, 'Large and Small States in International Organization', *International Affairs*, October 1954 and January 1955.

Sloan, F. B., 'The binding force of a recommendation of the General Assembly of the United Nations', *The British Yearbook of International Law*, 1948.

Vallat, F. A., 'The General Assembly and the Security Council of the United Nations', *The British Yearbook of International Law*, 1952.

4 THE SECURITY COUNCIL

Inis L. Claude, Jr.

The Security Council has undergone very significant changes in character and function since it began to operate almost two decades ago; it is certainly not, today, the organ defined in Article 24 of the United Nations Charter as the body bearing 'primary responsibility for the maintenance of international peace and security'. The alteration of the Council is but one aspect of the general transformation of the larger organizational system of which it is a part, and it can be understood only within the context of that broader pattern of change. It is not at all surprising that the general Organization, and each of its components, should have been caught up in a process of drastic change; for change is a law of life no less for international than for domestic institutions. Given the fundamental changes that have taken place in international politics since the Second World War, the United Nations would surely have become totally irrelevant if it had not been transformed. Moreover, change is a *sign* of life, and the changingness of the world organization may be taken as a symptom of its vitality. While most competent students would probably agree to this observation with respect to the United Nations, considered as a whole, its application to the Security Council might engender controversy, for it is generally believed that this particular organ has changed, more or less steadily, for the worse—that it has declined, decayed, fallen into decrepitude and desuetude, lost its vitality. It will be one function of this Chapter to subject this thesis to critical examination.

It is not my intention to present a comprehensive and systematic history of the Security Council, but rather to draw attention to some of the major aspects of its development as a functioning organ, concentrating on the effort to show how and why the Council has deviated from the intentions and expectations registered in the formulation of the Charter. This requires, first, an analysis of the original conception of its nature and role.

The Charter assigns a place of particular importance in the Council to the major powers, by giving them permanent seats and attributing to them, and to them *exclusively*, a capacity to veto all but procedural decisions. Moreover, it rigidifies this arrangement by listing the privileged Big Five by name, and by adopting an amendment procedure that enables any one of them to prevent a constitutional revision of that list or of the veto power. In objective terms, this commitment to rigidity adopted at San Francisco was most unfortunate, but it was clearly a political necessity. As students of world politics, the founding fathers must have known how transient is the glory of great-power status, how essential it is that a list of the major states be subject to addition and deletion. As students of international organization, they must have realized how damaging it is to prospects for the progressive development of institutions to equip the beneficiaries of special privileges with the capacity to perpetuate those privileges. But, as practitioners of the political craft of organization-building, they had to acknowledge the necessity of giving the major powers a basis for confidence that their strongly demanded and hard-won special status within the Council would not be shortly stripped away by the majority that conceded this status to them with such obvious reluctance and resentment. The great powers would have been foolish to expose themselves to the danger of the prompt reversal of the diplomatic victory which they had won at San Francisco; giving them a reliable safeguard against this danger was a political requirement for the establishment of the United Nations.

The Security Council was conceived as the dominant organ of

the United Nations in the centrally important field of high politics and security, that is, in regard to the matters deemed most directly and urgently pertinent to the issue of war and peace. This was made clear in the assignment of other matters to other organs, leaving the Security Council free, as the League Council had not been, to give single-minded attention to this crucial problem-area. It was evidenced by the explicit provisions of Articles 24 and 25, stressing the Council's 'primary responsibility' in this field and its capacity to act on behalf of all member states and to command their collaboration, as well as by the elaboration of its peace-keeping functions in Chapter VII of the Charter. It was emphasized by the provision, in Article 28, that the Council should be always ready to meet, available on short notice to deal with crises. Above all, it was indicated by the scheme, already described, for making the Council in a special sense the preserve of the major powers. While the Big Five were to share the Council chamber with six elected members, and at least two votes from the latter group were to be required to produce the decision-making majority of seven, these provisions did not radically qualify the proposition that the Council was to be, in essence, an instrument of the great powers. It was by no means pure happenstance that the Council was designated as the dominant political organ of the United Nations, and that the great powers were granted a dominant position within the Council; the linking of these two features was a crucial element in the political logic of the Charter.

Taking note of the points that the great powers were put in charge of the Security Council, and that they could operate it only on the basis of unanimity among themselves, many students of the United Nations have asserted that the Charter was built upon the fundamental assumption of great-power harmony. In this view, the founding fathers staked everything upon the sublime confidence that the major allies of the Second World War would have no serious falling out among themselves. I beg to differ with this interpretation of the Charter and of the negotiations which produced it. In my view, the framers of the Charter assumed rather that the new organization could prove effective as a device for dealing with the danger of war only if, and in so far as, and so long as, the major powers were in basic agreement, or could reach such agreement, among themselves. In short, they held that great-power harmony was certainly necessary, *not* that it was necessarily certain.

This, I think, is the clear import of the veto rule in the Security Council. This grant of extraordinary decision-blocking competence to individual great powers testifies not to the conviction of the founding fathers that unanimity among the Big Five was a reliable prospect, but to their belief that *dissension* among those powers was a distinct possibility, and that such dissension, when it occurred, would have to be treated as the decisive element in the political situation. When men go out of their way to contrive a special acknowledgment of the implications of dissent, I can only conclude that they are preparing for the contingency of discord, rather than asserting the firm expectation of concord.

It seems to me that this understanding of the meaning of the veto rule is absolutely vital to a realistic interpretation of the original conception of the nature and role of the Security Council. It is a paradox that the veto has attracted so much attention – too much, I should argue – but that it has been so little taken into account in analyses of the intended, the actual, and the possible character of the Security Council. Many of the absurdities that have appeared in interpretations of the United Nations as a political institution, and in projections of its political potential, are traceable to the ignoring of the veto rule or the failure to grasp its implications. No provision of the Charter relating to the Security Council should ever be read except in conjunction with Article 27. I should like to see Chapter VII printed with paragraph 3 of Article 27 inserted parenthetically at the end of each of its articles. Perhaps then we might be spared such analyses as those which suggest that the Security Council was designed with the intention and expectation that it would serve as a collective security agency to cope with any aggression, anywhere in the world.

The Council was conceived as an organ by means of which the great powers could exercise a joint directorate over international political affairs, in so far as they could agree upon joint policy and action. By the same token, it was designed to be inoperative in the absence of such agreement. The central implication of the veto rule is that the Council should be incapacitated for use as an instrument of some great powers against, or in opposition to the will of, one or more other great powers. More concretely, this means that the Council was to be constitutionally disabled for service to either side in a clash of policy or purpose between the United States and the Soviet Union. The veto says that you cannot outvote a great power, and you must not treat the explicit opposition of a great power as something that can be safely ignored or prudently overridden. In the scheme of the Charter and the theory of the founding fathers, this negative aspect of the Council's functioning loomed as no less important than the positive responsibility ascribed to that body; the Council could contribute to the maintenance of peace and order if it served as a vehicle for joint action *by* the Big Five, but it might disrupt the peace if it lent itself to the cause of one side or the other in a conflict *among* those powers.

It may be helpful to distinguish between two roles that are comprehended in the functional scope of the Council: the executive role and the diplomatic role. To put it differently, the Council can, in principle, serve as an agency for action and as a forum for negotiation, as an operative body and as a talk-shop. The veto power affects these two functions differently. With respect to the first, it inhibits operation. In this respect, the veto may be likened to a fuse in an electrical circuit; it is a circuit-breaker, designed to forestall disaster by interrupting the flow of action, a safety device justified by the proposition that the inconvenience caused by its operation is preferable to the risk of catastrophe that would otherwise be entailed. With respect to the second function, the veto rule serves, in principle, as a stimulant; in this case, it is better called by its quasi-official name, 'the rule of unanimity', for the demonstration of the implications of disagreement should motivate a quest for consensus. Ideally, the 'blowing out' of a fuse not only breaks the electrical circuit, but also stimulates an effort to discover and remedy the trouble that made the breaking of the circuit necessary and desirable. So it is with the veto; it has the negative function of preventing action in the face of great-power dissent, and the positive one of encouraging serious diplomatic work on the problem of dissension. These two functions, however different, are obviously connected; the exercise of the veto, blocking action, should instigate the negotiation of an agreed position, making joint action possible. This analysis suggests that the drafters of the Charter conceived the Security Council as a body which the great powers should use as a vehicle for joint action in so far as they were in agreement, and as a forum for negotiation in so far as they found themselves in disagreement.

So much for the original conception of the Council. Now, what has in fact happened to the Council? How has it functioned? How has it evolved?

The standard analysis tends to concentrate in rather broad terms on the theme of 'The Decline and Fall of the Security Council', emphasizing its displacement by the General Assembly as the central organ of the United Nations, even in its special field of political and security affairs. Attention is ordinarily drawn to the data indicating a diminution, after the first few years, in the numbers of meetings held and of substantive matters considered by the Council, and the corresponding increases in the activity of the General Assembly. The Uniting for Peace Resolution of 1950 is cited as the dramatic act by which the 'Down with the Security Council; Up with the General Assembly' trend was institutionalized. The creation of the North Atlantic Treaty Organization and the subsequent elaboration of other regional security or collective defence mechanisms are taken as evidence of the collapse of the Security Council and the retreat of statesmen from reliance upon it. With much of this line of analysis I have no quarrel, although I shall indicate some reservations. However, I should like to attempt a somewhat less grossly quantitative analysis, one based upon the two categories of function – executive and diplomatic – that I have distinguished.

In this connection the general tendency to substitute broad quantitative judgements for specific qualitative ones in evaluating the work of the United Nations is disturbing. How often one hears it said that 'The United Nations cannot do much about international problems'. From my point of view, the question should be not how much the organization can do, but *what* it can do. This applies to the Security Council as well as to the organization as a whole.

First, let us consider the course of development of the Council as an executive agency, a body capable of launching and conducting active operations in the political and security field. The record is mixed, but it must be recalled that the intentions and expectations of the founders were also mixed. The Council has displayed no real capability – and no promise of developing a capability – for organizing and managing international military action to suppress aggression undertaken or supported by a major power. It is on this basis that the claim is raised that the shift to reliance upon NATO and other regional security arrangements was a reaction to the failure of the Security Council. But this convicts the Council of failure to do what it was never intended to do. It is only by reading the Charter without paying attention to the veto provision that one can conclude that the Council was designed to provide collective security against Soviet or other great-power aggression. In fact, when it becomes inoperative in cases involving such aggression, the Security Council functions as it was designed to function. In these instances, its paralysis represents the fulfilment, not the frustration, of the scheme formulated at San Francisco. Moreover, the resort to extra-United Nations alliances can be characterized as action in conformity with the advice embedded in Article 51 of the Charter. Articles 27 and 51 should be read together; they say that when the major powers clash, the Security Council should be debarred from operating as an agency of collective security, and member states should contrive their defensive arrangements outside the United Nations.

To some extent, the collective reaction sponsored by the Council to the invasion of South Korea in mid-1950 appears to qualify my assertion that the Council has demonstrated no capacity to act against aggression backed by great powers. In this instance, the Charter's circuit-breaker failed to operate; the USSR did not reverse its current policy of boycotting meetings of the Council soon enough to prevent the initiation of military resistance to the attack, and the effective government of China had not been – as it still has not been – permitted to take its seat in the Council. Because of these unusual circumstances, neither of the two major powers which were assumed to be at least sympathetic with the North Korean cause was in a position to exercise the veto power. While this case produced an ephemeral surge of enthusiasm for the idea of institutionalizing collective security, the vicissitudes to which it ultimately led tended to reconfirm the conviction of the founding fathers that collective military measures could not safely be directed against one of the cold war camps, rather than to sustain the ambition to circumvent the fuse-box represented by Article 27.[1] Moreover, even when that ambition was at its peak, there was no expectation that the Security Council could become a reliable agency for taking enforcement action against or over the opposition of major powers; in so far as United Nations involvement in future cases of the Korean type was contemplated, the scheme – as spelled out in the Uniting for Peace Resolution – was to make the General Assembly, not the Security Council, the agency of such involvement. The Council's role in the Korean case, whether regarded with enthusiasm or with misgivings, was rightly considered exceptional if not downright freakish. Korea, in short, did not institute a trend toward the development of a general collective security role for the Security Council. So far as the Council was concerned, Korea represented an aberration rather than a precedent.

In the final analysis, the Korean case *diverted* attention from the Council as an agency for maintaining peace and security, despite the fact that, in this instance, the decision to launch collective measures had been taken by that body. Only in a superficial sense was the General Assembly the beneficiary of the shift away from the Council, because the provisions of the Uniting for Peace Resolution that purported to put the Assembly into the business of sponsoring collective resistance to aggression by great powers or their protégés proved to be untranslatable into practice, under the political circumstances that developed. More fundamentally, the shift went towards collective defence arrangements, effectively detached from the United Nations. Concretely, this meant NATO, in the first instance. The attack upon South Korea was a turning-point in the cold war, for it provided unambiguous evidence that the communist powers were prepared to resort to military invasion in order to expand their domain. The United States, as leader of the anti-communist cause, reacted by undertaking to construct collective military mechanisms to deter or defeat such initiatives. This involved not only the development of NATO, upon the foundation previously laid by the North Atlantic Treaty, but also the general elaboration of an American alliance network, and a heavy emphasis upon emancipating Western defence arrangements from any meaningful connection with the United Nations.

In subsequent years, the United States used cases involving the Organization of American States to demonstrate its insistence that Western regional agencies should operate autonomously; it not only refrained from relying upon the Security Council to act in security matters, but it also refused to tolerate any assertion by the Council of competence to concern itself with action undertaken by the O A S.[2] As this indicates, the American view has been that the Council is *worse than useless* when resistance to expansive communist moves is required; the Council cannot itself act, and it may be used to embarrass the Western coalition's countermoves.

To put it in documentary terms, the actual result of the Korean case was neither the resuscitation of Chapter VII of the Charter nor the substitution of the Uniting for Peace Resolution, but the placing of fundamental reliance upon Article 51, and, through it, upon the North Atlantic Treaty and other collective defence arrangements, buttressed by the virtual deletion of the provision, in Article 53, paragraph 1, which makes enforcement action by regional agencies subject to the authorization of the Security Council. Thus, on balance, the Korean affair actually contributed to the diminution of the role of the Security Council – or, more broadly, of the United Nations – with respect to the problem of conflict among the major powers.

While the authors of the Charter designed the Security Council to be inoperative in cases of conflict among the great powers, they evidently intended it to function as an agency of collective security in other cases. The scheme elaborated in Chapter VII suggests that the major powers were to serve, jointly, as the agents of the United Nations in maintaining the peace in instances not involving a clash among their own interests, or, to put it differently, that they should use the United Nations – in particular, the Council – as the vehicle for their collaborative endeavour to keep order in international relations. There was to be no collective security action *against* a great power, but there was to be such action, through the mechanism of the Security Council, *by* the great powers in combination. The heart of this scheme is to be found in Article 43, under which members were to make arrangements to supply the Council with forces to be used to combat aggression. The general provision of Article 43 was modified, in invisible ink, to say that the Big Five should provide the Council with the bulk of its striking power, while the lesser member states might make supplementary contributions.

The great powers lost little time in cutting out the heart of this scheme. In 1947, they engaged in one round of serious negotiations concerning the bringing into effect of Article 43, and, in fact, applied their blue pencil to the entire provision, including that part which had been invisibly inked in. In these talks, the great powers quickly reached and revealed the conclusion that they did not trust each other to intervene in troubled situations under the mandate of the Security Council.[3] Briefly, those who had been designated as the official spreaders of United Nations oil upon troubled international waters suspected each other of the intention to *fish* in those waters; East and West accused each other of planning to supply trawlers rather than tankers for the Council's fleet. This mutual suspicion eliminated any real prospect that the limited scheme of collective security enforced by the great powers, collaborating within the context of the Security Council, would be translated from Charter design into actual practice. For purposes of enforcement action, the Council had been conceived as the instrument of great-power collaboration; under the political conditions that rapidly developed in the postwar era, no such collaboration was forthcoming.

In terms of the classic categories of political action by international institutions, this reduced the Council to the function of promoting the pacific settlement of disputes. It is extremely difficult to evaluate the work of any international organ in this field, for so much depends upon the attitudes and policies of the parties to disputes, of interested parties on the sidelines, and of states which may be described as disinterested in the disputes themselves but interested in the effect of the disputes upon the general stability of international relations. When a dispute is settled after the intervention of an international agency, who can say whether that intervention was successful or superfluous – whether it succeeded in producing the changes in policy and in mobilizing the pressures requisite for the settlement, or whether its apparent success was fostered by developments that would have occurred in any case? When such intervention fails, who can say whether or not the political situation had left open any possibilities of success? All judgements in this realm must remain speculative or, at least, controversial. Evaluation is further complicated by the relativity of success and failure; the almost-peaceful-but-somewhat-violent settlement of disputes, and the peaceful perpetuation or successful encapsulation of disputes, deserve some measure of credit.

Beyond these general difficulties of measuring the effectiveness of pacific settlement efforts, there is a special problem in evaluating the work of the Security Council, posed by the fact that the Council has so seldom monopolized United Nations activity bearing upon a given dispute. Typically, the General Assembly or the Secretary-General, or both, have become involved in the management of efforts to promote peaceful solution of problems initially brought before the Council, thus complicating the task of determining how much credit to assign to the latter body for whatever success may have been achieved. One may evade the problem by talking in terms of the United Nations as a composite institution. It is tempting, and perhaps justifiable, to single out the Secretary-General as the hero in these affairs, and to consider the Council as the least effective of the organs involved. It should not be too readily assumed, however, that the intrusion of institutional reinforcements always indicates the incapacity and failure of the Council, rather than the working of a pragmatic wisdom that seeks to exploit the value of meshing the capabilities of the political organs of the United Nations.

With these reservations, I would endorse the continuing validity of the judgement expressed in 1958 by Leland M. Goodrich, that 'the Security Council has had very limited effectiveness' in the realm of pacific settlement.[4] It is all too clear that the Council has been used more to provide a battleground than to supply facilities for peace-making in the cold war, and that conflict among its major members has minimized their role as a peace-making team in cases involving other states.

Moving outside the classic categories of collective political action, we find that the United Nations has evolved a new category – that described by Dag Hammarskjöld as 'preventive diplomacy'. This kind of action is an outgrowth of the function of pacific settlement, but it deserves to be treated as a distinct development, an innovation in large degree, because it reflects and undertakes to implement the central concern to assist the cold war antagonists in avoiding a collision within a trouble zone, rather than simply to promote a settlement by the parties locally involved. I should describe it as a technique for containing the cold war, rather than for pacific settlement in the classic sense. In striking contrast to the scheme of the Charter, preventive diplomacy involves, in principle, the *exclusion* of the major powers from its operation; it represents the effort to keep the giants *apart* through the workings of the United Nations, instead of to harness them *together* to do the work of the organization. It relies upon the lesser states, and those least committed to cold war alignments, to serve as the work horses of the United Nations; they become the chief producers, and the great powers the foremost consumers, of the United Nations brand of security.[5]

As in the case of pacific settlement, the record of the Security Council in initiating and managing the exercise of preventive diplomacy is entangled with that of the General Assembly and the Secretary-General. Thus far, it is probably fair to assign first place in the exercise of this function to the Secretary-General, and last to the Council; certainly preventive diplomacy cannot be described as a type of political action associated primarily with the Security Council.

Nevertheless, there are compelling reasons for asserting that it *should* be intimately associated with the Council – and with the principle of unanimity enshrined in the Charter's provisions concerning that body. Preventive diplomacy is pre-eminently a service that may be rendered by the United Nations to the major cold war competitors, but only with their consent or acquiescence, only if they are sufficiently impressed by the dangerousness of hot war to recognize the mutuality of their interest in keeping the cold war cold, only if they are inspired, by confidence in the political impartiality of the executive mechanism of the United Nations, to welcome its management of peace-keeping operations, and only if they are reassured by the possession of safeguards against the diversion of such operations to serve interests which they regard as inimical to their own. This is to say that the veto principle is very nearly as essential to the control of preventive diplomacy as to the control of collective enforcement action – which is to say that political realism demands that the Security Council function as the central decision-making apparatus in relation to preventive diplomacy. This means, of course, that the disagreement of the great powers must be taken as seriously for decision-making purposes as their unanimity; opposition among them must be treated as a limiting factor to be respected, not as an impediment to be hurdled.

This view is not derived exclusively from theoretical analysis, but represents also my reading of the lessons implicit in the experience of the United Nations in the two major cases of preventive diplomacy, Suez and the Congo. The latter case, in particular, is at least as valuable for its revelation of the dangers and difficulties of preventive diplomacy as for its demonstration of the usefulness of that kind of action. The troubles which stem from the Congo case – and they have been, and remain, severe ones – seem to me to be traceable primarily to the illusion that the disaffection and opposition of great powers can be ignored or overridden in the exercise of preventive diplomacy. It was all very well for the Secretary-General to defy the Soviet charge that he ran the Congo operation as a pro-Western enterprise, but he broke his political back and gravely endangered the future of his office in so doing. It is all very correct for the United States, backed by official expressions of the views of the World Court and the General Assembly, to insist that the USSR, France, and other delinquents be held responsible for paying their shares of the costs of UNEF and ONUC, but, whatever effect this may or may not have upon the settlement of old debts, it is unlikely to promote the further development of the capacity of the United Nations to implement preventive diplomacy. Whatever the *legal* position may be with regard to the location of financial authority within the United Nations, the *political* position is that no state will pay for major United Nations activities which it regards as inimical to its interests. As an American, I must say that I do not expect my country to be the first major power to renounce that position – nor do I expect it to have much success in pressing the Soviety Union to be the first.

These difficulties suggest that, while there may be legal and constitutional evasions, there is no realistic escape from the necessity of great-power consensus if the United Nations is to become a reliable practitioner of the art of preventive diplomacy. This is the basis for my contention that the Security Council, an organ founded explicitly upon the recognition of the decisive importance of dissent by a great power, is the appropriate focal point for the control and direction of this new and promising form of peace-keeping action. The Assembly and the Secretary-General may be usefully involved in the operations – but to assist in securing and implementing great-power consensus, not to evade the necessity for formulating and maintaining that consensus.

This emphasis upon consensus reintroduces the subject of the diplomatic role of the Security Council, which now demands attention. As I have suggested, the Council was designed to serve as an instrument of action whenever a unanimous vote of the great powers revealed the existence of a consensus, and as a forum for negotiation whenever the use of the veto revealed the absence of a consensus. In the era of the cold war, the Council has had more frequent occasion to function in the latter capacity than in the former.

It cannot be said that the Council has been notably successful, or even particularly prominent, as a negotiating body. Again, as in the case of pacific settlement, precise evaluation of the role of the Council is difficult. Points of agreement that appear to have been worked out in the Council may in fact have been simply registered there, after having been negotiated elsewhere; on the other hand, agreements and understandings – formal and informal, explicit and tacit – that have been reached between the major cold war antagonists may owe more than any analysis of the record could demonstrate to the effects of debates and consultations within the context of the Security Council. Nevertheless, it does not appear that the Council has functioned very impressively as a focal point of consensus-building among the great powers.

We may regard this as understandable; after all, we are sufficiently familiar with the toughness of the issues that have divided the powers since the Second World War to look with some tolerance upon the fact that they have not yielded to the ministrations of the Council. What may require more explanation is the relative lack of prominence of the Council as a diplomatic centre for the great powers.

This is attributable, in part, to attitudes exhibited by the United States. Although the veto formula was largely made in Washington, the United States lost little time after San Francisco in repudiating the philosophy of the veto. On the whole, the United States has treated the exercise of the veto power by the USSR as a challenge to be overcome, rather than a signal indicating the need for negotiation. The general American reaction to Soviet opposition in the Security Council has been to find a means of circumvention, not to launch a quest for consensus; the United States has frequently refused to accept the proposition that the Soviet Union cannot be outvoted, or that its opposition cannot be overridden. Hence, parliamentary victories in the Assembly have been preferred to diplomatic efforts to dissolve disagreements in the Council.

In the last few years, the American urge to score triumphs of this sort has been supplemented and even overshadowed by a passion for making the United Nations an agency for action; it is not enough to secure the adoption by the Assembly of resolutions that have run afoul of the Soviet veto in the Council, but the United Nations must undertake executive operations, whether the USSR approves them or not. The organization must not be permitted to deteriorate into a mere debating society; its 'capacity to act', its ability to 'make internationalism operational' must be developed, and the criterion for every action affecting the United Nations must be, 'does it enhance, or does it tend to destroy, the Organization's capacity to take executive action?'[6] Whatever the merits of this emphasis, it should be noted that it tends to subordinate the diplomatic function of the Council to the executive function. Indeed, it almost suggests that there is something ignoble about haggling with a dissenting great power; the great thing is to get on with the action, despite opposition, not to permit dissent to reduce the United Nations to the level of a talk-shop, a mere diplomatic conference. It is this sort of enthusiastic activism that leads the United States to say to the Soviets, in effect, 'The Congo operation frustrated communist plans to take over the heart of Africa, and you should of course be willing to pay your share of the cost'.

It would seem to me a much sounder position to recognize that the diplomatic function must be linked to, not subordinated to, the executive function; in my view, the usefulness of the United Nations as an agency for action is dependent upon its capacity to promote agreement, rather than to override disagreement, as to the nature of the action which it should undertake.

The relative lack of prominence of the Security Council as a centre for negotiation is not by any means attributable wholly to American attitudes and policies. If the United States has lacked incentive to use the Council for this purpose, other states have felt that the Council was inappropriate for this purpose. This view has its merits; the composition of the Council has not been, and is not, such as to commend it for utilization as the supreme organ of global diplomacy. It should surprise no one that the Soviet Union has found the Council unattractive as a negotiating forum, given the fact that Western and pro-Western states have consistently held such a preponderant number of its seats. The USSR enjoyed the company of one other communist state in the Council from 1946 through 1949; in the 1950s, the only communist state other than the USSR to serve in the Council, for a total of three years, was Yugoslavia – not precisely a member of the Soviet bloc! Only since 1960 has it been possible again for members of the Soviet bloc to win election to the Council, and then in each case only for half of the normal two-year term. The second communist government to assume power in a major state, the Chinese communist régime, has been required to stand aside for a decade and a half, while its predecessor, surely one of the lamest ducks in the history of international affairs, has continued to occupy the Chinese seat. In recent years, the United States has displayed some anxiety concerning the possibility that it might lose its accustomed capacity to mobilize, with reasonable assurance, the critical minimum of seven votes in the Council. By contrast, the Soviet Union has more often than not been the lone communist wolf in the Council, enjoying occasionally the small blessing of being allowed one comrade. Under these circumstances, it is small wonder that the USSR has not taken the Council seriously as a focal point for negotiation.

A somewhat similar dissatisfaction with the Security Council has developed among the new states, as they have crowded into the Assembly and discovered that the Council is too small to afford them adequate representation. Their reaction to this situation took the form of a proposed Charter amendment, approved by the Assembly at its Eighteenth Session, providing for the creation of four additional places in the Council.[7] It is clear that the Council, as it now stands, fails to inspire a general conviction that it is a suitable body for use as the highest diplomatic organ of the United Nations.

Despite all this, there is some evidence that the Council is in process of gaining a new diplomatic significance. The Secretary-General recently asserted that 'The Security Council, which for some years seemed in danger of paralysis from the stresses and strains of the East–West struggle, has re-emerged recently to resume the key role in dealing with matters affecting peace and security which was allotted to it by the Charter . . .'.[8]

In part, this reflects a retreat from the General Assembly, which, regardless of its merits as an increasingly comprehensive collection of spokesmen for the world's governments, is being transformed by the expansion of its membership into a less predictable and manageable voting machine, a less workable instrument for the direction and control of executive operations, and a less likely setting for serious diplomatic consideration of delicate and complicated issues. Even though the Council has the structural defects that we have noted, it provides a convenient and readily available context for negotiation within the framework of the United Nations. The key to the explanation of the trend towards greater utilization of the Council is to be found, I suspect, in the increasing negotiability of many of the issues between East and West, and growing awareness by the major powers of the essentiality of agreement among themselves. The American disposition to override Soviet dissent is more instinctive than rational; in the concrete case, when the dangers are grave or the opportunities seem great, the United States tends to turn, however reluctantly, to confront the necessity of coming to terms with the Soviet position. The lesson of the postwar era is not that the framers of the Charter were mistaken in the view, expressed in Article 27, that decisive significance should be attributed to disagreement among the great powers; rather, everything that has happened since 1945 has confirmed and emphasized the correctness of that view. Responsible statesmen have gradually come to the realization that indulgence of the urge to ignore that lesson is a luxury that they cannot afford.

For all its success in reducing the negative effect of the Soviet veto in the Security Council, the United States has discovered that there can be no ultimately successful evasion of the implications of Soviet dissent. That dissent derives its importance not from provisions of the Charter, but from the facts of world politics; it may be deprived of decisive effect in the United Nations, but not of decisive significance in international relations. In short, the dissenting great power must be taken into account, just as Mount Everest must be climbed, simply because it is *there*. The weight of this point, as it applies to the USSR, is coming to be widely appreciated, and the denial of its application to communist China is becoming more and more difficult for the United States to maintain. If the usefulness of the Security Council is increasing, and is to be maximized in the future, the West's growing recognition of the necessity for doing diplomatic business with the East will figure prominently in the analysis of that trend.

It seems to me fundamentally erroneous to suggest that the

scheme of the founding fathers regarding the role of the Council as an executive agency has been proved seriously defective, and that the Council has had simply to fall back upon the secondary function of providing a diplomatic forum. On the contrary, the Council has conformed to the original plan in so far as it has been reduced to inactivity by disagreement among the major powers. Its greatest deviation from initial expectations has been its failure to serve effectively as a diplomatic device for promoting the resolution of such disagreement. The diplomatic function is of *primary*, not secondary, importance – and it is not a function upon which the Council can merely 'fall back', an alternative role which is available when action proves unattainable. Rather, it is a crucial function which poses difficult requirements of its own. The value of the Council has been most significantly limited, thus far, by failure to meet the requirements for meaningful negotiation. Its greatest promise for the future lies in the hope that the present trend towards satisfaction of those requirements will be fully realized.

As I hope this analysis has made clear, the Security Council has not developed significantly as a corporate entity, displaying an emergent will and purpose that can be identified with it as a collective organ, or even a corporate jealousy of its status and jurisdiction within the United Nations system. Champions of international organization may be inclined to deplore the former aspect of the Council's development, and to welcome the latter. Actually, the two aspects of the evolution of corporateness go hand in hand, and the failure of the Council to assert a kind of institutional vested interest is but a symptom of its failure to achieve collective identity in the positive sense. Selfishness, however deplorable, is evidence of selfhood; the Council's lack of the former quality indicates its deficiency in the latter respect.

This deficiency is not difficult to explain. The Council might have become the collective guardian of the international order, as the framers of the Charter evidently intended, if the major powers had maintained an essential harmony of interest and unity of global purpose. Functioning as the acknowledged directors of the international political system, they might have seen their agreed purposes translated through the institutional medium of the Council into the collective will of an international Board of Directors. This possibility was revoked by the cold war. As the deep-seated conflict between East and West emerged, it became clear that the Security Council was destined to serve not as the instrument of a global condominium by the great powers, but as one of several arenas within which they would do political and ideological battle. The giants came to regard the Council less as their joint property, whose value they had a common interest in enhancing, than as a battlefield which they might or might not choose, depending upon pragmatic calculations of advantage. More often than not, their calculations led them to prefer other institutional locations for the waging of the cold war; within the United Nations, the General Assembly was the primary beneficiary of the urge for a change of venue. This shift to the Assembly was abetted by the smaller states, which found that body far superior to the Council as a mechanism for the exercise of their growing influence in world affairs.

In short, throughout most of the history of the United Nations, there has been no substantial group of states displaying consistent interest in developing the status and role of the Security Council within the United Nations system. The Western powers have sought other forums, to escape the frustrating impact of the Soviet veto. States without guaranteed membership in the Council have favoured the Assembly, with its seats and votes for all. The Soviet bloc might be thought to form an exception, and this view is supported by the fact that the USSR has obviously valued the unique opportunity to safeguard its interests which is provided by the unanimity rule in the Security Council. However, not even the Soviet Union has consistently preferred the

Council; when its preoccupation with defensive tactics has given way to the urge to win political victories, it has looked to the larger, more public, forum of the Assembly. In any case, the maxim that it takes two to make a fight carries with it the implication that it takes two to confine a fight to a particular location; the role of the Security Council has remained under-developed because political antagonists have seldom found it mutually acceptable as the locus of their confrontation. The incentive of one party to use the Council has frequently served as a disincentive for the other.

The stunting of the Council's institutional stature is ultimately attributable to the political motivations and diplomatic tactics of the various states and blocs that constitute the United Nations, not to the organization's constitutional provisions or to broad principles of institutional development functioning independently of national foreign policies. By the same token, the Council may yet gain a new prominence. In so far as the major powers come to act upon the growing conviction that the United Nations can serve each of them best by facilitating the stabilization of their relationships with each other, they may well turn increasingly to the Council, exploiting its potentiality as a centre for meaningful negotiation. In so far as other states, particularly those newly carved out of colonial empires, come to believe that their stake in general international order exceeds their interest in pressing the multifaceted process of change which has been their primary concern, they may give greater emphasis to the development of their potential contribution to the functioning of the Council as a supreme diplomatic organ. The Security Council is unlikely to become the corporate expression of the will of a joint directorate of the international community. It may become a more useful and significant part of the apparatus by which the major powers undertake to promote, and the lesser states to encourage and assist, the development of a less fragile basis for peace and order than the world has recently known.

TEXT REFERENCES

1. Inis L. Claude, Jr., 'The United Nations and the Use of Force', *International Conciliation*, No. 532, March 1961, pp. 357-64.

2. Inis L. Claude, Jr., 'The OAS, the UN and the United States', *International Conciliation*, No. 547, March 1964.

3. 'The United Nations and the Use of Force,' pp. 346-55.

4. Leland M. Goodrich, 'The UN Security Council', *International Organization*, Vol. XII, No. 3 (1958), p. 279.

5. For a fuller elaboration of the theory of preventive diplomacy, and commentary on instances of its application, see Chapter 14 in the third edition of my *Swords Into Ploughshares*, New York, 1964.

6. The quotations are from a speech by Assistant Secretary of State Harlan Cleveland, Department of State Press Release No. 129, 11 March 1961.

7. UN General Assembly Resolution 1991A (XVIII), 17 December 1963.

8. U. Thant, 'Strengthening of the United Nations', *UN Chronicle*, May 1964, p. 83.

BIBLIOGRAPHY

Burns, A. L. and Heathcote, N., *Peace-Keeping by UN Forces*, New York, 1963.

Dallin, A., *The Soviet Union at the United Nations*, New York, 1962.

Goodrich, L. M., 'The UN Security Council', *International Organization*, Summer 1958, pp. 273-87.

Goodrich, L. M., and Simons, A. P., *The United Nations and the Maintenance of International Peace and Security*, Washington: The Brookings Institution, 1955.

Hasluck, P., *Workshop of Security*, Melbourne, 1948.

Jiménez de Aréchaga, E., *Voting and the Handling of Disputes in the Security Council*, New York: Carnegie Endowment for International Peace, 1950.

Lee, D. E., 'The Genesis of the Veto', *International Organization*, February 1947, pp. 33-42.

Moldaver, A., 'Repertoire of the Veto in the Security Council', *International Organization*, Spring 1957, pp. 261-74.

Nicholas, H. G., *The United Nations as a Political Institution*, London, 1959.

Padelford, N. J., 'The Use of the Veto', *International Organization*, June 1948, pp. 227-46.

5 THE UNITED NATIONS SECRETARIAT

Sydney D. Bailey

During the twenty years since the San Francisco Conference, the United Nations has been adapted to meet new needs. The most important development in the political field has been the concept of peace-keeping by consent. Part of the credit for this change must be accorded to the UN Secretariat.

The founding fathers of the United Nations, with the failures of the League of Nations in mind, were naturally preoccupied with the problem of aggression and the need to provide for collective enforcement action. It was Mr Hammarskjöld's particular contribution to realize that, as the Cold War waned, the most pressing international problems did not always arise from threats of direct aggression by the super-powers. He knew, moreover, that the United Nations had little possibility of exerting a direct and immediate influence on major problems between the power blocs, but he believed that the UN could be successful in insulating difficulties arising in the Third World.

In the introduction to his annual report in 1960, he elaborated this concept of 'preventive diplomacy'. The main efforts of the United Nations, he held, should 'aim at keeping newly arising conflicts outside the sphere of bloc differences'. If a power vacuum should arise between the blocs, the aim of the United Nations should be to fill the vacuum.

> The ways in which a vacuum can be filled by the United Nations . . . differ from case to case, but they have this in common: temporarily, and pending the filling of a vacuum by normal means, the United

Nations enters the picture on the basis of its non-commitment to any power bloc, so as to provide to the extent possible a guarantee in relation to all parties against initiatives from others.

This was to challenge traditional ideas about the role of power. The diagnosis was clear: a power vacuum between the blocs. The remedy was vague in the extreme: 'the United Nations enters the picture on the basis of its non-commitment . . .'. A power vacuum was to be filled with a moral symbol.

The genius of Hammarskjöld was that, through his office of Secretary-General, he made this idea work, not in all cases, it is true, and often with only partial success. He adapted for international purposes the methods used by Gandhi before him and Martin Luther King since. He sought to persuade people and governments to act in ways they had not originally intended, not by the threat of physical coercion, but by the presence of a moral symbol. Even the most powerful forms of UN 'presence' were to use force only as a last resort and when all other methods had failed. Although Hammarskjöld did not have at his disposal any of the usual instruments of power, he exercised an extraordinary influence on the course of events, and he was able to communicate to others his own conviction that the United Nations represented a new form of power, which could be used to advance the universal common good.

The idea of peace-keeping by consent had not been explicitly provided for in the Charter, but it had not been explicitly forbidden either. The difficulty was that the Secretary-General was increasingly brought into the political arena and, in the case of the Congo, Hammarskjöld and his colleagues were forced to take political decisions when the policy-making organs were unable to agree.

It had always been intended that the Secretary-General should be more than simply an administrator. The Secretariat is responsible for preparing the ground for meetings of the policy-making organs and implementing their decisions. But the responsibilities of the Secretary-General and staff do not end there.

The Secretary-General, under Article 99 of the Charter, is empowered to bring to the attention of the Security Council any matter which in his opinion may threaten world peace. He is, in a sense, to act as the eyes and ears of the organization and its members. If a threatening situation arises and no member state brings the matter to the attention of the Security Council, the Secretary-General can insist that the Council consider the matter. He thus needs to be fully informed about difficulties before they actually arise, so that he will be in a position to decide whether to exercise his formal rights under Article 99. Hammarskjöld explicitly invoked this concept of Article 99 to justify his visit to Tunisia in 1961.

> It is obvious that the duties following from this Article cannot be fulfilled unless the Secretary-General, in case of need, is in a position to form a personal opinion about the relevant facts of the situation which may represent such a threat [to international peace and security].

It was only in relation to the Congo that Hammarskjöld resorted to Article 99 in order to draw the Security Council's attention to a potential threat to world peace.

From a legal point of view, Article 98 of the Charter has proved more interesting than Article 99. Article 98 requires the Secretary-General to undertake certain routine administrative duties, and adds that he shall perform 'such other functions as are entrusted to him' by the policy-making organs. The functions entrusted to the Secretary-General under Article 98 need not be administrative in any narrow sense; they can be diplomatic or operational. It was presumably this Article which provided the legal basis for the authority granted to the Secretary-General in connection with the UN Emergency Force in the Middle East.

The crucial role now played by the Secretariat, and in particular by the Secretary-General, arises from weaknesses in the functioning of the United Nations. The founders intended that the Security Council should have primary responsibility for maintaining world peace. The Council was to have at its disposal an international military force to give effect to its decisions. The great powers were to have permanent membership of the Council, with the right to veto most substantive decisions.

It may well be that an enlarged Security Council, in which the Chinese seat is occupied by a representative of the People's Republic of China, will in the future perform the functions which had been envisaged for it at San Francisco. During the early years of the United Nations, however, it was a major aim of United States policy to devise procedures for transferring responsibility to the General Assembly should the Security Council be deadlocked. These attempts culminated in the Uniting for Peace Resolution of 1950, and the Assembly has now met in emergency session four times under the terms of this resolution.

To call on the Assembly for prompt and decisive action in an emergency is to ask it to perform functions for which it was not designed, and the passage of time adds to the difficulties. The Assembly has become increasingly unwieldy as the number of members has grown; it has more business to discharge every year; oratory is too often mistaken for diplomacy, and votes for agreement; and in most respects the Assembly lacks the legal authority to take binding decisions.

The General Assembly is as likely as the Security Council to find itself unable to act promptly and decisively, though usually for different reasons. The difficulties which have arisen over the financing of peace-keeping operations emphasize the fact that procedural gimmicks are not of themselves sufficient to persuade a great power to act in a way which it believes to be contrary to its interests.

The authority which Hammarskjöld exercised was due, in part at any rate, to the inability of the policy-making organs to reach clear and detailed decisions. In such circumstances, it was convenient to conceal the fact that agreement on details was lacking by asking the Secretary-General, in the most general terms, to pursue aims which were unobjectionable by means which were unspecified. A good example of a decision of this sort is that taken unanimously by the General Assembly in August 1958, asking the Secretary-General to make forthwith, in consultation with the governments concerned and in accordance with the Charter, such practical arrangements as would adequately help to uphold the purposes and principles of the Charter in relation to Lebanon and Jordan, and thereby facilitate the early withdrawal of foreign troops from the two countries.

While there has been a steady development of the functions conferred on the Secretary-General by the policy-making organs under Article 98 of the Charter, there has also been an increase in the duties of the Secretary-General as a result of initiatives taken by him without such explicit authority. Action of this kind may be undertaken at the request of one or more governments, or because the Secretary-General himself considers that some initiative on his part would promote the aims of the Charter. On a number of occasions, for example, the Secretary-General has designated a special representative to assist two governments to compose their differences, without seeking explicit authority for such action from a policy-making organ.

It is inevitable that some decisions of this kind should contain the seeds of difficulties in the future. The Secretary-General may be told to accomplish certain tasks and then be denied the men, money and diplomatic support necessary for success. The governments on whose behalf the operation is undertaken may withhold co-operation, or seek to exploit the presence of the United Nations for purposes incompatible with the original decisions. The Secretary-General may encounter problems which were not foreseen when the original mandate was conferred, and yet may find it impossible to secure from the policy-making organs a clarification or extension of his instructions. In such circumstances, he will naturally seek for guidance in the Charter or in previous decisions of organs of the United Nations or in generally accepted principles of international law. In the absence of such guidance, however, the Secretary-General cannot refuse to act merely because someone will object if he does something. Inaction may be as decisive in its consequences as action. When it comes to the crunch, he has no alternative but to act 'on his own risk', as Hammarskjöld put it. An international policeman's lot is not a happy one.

Changes in the role of the Secretariat have been accompanied by changes in its composition. If the Secretary-General and staff are to play an active and positive role in the affairs of the United Nations, it is essential to maintain the highest standards for recruiting and promoting staff. The founders did not leave the composition of the Secretariat to chance. It was laid down in the Charter that the Secretary-General should be 'appointed by the General Assembly upon the recommendation of the Security Council'. The recommendation of the Security Council requires the affirmative votes of the five permanent members; it is, in other words, subject to veto. The practice has been for the Security Council to meet in private until it is in a position to recommend one candidate for appointment, and for the Assembly to approve the recommendation.

All other members of the Secretariat are appointed by the Secretary-General, in such a way as to meet the requirements of Articles 100 and 101 of the Charter and subject only to 'regulations' established by the General Assembly. Article 100 of the Charter states that the responsibilities of the Secretariat are 'exclusively international'; staff members are to be 'responsible only to the Organization' and shall neither seek nor receive instructions from any government or authority external to the United Nations. Article 101 seeks to establish priorities for selecting staff. The paramount consideration is to be the need to secure the highest standards of efficiency, competence and integrity; but due regard is also to be paid to the importance of recruiting on as wide a geographical basis as possible.

The requirement that the staff shall be independent and international has always been difficult to implement. It depends on a distinction being made between a man's inward thoughts and his outward actions. This distinction is made by a judge wherever the rule of law operates; it is also made by an umpire in cricket. But the UN Secretariat is not composed of judges, and the nations of the world are not playing cricket. Many members of the Secretariat are either on loan from national governments or are former national civil servants, and in a national civil service it is taken for granted that its members promote the national interest. An international official is not expected to give up his private opinions or national prejudices, but he is asked to subordinate these to the interests of the United Nations so long as he is a member of the Secretariat.

The requirement that due regard should be paid to the importance of selecting staff on as wide a geographical basis as possible was especially difficult to apply in the early days, and Trygve Lie had no alternative but to recruit largely from Western countries. In 1946, two-thirds of the internationally-recruited staff at UN headquarters in New York were drawn from the United States, Britain, and France. The Secretary-General was Norwegian; of the eight senior posts in the Secretariat, three were held by West Europeans and one by a citizen of the United States.

There were obvious practical reasons for this state of affairs. During the initial period of post-war reconstruction, all governments were reluctant to release their best people for service with international agencies. Lie relates in his memoirs how difficult it was to find able people. The Big Five had agreed that a national of each of them should have a senior post, but Lie comments that the British government 'took an approach which was so solicitous of my right to appoint whatever British subject I chose . . . as to be not quite helpful'.

In 1948 a formula was devised whereby each member state was allocated a 'desirable range' for the number of its nationals in the Secretariat. This formula was based on budgetary assessments, not because it was thought that wealth should be the determining factor, but because the budgetary assessments were themselves fixed by reference to a combination of relevant criteria. Flexibility was provided by allowing an upward or downward variation within 25 per cent of the budgetary assessment, except that there was no upward variation for countries contributing more than 10 per cent of the budget. The absence of an upward variation originally applied to the United States and the United Kingdom, but in 1953 the Soviet assessment rose above 10 per cent, and the following year the British assessment fell below that figure. No country with fewer than four nationals in the Secretariat was to be regarded as over-represented. Gradually the original staff were screened, and the best people offered permanent appointments.

The great influx of new UN Members began with the 'package deal' of 1955, by which sixteen states were admitted. There have been a further forty new admissions since 1955. The new member states want to see their nationals in UN employment and are often frustrated to discover that, so long as it is regarded as improper to terminate the contracts of competent staff merely to create vacancies, the process of changing the overall geographical composition of the Secretariat is bound to be slow. With a total staff of about 1,500 subject to geographical distribution, there are about 150 vacancies in any one year, many of which are to replace short-term staff from Eastern Europe, the Middle East, Africa, Asia and Latin America. It is only in filling the remaining vacancies that the Secretary-General can change the overall geographical balance within the Secretariat. In the period 1962–65, for example, only 108 probationary or long-term appointments were made; the other appointments, totalling 374, were for short terms and mainly to replace other short-term staff.

In 1962, the General Assembly adopted a new formula for fixing the 'desirable range' of staff members from each member state. Each country has a minimum range of one to five posts, and population is given greater weight than was formerly the case. The effect of the new formula has been to increase the 'desirable range' for the countries of the Afro-Asian area and Latin America, and to reduce it for both Eastern and Western Europe and for North America. The number of British nationals in the Secretariat declined from 152 in 1956 to 110 in 1965 (of whom six were from non-self-governing territories). In course of time, the number of British nationals in the Secretariat is likely to fall to about 80.

There has been a general disposition in the West to aim at limiting the number of short-term staff in the Secretariat. Some assignments are temporary and must necessarily be filled by short-term staff; but on balance the advantage lies in limiting the percentage of short-term staff to something like one-fifth or one-quarter of the total. The process of adjusting to the special conditions of an international Secretariat is not easy, and some staff members serving for only two years never succeed in making a useful contribution to the work of the Secretariat. The proportion of non-career staff increased from 11 per cent in 1956 to 28 per cent in 1965; it is to be hoped that the proportion of short-term staff can fall.

The need for a first-rate career service is now even greater than was envisaged at San Francisco twenty years ago. The idea of war as merely an extension of diplomacy is too hazardous in the nuclear age. States are having to live indefinitely with situations which in earlier generations would have seemed intolerable. Peace-keeping techniques are being devised which depend to a great extent on the skill and wisdom of international officials.

How far has the role of the Secretariat evolved with time, and how much more may it need to do so in the future?

The provisions of the Charter in relation to the Secretariat have in general stood the test of time. There have been sporadic pressures to abandon the principle of the neutrality of United Nations staff, particularly in the 'troika' proposal of 1960-61. This would not only have introduced the veto into the administration, but also have made members of the Secretariat into representatives of national or ideological points of view. The 'troika' proposal is not now actively promoted, though some of the malaise of which it was a symptom remains.

The importance of the office of Secretary-General has increased beyond what was envisaged at San Francisco, though without contravening the Charter. The enhancement of the role of Secretary-General during the late 1950s was to some extent due to the genius of the holder of the office, but a major factor was the state of international immobility and deadlock which had begun to become apparent. The major powers had achieved a rough strategic balance and were increasingly aware of a common interest in preventing conflicts in the Third World from escalating. Attempts to circumvent the veto in the Security Council had proved irrelevant, since the power realities were not changed merely by procedural devices. It was in this situation that Dag Hammarskjöld became the main instrument of the UN in its efforts to contain and insulate local conflicts, thus giving the great powers a respectable excuse for limiting or even foregoing intervention, and for giving aid under multilateral auspices.

By a series of improvised responses to diverse emergencies, the United Nations has begun to develop a code for peace-keeping. An important advance occurred in the Cyprus case, when the mediation and police functions were separated, although both remained under the direct authority of the Secretary-General. Peace-keeping hath her victories no less renown'd than war, but it is paradoxical that the more effective the United Nations is in its peace-keeping functions, the less the incentive to achieve peaceful settlements. Disputes like that between Israel and her Arab neighbours fester year after year.

U Thant, like his predecessors, has appointed Under-Secretaries and other staff on a wide geographical basis, while maintaining the principle that the staff are responsible only to the United Nations. With the many additions to the number of member states during the past decade, it has become increasingly difficult to ensure the necessary geographical distribution within the Secretariat. The number of staff members from Eastern Europe is still below the 'desirable range' for the region, but this is not because of any discrimination on the part of the Secretary-General or the Office of Personnel. It is impossible to make long-term career appointments from Eastern Europe, so that a sustained effort is needed merely to maintain the number of East Europeans at the present level. In any case, candidates nominated for temporary appointment by the governments of the region, the only method of recruiting East Europeans, may not have the particular technical skills which are in short supply in the Secretariat.

An important task now is to strengthen the senior echelons in the Secretariat (Under-Secretaries, Directors, and Principal Officers). If the United Nations is to respond to the demands which will be made in the years ahead, it will be essential for member states to have confidence in the integrity and competence not only of the Secretary-General, but also of senior staff in all departments. The United Nations needs those who are also in demand in their own countries.

Two members of a committee appointed by the League of Nations reported in 1930 that there could be no 'international man' without a super-state. Today the United Nations and its agencies employ tens of thousands of professional men and women in the secretariats and in field operations. These persons, at their best, are citizens of the world, seeking to substitute large for narrow interests. The 'international man' now exists.

BIBLIOGRAPHY

Bailey, S. D., *The Secretariat of the United Nations*, second ed., London and New York, 1964.

Hammarskjöld, D., *The International Civil Servant in Law and in Fact*, Oxford, 1961.

Hammarskjöld, D., *Markings*. Trans. by Sjöberg, L. and Auden, W. H., London and New York, 1964.

International Civil Service Advisory Board. Reports: 'Recruitment Methods and Standards for the United Nations and the Specialized Agencies' (1950), 'In-Service Training in the United Nations and the Specialized Agencies' (1952), 'Standards of Conduct in the International Civil Service' (1954).

Langrod, G., *The International Civil Service*, Leyden, 1963.

Lie, T., *In the Cause of Peace*, New York, 1954.

Ranshofen-Wertheimer, E. F., *The International Secretariat*, Washington, 1945.

Review of the Activities and Organization of the Secretariat. Report of the Committee of Experts and Comments of the Secretary-General. General Assembly Official Records, Sixteenth Session, Annexes Agenda item 61, A/4776 and A/4794, 1961.

Schwebel, S. M., *The Secretary-General of the United Nations*, Cambridge (Mass.), 1952.

Scott, F. R., 'The World's Civil Service', *International Conciliation*, No. 496, New York, 1954.

The Internal Administration of an International Secretariat, London, 1945.

The International Secretariat of the Future, London, 1944.

The United Nations Secretariat, New York, 1950.

6 THE ADMINISTRATIVE COMMITTEE ON CO-ORDINATION

Martin Hill

The remarkable development of international economic and social action through the United Nations system has been accomplished as a result of the individual and concerted efforts of a large number of autonomous agencies, each having responsibilities in particular fields. This functional decentralization, with wide freedom of action for the individual agencies in their respective technical tasks, has been a source of great strength and vitality: it has also given rise – as the Charter foresaw – to a quite crucial need for co-ordination. Because the major problems of economic and social policy are so closely interrelated, the terms of reference of many of the agencies overlap, and much of the work of each of them closely affects – and may be indeed essential to or dependent upon – that of others. Hence the emphasis that has been placed over the years on the need for co-operation and co-ordination and the development in certain cases of concerted action. A considerable network of institutional arrangements, as well as considerable and continuing efforts, would in any circumstances have been needed to ensure that the various United Nations organizations worked towards common ends, acted where necessary as a team, and maintained a high degree of administrative co-ordination in the interests of operating efficiency and economy. With the rapid increase in the range and scope of international work and in the complexity of the structure of international organization, these tasks became both more important and more difficult.

This chapter will not attempt to review or appraise the co-ordinating activities of the organs which have responsibilities for co-ordination under the Charter – the General Assembly, with its Advisory Committee on Administrative and Budgetary Questions, and the Economic and Social Council, with its Co-ordination Committee and other subordinate organs; still less will it attempt to discuss co-ordination in international organization in its wider aspects.[1] It will concentrate as closely as possible on the evolution, functioning, achievements and limitations of a little-known body, for which the Charter made no provision, namely the Administrative Committee on Co-ordination, referred to in the jargon of the United Nations as the ACC.

The ACC consists of the Secretary-General of the UN as Chairman and the executive heads of the specialized agencies (ILO, FAO, UNESCO, ICAO, WHO, IBRD (with IFC and IDA), IMF, UPU, ITU, WMO and IMCO) and the International Atomic Energy Agency. Others who attend its sessions include the Executive Secretary of the GATT, the UN Under-Secretary for Economic and Social Affairs, the Secretary-General of the UN Conference on Trade and Development (UNCTAD), the Managing Director of the Special Fund,[2] the Executive Chairman of the TAB, the Executive Director of UNICEF, the High Commissioner for Refugees, the Commissioner-General of the UN Relief and Works Agency (UNRWA), the Executive Director of the World Food Programme, the Executive Director of the UN Institute For Training and Research (UNITAR), and the Chairman of the ACC's Preparatory Committee.

The ACC has come to play a central role in the United Nations system, complementary to that of the Economic and Social Council, to which it reports. Apart from activities undertaken in response to direct requests by the Council or the General Assembly, it provides point of contact among the organizations of the United Nations family at the top executive level. It encourages and facilitates the exchange of information and views on matters of common concern, as well as co-ordinated action, as required. Not less important, it sees to the establishment and functioning of arrangements to ensure co-ordination among the staffs of the different agencies at the working level. Finally, it is through the ACC that reports, proposals or action on any subject touching upon the competence or interest of a number of agencies (a very wide range of activities relating to economic and social matters and to human rights, as well as to administration and finance, fall within this category) are normally prepared or cleared.

To these statements, the sections that follow will attempt to give some substance. The historical part is divided into three phases corresponding roughly to changes in the demands made on the Committee and in the conditions affecting it. The first phase covers the early years until 1952-53; the second, the remainder of the 1950s; and the third, the first half of the Development Decade. These periods also correspond rather closely to the periods of office of the three Secretaries-General of the United Nations, whose personalities and policies have inevitably exercised a very considerable influence on the Committee.

The Charter speaks of co-ordination 'through consultation and recommendation'; it is in this sense, and not in the sense of '*coordonner c'est ordonner*', that the term must be understood throughout this chapter. It will be used, moreover, to cover a wide variety of efforts, from those aimed at avoiding duplication and overlapping, at the adoption of uniform or comparable regulations, practices and methods, at arrangements for co-operation and the appropriate division of work, to agreements on lines of policy and generally on the manner in which the aims of Article 55 of the Charter may best be pursued. Whatever the immediate task confronting it, the ACC has always interpreted co-ordination in a dynamic sense and never as the 'dead hand'; it has sought through co-ordination to increase the effectiveness of international efforts and never to impede such efforts.

Acting on a recommendation of the Preparatory Commission of the United Nations, the Economic and Social Council, at its third session in October 1946, 'being desirous of discharging effectively its responsibility . . . to co-ordinate the activities of the specialized agencies' requested the Secretary-General:

> to establish a standing committee of administative officers consisting of himself, as chairman, and the corresponding officers of the specialized agencies brought into relationship with the United Nations, for the purpose of taking all appropriate steps, under the leadership of the Secretary-General, to ensure the fullest and most effective implementation of the agreements entered into between the United Nations and the specialized agencies.

By the Agreements between the United Nations and ILO, FAO and UNESCO, which had been negotiated during the summer and entered into force in December 1946,[3] these agencies undertook (Article IV) to co-operate in 'measures necessary to make co-ordination of the activities of the specialized agencies and those of the United Nations fully effective' and in particular 'to participate in and to co-operate with any body or bodies which the Council may establish for the purpose of facilitating such co-ordination'.

Such were the formal origins of the ACC[4], which held its first meeting in February 1947. An unwritten convention was established at the outset that meetings of the Committee would continue to be attended by the Secretary-General and the executive heads of the specialized agencies themselves,[5] and that it would meet in private. These practices, which reflect primarily the importance attached by its members to having a centre for contacts and the confidential exchange of information and views at the highest level, have had a decisive influence in building up the authority of the Committee and in determining its character. In particular, it made it inevitable that the Committee would (*a*) take initiatives and propose solutions and not merely carry out the requests of the Council or other inter-governmental bodies; (*b*) concern itself with broad issues of policy and any matters affecting the United Nations system as a whole, and (*c*) be able to meet at most two or three times a year and for very short periods, relying on subordinate bodies to dispose of routine matters and to prepare the ground for its consideration of other matters up to the point where policy decisions were needed.

The Committee was mainly concerned in its first year or two, assisted by inter-secretariat consultative committees, with laying the basis for co-ordination in public information and statistical activities and, so far as feasible, in administrative and financial matters. But the characteristics just referred to soon became apparent. As early as November 1947 the General Assembly asked the Secretary-General, in consultation with the specialized agencies through the ACC, 'to report and make recommendations on the establishment of priorities for international action'. In the course of the same year and 1948, the Committee established the terms of reference of the International Civil Service Advisory Board (ICSAB), appointed its members and assigned the Board its first tasks. In December 1948 the Committee, which had earlier established a Preparatory Committee of deputies, decided that it would delegate questions of detail to technical co-ordinating bodies, bringing together those professionally responsible in the agencies directly concerned, under the general supervision of the Preparatory Committee, in order to allow the members of ACC 'to give adequate attention to the major questions of programme co-ordination, including the question of priorities'. While the Committee's earliest reports testify to its concern with the promotion of co-ordination in work programmes, the nature of this concern developed rather rapidly. To quote the Committee's fifth report of June 1949:

> While attention will continue to be given to the avoidance of overlapping, emphasis will be laid on the more positive task of increasing, through co-operation, the effectiveness of international action in the various economic and social fields.

It had at first been assumed that the agreements concluded between the United Nations and the specialized agencies might need to be revised in the light of experience and in 1949, three years after the first agreements had been concluded, the Secretary-General prepared through the ACC machinery a study on how they had been applied. The conclusion of the study, which was endorsed by the Council and the General Assembly, was that no revision was needed,[6] the agreements as they stood providing a framework within which co-operation was developing satisfactorily. How co-operation was developing was brought out the same year in an 'Illustrative Account of the more important concrete results achieved through co-operation with the specialized agencies' (A/1029) submitted by the Secretary-General to the General Assembly at the Council's request. While the catalogue of arrangements for co-operation[7] drawn up through the ACC was thin by present-day standards, it was not inconsiderable. It was possible for the Secretary-General to state that 'almost every economic and social activity undertaken by the United Nations or a specialized agency involves co-operation at some stage and in some degree with other United Nations bodies'.

The same year the Secretary-General submitted to the Council a plan which had been worked out with the specialized agencies for an expanded co-operative programme of technical assistance for economic development. There had been some difference of opinion between the Secretary-General who wanted:

> the establishment of a single common fund into which all special contributions from Governments would be paid and out of which allocations would be made to the several international organizations . . . subject to such broad policies as might be laid down by the Economic and Social Council and the General Assembly, . . . and the majority of his colleagues from the specialized agencies who were not able to subscribe to this position.[8]

But a compromise was agreed which the Council accepted. The

funds contributed for the Programme were to be divided among the various organizations according to predetermined percentages, and an executive inter-agency body to administer the Programme, the Technical Assistance Board, was established by ACC and brought under ACC's general supervision. On ACC's proposal, some major changes were made in the Programme in December 1951, including the appointment by the Secretary-General, after consultation with the executive heads of the specialized agencies, of a full-time Executive Chairman of the Technical Assistance Board. It then decided also to undertake a special review, twice a year, of policy aspects of the technical assistance programme. Such a review has since been undertaken at each of its regular sessions, and it has also regularly approved the TAB's annual reports to the Council's Technical Assistance Committee.

In 1948 the ACC set up a single Consultative Committee on Administrative Questions to replace its earlier committees on personnel and on administrative and budgetary questions respectively. By the early 1950s it had succeeded in reaching a fair degree of harmony in the staff and financial regulations of the various organizations.[9] It has not yet been able to reach agreement on a common form of budget or on a common audit. On the other hand, it did agree on common principles for external audit and set up a panel of auditors of which the auditors of each organization became members. It succeeded in working out and applying a uniform classification system for salary purposes but failed to define common standards for classifying jobs within that system. Following the report of the 1949 Salary Review Committee, set up by the General Assembly, the ACC brought about agreement on a modified version of the Committee's recommendations which were accepted by all the organizations concerned. This was the origin of the present common system of salaries and allowances. The pensions system, jointly administered by representatives of the various United Nations organizations participating in it and providing uniform entitlements to all members, was set up with the help of ACC in late 1948.

Mr Trygve Lie consulted the ACC in May 1950 on his proposed Twenty-Year Peace Programme. The Committee issued a formal statement urging the importance for the future of the United Nations and the specialized agencies of finding an early solution to the political deadlock[10] that then existed in the United Nations and reaffirming the validity of the principle of universality in the membership and programmes of the United Nations and those of the specialized agencies which are founded on that principle. This was the first of a number of occasions on which members have sought the support of ACC for particular proposals which they intended to place before the governments. It was also one of the rare occasions on which the ACC has taken position on a political issue. Another such occasion arose in 1965. At its Vienna meeting in May of that year, information and views were exchanged about the long and heated proceedings that had been taking place in several agencies on the subject of the participation of South Africa – and in some cases also Portugal – in meetings called by them. The Introduction to the latest Annual Report of the Secretary-General to the General Assembly[11] makes the following reference to that discussion:

> ... it is the feeling of the Executive Heads of all the organizations that a precondition for the continued success of economic, social and cultural co-operation on an international plane is the preservation to the greatest possible extent of the essentially technical character of such action. I have previously had occasion to observe that it would be a matter for regret on the part of the entire international community if important meetings dealing with these questions, and depending for their success on the vital element of international co-operation, were to fail to yield solid results because of the introduction of highly contentious political issues into the discussions and deliberations.

In the early 1950s the Expanded Programme of Technical Assistance got under way and most of the United Nations agencies began the dramatic shift in their activities away from research, exchanges of views and experience, and standard-setting, towards field operations. This opened up broad new areas in which measures for co-operation had to be worked out and ushered in the second phase of the ACC's work.

New arrangements at the regional level were explored and developed,[12] mainly around and in conjunction with the United Nations Regional Economic Commissions.[13] These arrangements ranged from the posting of officers of the agencies at the Commissions' headquarters to the undertaking of joint studies and field assignments. In a number of the countries receiving technical assistance, a resident representative was early entrusted with the task of consolidating action in the field by the different agencies under the Expanded Programme; but the major effort to build up his authority and render the activities of the United Nations family more closely integrated country by country came much later. At the time most emphasis was placed on ensuring as far as possible that coherent policies were followed at the centre.

As the culmination of prolonged efforts in which the ACC played a major part, the Council in the summer of 1952 adopted a framework of priorities for international action in the economic and social field, the overriding priority being the promotion of the economic and social development of the under-developed countries. A series of technical working groups and working parties, to determine which agency should do what and how, began to take shape under the Preparatory Committee of the ACC. Largely on the basis of their work, the Council laid down the broad lines of an International Programme of Concerted Practical Action in the Social Field in the summer of 1953. The ACC called the Council's attention to the need for better co-ordination of the planning and supervision of projects at the community level and an *ad hoc* meeting arranged by it worked out definitions of the terms employed, as well as the roles and objectives of the various agencies in that area. This was the first practical step in a complicated process of attaining co-ordination among the related social programmes of different agencies, established under different titles and with different ends in view. It led to numerous agreements on specific issues such as the practical relation between the FAO programme for agricultural extension and the ILO's programme of vocational training; and it gradually brought together the United Nations community development programme, the UNESCO programme of fundamental education, the FAO's work on rural development, the ILO's Andean Indian project, as well as the related work of WHO. All such activities, and problems of co-ordination ensuing in connection with them, have since been reviewed at an annual meeting of a rural and community development working group under ACC.

The need to reach detailed understandings was naturally felt in other fields of work also. As a result partly of its own decisions and partly of requests by the Council, the ACC in the course of the 1950s set up machinery to bring about co-ordination and co-operation in respect of a number of specific topics, including land reform, urbanization problems, commodity problems, and oceanography, as well as broad programmes such as those of industrial development, water resource utilization, education and training, and public administration. These broad programmes, calling for concerted efforts among several members of the United Nations family, reflected a deliberate policy of the General Assembly and the Council, as well as some of the specialized agencies, to concentrate efforts that had hitherto been too dispersed on small individual projects. These bodies were also coming to demand that issues in their own fields (for example agriculture, education, manpower) be considered in relation to other elements of the world or the national economy, and not, as previously, in relative isolation from them. Both of these tendencies, which still prevail, naturally increased the possibilities of overlapping, the need for co-operation in the planning as well as the carrying out of work, and consequently the work falling on the ACC.

The development of the field programmes also greatly increased the number of points at which the autonomous administrative systems of the different agencies came into contact, and made it more difficult to tolerate discrepancies in conditions of service. Staff working for different agencies in the same place had to have at least roughly comparable treatment. The various United Nations organizations informed the United Nations Salary Review Committee in 1956 that reconciliation of divergent conditions was one of its most pressing problems. The ACC, with the help of CCAQ, and the Salary Review Committee between them succeeded in achieving such a reconciliation. TAB soon afterwards decided to leave CCAQ to deal with co-ordination of conditions in the field as well as regular programmes.

It would be misleading to suggest that the changes just described brought about any noteworthy change in the functioning of the ACC itself. By the early 1950s the ACC was normally meeting for two days twice a year, in Geneva in April/May and in New York in the autumn, and consultations by correspondence, when some ACC action was required between sessions, were already an established procedure. Those parts of the sessional agendas which were not of a political character, or for other reasons not reserved for the exclusive consideration of ACC itself, were prepared, and passages intended to form the basis for the ACC's report to the Council drafted, by the Preparatory Committee. The Preparatory Committee met a week or so before the ACC, to review the follow-up of past ACC decisions, to consider such new problems as might have arisen as well as proposals and drafts submitted by the United Nations or one of the agencies, to examine the reports of the consultative committees, the technical working groups or *ad hoc* working parties it might have designated for particular tasks and to take such decisions as seemed called for and which did not require action by the ACC itself. The Committee's secretary was chief of the specialized agencies section in the Office of the Director of Co-ordination for Specialized Agencies and Economic and Social Affairs, an Office which was located in the Executive Office of the Secretary-General of the United Nations. The Director, who combined this function with that of Deputy Executive Assistant to the Secretary-General, was both Chairman of, and the Secretary-General's representative on, the Preparatory Committee. He also acted as Rapporteur of the ACC to the Council and Committees II and III of the General Assembly.

The proceedings of the ACC have always been informal. From the beginning, the Committee took its decisions by consensus, without recourse to voting; it never adopted Rules of Procedure. This informality was facilitated by the small numbers of persons involved, the private character of the meetings and the fact that the Committee worked almost exclusively in one language, English. As the years went by, the attendance became less homogeneous and naturally grew owing not only to the growth in actual membership resulting from the creation of new specialized agencies[14] but also to the establishment of new United Nations programmes whose activities and responsible officials needed to be brought within the ACC's arrangements for consultation. Those officials who came to be regularly invited to attend ACC meetings as observers have been mentioned in the early pages. The participation of the executive heads of the Expanded Programme of Technical Assistance, UNICEF and, later, the Special Fund, became increasingly important as an ever larger proportion of the activities of many agencies came to depend on the funds they administered. Other officials of United Nations bodies, such as the Chairman of the International Civil Service Advisory Board (ICSAB), were from time to time invited to particular meetings to discuss specific issues as were the executive heads of the OEEC (which was later transformed into the OECD), the Council of Europe, the European Coal and Steel Community, and the Organization of American States.

Among the administrative changes in the United Nations Secretariat which Dag Hammarskjöld introduced soon after his election to the post of Secretary-General, there was one that directly affected the ACC Secretariat and, to some extent, the *modus operandi* of the Committee. Co-ordination in economic and social matters within the United Nations Secretariat itself had been exercised by the Secretary-General's Office. The need for this was naturally diminished when the Departments of Economic Affairs and Social Affairs were brought under a single head in 1952 and formally merged two years later.[15] At the same time, as has been indicated, arrangements for co-ordinated or concerted action in broad economic and social programmes under the leadership of the United Nations were demanding increasing attention and had indeed come to represent the largest area of ACC work. While the central responsibilities in connection with the ACC and its subordinate bodies had to be exercised under the direct supervision of the Secretary-General himself, it became essential that those responsibilities should be exercised in full knowledge of the work of the Department mainly concerned. The Director of Co-ordination was accordingly made Deputy Under-Secretary for Economic and Social Affairs and the Secretary-General's Personal Representative to the Specialized Agencies, reporting directly to the Secretary-General in the second capacity. The Specialized Agencies Section was incorporated in the Secretariat of the Economic and Social Council, its size being greatly reduced, because of the desire, shared at that stage by Hammarskjöld and the ACABQ, to reduce routine and liaison functions performed by the Secretariat to a minimum. Much of the documentation prepared by the Section to assist the processes of co-ordination, including the compilation of an annual Catalogue of Economic and Social Projects, was discontinued.

Apart from the 'streamlining' of internal organization, it was one of Hammarskjöld's personal preoccupations during his early years of office to stimulate the economic and social work of the United Nations family. He expressed in the phrase 'unity within freedom' his general philosophy of co-operation within the family, the responsibility for providing leadership devolving on the United Nations itself. The ACC seemed to him a potentially important instrument through which policy proposals for economic and social action could be worked out jointly and a constructive dialogue maintained with the governments, as represented in the first instance by the Economic and Social Council. He sought to give the ACC a more dynamic role than it had previously played, a role more nearly comparable to that of an international cabinet.

Hammarskjöld's broad aims were shared by the heads of several of the major agencies. They were never fully achieved, partly because of limiting factors inherent in the composition and structure of the ACC itself, partly perhaps because of differences of view, which gradually became apparent, as to the meaning of 'United Nations leadership', partly also because, particularly from 1956 onwards, problems of peace and security came to absorb more and more of the Secretary-General's time and energy.

The ideas put forward in 1953 and 1954 did, however, have a considerable and lasting influence on the character of the ACC's work and its relations with the Council. For the purpose of facilitating free and spontaneous consideration of major problems and policies in their political context, it became part of the established practice to hold part of each session in strict privacy, without advisers or précis-writers, and without records. The Council decided in July 1954 to combine henceforth in a single annual General Review its consideration of co-ordination and the broad development of the economic and social activities of the

United Nations family, the Secretary-General and the heads of agencies being formally invited to participate in this Review.

The first half of the 1960s, the United Nations Decade of Development, may be said to constitute a third phase in the evolution of the ACC. It has been, for political reasons that are well known, a period of stringency for the budget of the United Nations itself; but it has seen a very rapid growth in the economic and social work of the United Nations family as a whole. The increased resources have come not only from voluntary contributions (the combined annual contributions to the Special Fund, EPTA and UNICEF having risen from $79 million in 1959 to $178 million in 1965), but also through the regular budgets of the specialized agencies[16] and IAEA, which rose from $60·6 million to $110·8 million[17] over the same period. Almost all of this international activity has been directed towards assisting in the processes of development, and a considerable part of it has required co-operation among several agencies. It has been the ACC's task to promote and facilitate these concerted efforts. Through it agreement was reached in 1962 on the text of what is called the 'Blue Book' on the Development Decade – the 'Proposals of the Secretary-General',[18] which have provided a common basis for the Decade programme of the United Nations system. With the help of the ACC again, the United Nations Conference on the Application of Science and Technology to Development, held in February 1963, was organized and followed up as a co-operative undertaking of many agencies of the United Nations family. To carry forward the work begun by the Conference, the ACC recommended the establishment by the Council of an Advisory Committee, the members to be nominated by the Secretary-General in consultation with the agencies, and it set up its own Sub-committee to assist the Advisory Committee and ensure co-ordination of the programmes of the various United Nations organizations concerned. The Advisory Committee was duly established and it is now preparing a broad international programme of action, based on proposals laid before it by the ACC's Sub-committee.

Such evidence of co-operation should not obscure the fact that the expansion of international activity and the concept of the Development Decade, with its emphasis upon the concerted effort of the United Nations as a whole, made an overhaul of existing arrangements for co-ordination essential. In particular, the activities of the various organizations had to be brought into closer relationship in the field, and the complicated structure and procedures of the technical co-operation programmes of the United Nations family simplified.

To meet the first of these aims, an accommodation had to be found between, on the one hand, the need for a clearer image and unified representation of the United Nations family in each country and, on the other, the retention by each agency of full substantive control over the activities for which it was responsible. A set of principles was agreed in the ACC in October 1961 among the organizations participating in the EPTA which, while safeguarding the technical competence of the different agencies' field staff and the direct contacts between the agencies and their own member states, recognized the central position of the Resident Representatives of the TAB (who now number almost eighty and act also as country directors of Special Fund programmes and agents of the UN/FAO World Food Programme). It also built up their authority as co-ordinators of the activities of the United Nations family within each of the countries receiving aid.

In pursuit of the second aim, a proposal was kept for several years under consideration to combine the Expanded Programme of Technical Assistance and the Special Fund in a single United Nations Development Programme. This proposal, launched by the United States and certain other major contributors, was early endorsed by the Secretary-General and agreement was reached through the ACC in 1964 on a set of recommendations which, by and large, were the basis of those laid by the Council before the General Assembly. The agreement in ACC represented something of a landmark, for the merger, now approved,[19] will not only affect the individual interests of the different agencies, but it will also involve a major change in the context in which the ACC works. For authority as to the use of the operational funds at the disposal of the Special Fund and the EPTA is to be concentrated in the hands of a single inter-governmental committee of the United Nations and a single management; furthermore a single consultative inter-secretariat body – which, it is true, will participate actively in the processes leading up to the formulation of decisions – is to supersede the Consultative Board of the Special Fund as well as the Technical Assistance Board, to the executive character of which so much symbolic importance has hitherto been attached.

U Thant, who first chaired the ACC in the spring of 1962, has been particularly concerned to develop relations of confidence and solidarity with the executive heads of the agencies, to make the ACC a useful instrument of consultation on the common political problems facing the international organizations, and to help build with its assistance a more solid basis for the continued expansion of multilateral aid activities. There has been a tendency in recent years to delegate further the tasks of co-ordination in individual economic and social programmes as well as administration to the Preparatory Committee. This applies also to the Consultative Committees on Administrative Questions and on Public Information, the Sub-committees which now exist in respect of the application of science and technology, Education and Training, Commodity Problems, Oceanography, and Water Resources Development, and other bodies. By and large, these subsidiary bodies apart from the Consultative Committees are of an *ad hoc* character; they meet when called by the ACC and are disbanded when their work is done.

The United Nations staff working directly on inter-agency and ACC matters in New York and Geneva has been somewhat strengthened. The present Secretary of the ACC is the Secretary of the Economic and Social Council; in Geneva there is now an Office for Co-ordination and ACC Affairs working under the general direction of the Secretary-General's Personal Representative at United Nations headquarters. The ACC has met more frequently at the seats of Specialized Agencies and IAEA.[20] Brief supplementary meetings of the Committee were held in Geneva in 1964 and 1965 during the summer sessions of the Council.

On the administrative side there have been successes and disappointments. The main success has lain in the relatively smooth working, under the CCAQ, of the common system of salaries and allowances and its adjustment to meet changing circumstances. On the other hand, the process of dealing with the minutiae of administration through CCAQ has proved very time-consuming for the senior administrative officers of the different agencies. Moreover, there has been little progress in the direction of common recruitment or standards, and on certain important matters that fall outside the scope of the common system (such as the numbers and grading of senior staff), differences between organizations would seem to have been accentuated rather than diminished over the years. The failure of the organizations mainly concerned to agree on the extent of salary increases for the general service (i.e. clerical and secretarial) staff in Geneva, as well as difficulties in reaching inter-agency agreement in other fields, led in 1962 to the ACC reinforcing the authority and enlarging the functions of the International Civil Service Advisory Board. In addition to advising, on request, on recruitment and personnel policies, the Board is now authorized to review and advise, through its own initiative, on conditions of service and divergences as between organizations in the application of the common system, and it has been provided with a full-time independent secretariat. While this enlargement of the role of ICSAB will no doubt prove helpful, it would be unrealistic to underestimate the difficulties of achieving, in a loose federation like the UN family, anything approaching the unified administrative arrangements that would be possible in a centrally-directed system.

Before drawing conclusions from this history, we must consider ACC's relations with ECOSOC and the General Assembly on the one hand, and with the individual agencies on the other.

The Economic and Social Council has frequently stated that the ACC is essential to it in carrying out its Charter responsibilities for co-ordination and for promoting the United Nations' economic and social objectives. The ACC has not only prepared the ground for a considerable range of ECOSOC's decisions, but it has tried to ensure that the Council's decisions were such as could be accepted and implemented by the governing organs of the agencies, to promote the necessary action by those organs (which, while very willing to co-operate with the United Nations, have been sensitive to any impairment of their autonomy) and to facilitate co-ordination of policies at the national level through the close contact of its members with the key officials of the different ministries handling the affairs of their respective agencies.

Responsibilities have been piled upon the ACC by ECOSOC both directly and by the practice of requesting the Secretary-General to undertake, in consultation or co-operation with the agencies, major tasks transcending the interest of the United Nations alone. At the ACC's suggestion the Council introduced into its Rules of Procedure in 1952 clauses requiring consultation with specialized agencies before action was taken by it on any proposal relating to matters of concern to them. The ACC's recommendations have sometimes been amended by the Council, but such amendments have usually been minor and it can safely be said that ACC has contributed much to determining the Council's economic and social programmes.

Nevertheless ACC's relations with ECOSOC have not been altogether smooth or easy. The ACC has not always been happy about the way in which, and the level at which, matters of prime importance to the agencies have been dealt with by Council bodies. It has sometimes uttered a discreet suggestion that more could be accomplished if stronger leadership were forthcoming from the Council. It has occasionally issued direct warnings about, or criticisms of, actions by certain of the Council's subsidiary organs and even of the Council itself. The ACC has thus tended to reflect the views of the agencies. It has taken particular umbrage at any attempt by a commission or committee of the Council to exercise the co-ordinating powers vested in the Council itself, and at any serious failure to carry out the obligation to consult with the agencies prior to adopting decisions affecting them.

The Council for its part has been jealous of its Charter responsibilities and restive at not being able to play a more direct part in the co-ordinating processes. The somewhat anomalous position of ACC has also been a source of friction. Constitutionally each member of the ACC, as the executive head of his organization, is responsible to his governing body, to which he reports the results of ACC's discussions, presenting – to the extent possible and considering the special requirements of his organization – proposals in harmony with the action taken by other organizations. It has not always been understood that the ACC, although established at ECOSOC's behest, is not one of its subordinate organs or that it derives its authority less from ECOSOC than from its members' position of influence and trust with their own governing organs.

Members of the Council have not infrequently expressed annoyance that the ACC should meet in private and report only as it thinks fit, and have complained that real problems of overlapping and duplication were being concealed from the Council and the world under cover of promises of consultation and co-operation. On one occasion the Council specifically requested the ACC to report on difficulties encountered[21] as well as on progress achieved – a request which the ACC has tried to meet in part, commenting, however, that 'there would not be advantage in making public differences of views that might arise in the course of inter-agency discussion leading ultimately to agreements in the ACC.'[22] A further complaint has been that neither in the course of a two-day debate in plenary session, consisting mainly of set speeches, nor in the Co-ordination Committee, was there any real consultation or confrontation of views among the Council representatives and the members of ACC. Finally, there has been some feeling among Council members that ACC has tended to be used by the agencies as an instrument to safeguard entrenched interests and limit interference by the Council.

There have been repeated requests by the Council that the ACC should give it more help, and that to this end it should review its machinery and procedures and strengthen its staff resources. At its summer session in 1963, the Council[23] asked the Secretary-General to arrange a meeting between the ACC and the officers of the Council, together with the Chairman of the Council's Co-ordination Committee. The meeting duly took place during the Council session in July 1964. A similar meeting in 1965 led to a major innovation. The Council had established three years earlier a Special Committee on Co-ordination with particular emphasis on the United Nations Development Decade which met before the Council's summer session and submitted conclusions and recommendations to the Council in regard both to the Development Decade and co-ordination issues arising from the reports of the ACC and the agencies. This Special Committee was now enlarged to comprise the officers of the Council and the Chairman of the Council's Co-ordination Committee, together with representatives of ten elected members of the Council. The Council decided that this reorganized Special

Committee 'shall participate in appropriate joint meetings with the Administrative Committee on Co-ordination' and the two Committees, in their joint meetings, were requested to:

(*a*) Examine the provisional agenda of the Council's sessions, and draw attention whenever necessary or desirable to the major questions that require the Council's urgent action;

(*b*) Keep under review the activities of the United Nations and its related agencies in the economic, social, human rights and related fields, particularly in respect of the United Nations Development Decade;

(*c*) Submit conclusions and recommendations to the Council on those questions as well as on problems in the field of co-ordination which call for special attention by the Council.

The ACC's relations with the General Assembly have been much less close and direct than with the Council; and the Assembly has so far been unwilling to accede to ACC's request that it provide in the Rules of Procedure, as the Council had done, for consultations in appropriate cases with the specialized agencies and IAEA prior to taking decisions. There was a time when the Second and Third Committees of the General Assembly met in joint session to consider the sections of the Council's annual report dealing with co-ordination and relations with the specialized agencies, and when these two Committees joined with the Fifth Committee to consider the reports of the Advisory Committee on Administrative and Budgetary Questions on the budgets of the specialized agencies and questions of administrative co-ordination. These practices were abandoned after 1952 because they made such a heavy call on the time of the General Assembly. The section of the Council's report dealing with co-ordination has since gone direct to the plenary meetings (which means that there is no discussion of it) and the report of ACABQ has been considered, usually in a very perfunctory way, by the Fifth Committee alone.

The joint meetings of the economic, social and budgetary

committees of the General Assembly were a cumbersome and inadequate device, but no easily available alternative has presented itself. With their abandonment, the programmes and the budgets of the United Nations family have been considered largely in isolation from one another by the Council and the Advisory Committee (for the General Assembly) respectively. It has proved difficult for these bodies to get together except through the Secretariats. In 1951 and 1954 meetings were arranged between the ACC and the ACABQ, but they were formal and *protocolaire* to a degree and proved to be of very limited value. More profitable have been the detailed on-the-spot studies of the different agencies' administration and budget, involving willy-nilly a study of programmes, which ACABQ undertook in 1956-58, and the appointment in 1961 of the former secretary of the ACABQ as 'staff officer' of the ACC's Consultative Committee on Administrative Questions, paid for by all the agencies in the 'common system', to help prepare the ground for agreement on various administrative matters. At the invitation of ACC the Chairman of ACABQ attended part of its session in Vienna in April 1965 to discuss how co-operation between the two bodies could be improved. From this meeting, which was quite informal in character, useful long-term results are expected.

In comparison with its relations with the central organs of the United Nations, ACC's relations with the specialized agencies have presented few problems. This is not surprising, since ACC provides the agencies with the means of maintaining, without compromising their independence and without hint of subordination, the close co-operation with the United Nations and with one another which is essential for the achievement of their own purposes. The executive heads of agencies have frequently been instructed by their own governing organs to consult on particular matters with the ACC and to report back. There have been few exceptions to the rule that views expressed by the ACC in its reports to ECOSOC are accepted as guidelines by the agencies, the executive heads themselves acting as spokesmen for ACC in their respective governing organs, supported as required – but only as required – by a representative of the Secretary-General.

The ACC has helped to ensure the smooth operation of the Charter procedures by keeping the Council and its subsidiary bodies, as well as the United Nations membership as a whole, informed of the views of the other United Nations organizations on important issues and of the institutional context in which those issues should be considered. It can safely be said that the broad support finally obtained throughout the United Nations family for launching the Programme Appraisals in 1959, for the action proposals for the Development Decade (1962) and for the proposed merger of the EPTA and the Special Fund (1964–5), to cite a few recent instances of United Nations initiatives which at first encountered some difficulties, would not have been forthcoming without the intensive consultations for which the ACC was well equipped to arrange. The Committee has likewise mobilized support behind many major undertakings of the specialized agencies such as the Freedom from Hunger Campaign and the Programme for Universal Literacy. The promotion of a sense of solidarity among the executive heads of the different organizations has been not the least important of the functions of the ACC, in which indeed the term 'the United Nations Family' was coined. Common membership in the committee has stimulated a positive attitude towards inter-agency co-operation and there is no doubt that this attitude has been decisive in bringing about much of the co-operation that exists.

Recent major developments in the economic and social activities of the United Nations, such as the growing proportion of total resources provided by the centrally administered voluntary programmes[24] and the trend towards decentralization and dispersion of authority in the United Nations itself, may have tended to reduce the direct influence of ACC in some cases, but they have also enhanced the importance of the consultations, and especially the top-level consultations on policy, for which the ACC provides the opportunity.

The ACC is, of course, only one of the channels through which the agencies maintain contact with the United Nations and one another. It is a supplement to, and not a substitute for, the relations which each agency maintains with the United Nations and other agencies. Numerous activities of the United Nations, the specialized agencies and the IAEA which directly concern two or more of them, are co-ordinated by direct agreement among the agencies concerned. Apart from the regular representation and liaison maintained with the help for example of the permanent offices of several agencies in New York, special arrangements have not infrequently been resorted to. An interesting example of the inter-action of the ACC and such *ad hoc* arrangements is provided by the measures taken by the ILO in 1963. In view of the difficulties to which the continued participation of South Africa was giving rise, the Governing Body decided to send a delegation to New York to consult with the Secretary-General on how these difficulties might best be met. The consultations assisted the Governing Body in reaching an orderly solution. Their full benefits not only to ILO but also to other agencies faced with a similar problem have, however, depended on the consultations on the subject which have since taken place at successive meetings of the ACC.

The striking differences in the size and character of the agencies, in the degree to which their work depends upon that of the United Nations and other Agencies and in the position of their executive heads *vis-à-vis* their inter-governmental organs, have naturally been reflected in the roles played in the ACC by its different members. The IBRD and the IMF, for example, have financial and administrative arrangements differing considerably from those of the other agencies and they have taken little part in that side of the ACC's work. Nor has either of them until recently[25] been greatly concerned with the activities in the social field which loom large in the programme of the United Nations, ILO, FAO, UNESCO and WHO. Again, although the range of problems common to all agencies is wider than might be suspected, the smaller and highly technical agencies, such as ITU, WMO, UPU and IMCO, are normally interested in only a relatively small segment of ACC's work. Such differences in the interests and responsibilities of its members have naturally tended to set certain limits to the scope of the responsibilities the ACC, as such, is equipped to discharge.

What general conclusions can be reached about the role of the ACC and the factors influencing it?

If its usefulness is obvious, so are its limitations. Because of its composition, it cannot easily take a position detrimental to the interests of any agency or in opposition to the wishes of its executive head; it can be used as an instrument for economizing staff and other resources but not as an instrument of budgetary stabilization; it has no authority to decide on the distribution of international resources as between different purposes, or to settle jurisdictional disputes (though it has usually been able to find practical solutions in cases of overlapping competences). It cannot eastablish, though it may influence, the policy decisions which are fashioned through the inter-governmental organs of the United Nations, the specialized agencies and the IAEA.

The role it performs is none the less indispensable. An appraisal of the programmes of the United Nations family, for the period 1959-64, published in 1960[26] by a distinguished committee of past Presidents of the Council and Chairmen of its Co-ordination Committee, dwelt on the difficulties of achieving common policies and co-ordination through the budgetary and policy-making bodies of separate and autonomous agencies. The difficulties arise partly from the lack of co-ordination among national ministries, which leads to governments speaking with different voices in different agencies. It also frequently happens that delegates, innocent of any instructions, express no views except their own. Such factors are compounded by others, among them the fact that the principal government representatives in certain specialized agencies are practitioners in the special fields in question and voting along professional lines irrespective of government instructions has not been unknown. It may be remembered too that one major agency, the ILO, is not inter-governmental but tripartite, representing the organized management and labour, as well as the government, of each Member.

If the ACC established itself early as a means of regular consultation, it came in time to represent something a good deal more, namely the framework and symbol of inter-agency co-operation. Furthermore, it came to partake of the nature of an executive organ, because of the actions taken severally by its members in the light of decisions reached within it. Thus its role was gradually increased. The actual meetings of the Committee remained important,[27] but the basic negotiations and even a large proportion of the agreements 'through the ACC' tended to be reached more and more through the ACC's numerous sub-committees and working groups or informally by correspondence or telephone throughout the year. The strength of the ACC reflects the phenomenon in international as well as national affairs that public policy is so largely determined by officials, and by successive administrative decisions rather than by legislation. It reflects furthermore the personal prestige which most of the executive heads of the United Nations organizations have succeeded in establishing *vis-à-vis* their governing organs. Nor should two other factors be ignored: the considerable degree of continuity in some of the key posts involved,[28] and the consistent pressure in favour of inter-agency co-ordination exercised by a number of countries, and especially the USA.

Because of the authority which it enjoys, the ACC, in the words of the Appraisals Committee,[29] 'cannot escape responsibility if there are serious flaws or deficiencies in co-ordination'. No one could claim that such flaws and deficiencies do not exist. In his report on consultations with the ACC in the summer of 1964, the President of the Council spoke of the 'scepticism and frustration within the Council about co-ordination, particularly as regards the overall policy of the United Nations family'.[30] Towards the co-ordination of overall policy, indeed, it cannot be claimed that the ACC has made more than a minor and intermittent contribution. The decisions of each agency that have led to the great recent development in international activities have been taken individually with little regard to any general priorities, and it has not always been easy to adhere strictly to the established division of functions among international organizations. One can point to cases where the secretariats have tried, but have not been able, to prevent legislative bodies, including the General Assembly, from taking a decision likely to cause overlapping or confusion; all too often, however, the secretariats have failed to carry out fully the 'prior consultations' to which they are committed.

The ACC's subsidiary machinery has been considerably enlarged, and its procedures have been somewhat adjusted to meet the growing demands made upon it; it has been influenced too by the personalities, policies and methods of different Secretaries-General, as well indeed as by the attitudes of other key members. By and large, however, its *modus operandi* has changed little from the earliest days. Suggestions for reform have been made from time to time. Could not the ACC act as a fully executive organ, it has been asked, carrying out certain responsibilities directly on the Council's behalf? Were not its proceedings rather too informal and loose to be fully efficacious? Should not the ACC staff be divorced from the United Nations Secretariat, like the staff of the TAB? Could not the different organizations second officials to it? Has not the policy of delegating responsibilities for preparing and executing ACC decisions to different agencies and divisions of the United Nations gone too far and should not the Committee have a stronger central staff? Should not the ACC itself meet for longer periods and leave less to the Preparatory Committee? Other suggestions have been more radical. Representatives on the Council have sometimes asked why ACC cannot work in public like a normal Council committee and why Council representatives are not permitted to participate as observers. At one stage, the suggestion was even made that it might be desirable to reduce or eliminate the role of the Preparatory Committee, replacing it by a single top-level official, responsible to the ACC under its Chairman, whose sole responsibility it would be to settle inter-organizational difficulties and develop plans of concerted action.

As indicated earlier in this chapter, some of these ideas – those, for example, relating to the strengthening of the staff – have left their mark; but those involving radical change did not meet the conditions under which alone the ACC can operate (or under which the membership as a whole felt it could operate) and have been shelved.

The structure, procedures and approach of the ACC have been very largely determined – and inevitably determined – by *internal* factors. One of these is the responsibility of its members to their own representative bodies, rather than to the Council; another the necessity of reconciling the roles of providing for intimate inter-agency consultation at the highest executive level and of carrying out – and reporting on – the manifold behests of the Council and the General Assembly; another again – and not the least important – the dominant role which the United Nations Secretary-General and his representatives have had to play, not only because of the constitutional position of the United Nations *vis-à-vis* the agencies but because by far the greatest part of ACC's work has lain in providing for co-ordination between the United Nations and the agencies rather than among the latter[31] and for smooth co-operation in carrying out United Nations decisions and programmes.

Experience has demonstrated not only that the ACC depends greatly upon the active leadership of the United Nations but also upon that leadership being exercised by the Secretary-General himself. This is a task, involving much time and attention, which, beyond a certain point, cannot be delegated. But the office of Secretary-General has become so burdened with continuing political and diplomatic responsibilities, which properly claim highest priority, that the time a Secretary-General can normally devote to economic and social programmes and relationships with the specialized agencies is necessarily limited.

These internal factors, therefore, suggest certain limits to the possible scope of ACC activities. But the possible long-run influence of current *external* factors on the ACC's role and functioning must, of course, not be overlooked. One such factor, sometimes restricting and sometimes providing opportunities for Secretariat influence, is the growth in the membership in the United Nations and the agencies, and in the practice of group discussions and group voting among member states. Another factor is the growth and vitality of non-United Nations organizations of a regional character, some of which are actively engaged in the same fields of work as the United Nations organizations and with which existing arrangements for co-ordination may well need to be strengthened.

A factor of key importance already referred to is the dispersion of authority within the United Nations itself, at the level of the Secretariat as well as that of the inter-governmental organs. For several years a process of 'decentralization' from Headquarters to the regional economic commissions has been in progress, while the importance of the independent authority exercised by the Special Fund has naturally increased with the growth in the resources the Fund administers. The United Nations Conference on Trade and Development, assisted by a Trade and Development Board of fifty-five states, has now been established as an organ of the General Assembly, the frontiers of its authority and that of the Council being left largely undemarcated and its secretariat separated from the Department of Economic and Social Affairs. The ACC has obviously only an oblique role in regard to questions of co-ordination among the various authorities directly dependent upon the General Assembly and the Council. A fourth factor, related to the one just mentioned, has been the weakness of the Economic and Social Council – a situation which it is expected the Charter amendment to increase its membership will help to rectify, but from which in recent years the ACC has necessarily suffered. Yet another factor is the impending establishment of the Inter-Agency Consultative Board of the United Nations Development Programme and the informal agreement that its meetings, unlike those of the Technical Assistance Board in the past, will be attended by the executive heads of the agencies themselves and synchronized as far as possible with the meetings of the ACC. Finally, account must be taken of the financial situation in the United Nations itself as well as the growing concern of the General Assembly with questions of co-ordination and with the expenditure and financing of the United Nations system.

At the latest (thirty-ninth) session of the Council, there were significant moves towards a closer linking of co-ordination with policy and programme formulation, towards making the Development Decade a broad policy framework for much of the work of the United Nations system, and towards developing a more active working partnership between the ACC and the Council. The ACC has responded by setting up a sub-committee to further the contribution of the international organizations to the Development Decade, and preparations are under way to make the forthcoming joint meeting of the ACC and the Council's Special Committee on Co-ordination as fruitful as possible.

This chapter closes therefore at a time of rather rapid evolution. The structure and *modus operandi* of the ACC itself are not likely to be radically altered, sinse they reflect the structure of international organization set up in 1945; but, to meet the expansion and change in the functions performed by the Committee (whose very name has indeed become misleading), the inter-agency arrangements for consultation and co-operation which have grown up under its aegis may well need to be not only developed but considerably recast in the years ahead.

TEXT REFERENCES

1. C. W. Jenks, *Co-ordination in International Organization, An Introductory Survey*, 1950. *Receuil des Cours de l'Académie de droit International*, Le Haye 1951, remains the standard study of this broad issue.

2. From 1 January 1966, the Administrator and Co-Administrator of the UN Development Programme.

3. These provisions were reproduced in the Agreements subsequently concluded between the United Nations and the other agencies (except the IBRD and its affiliates and the IMF). By Article XI of its Agreement with the UN, the IAEA specifically agreed 'to participate in the work of the Administrative Committee on Co-ordination and, as appropriate, of any other bodies which have been or may be established by the United Nations to facilitate such co-operation and co-ordination'.

4. Originally known as the Co-ordination Committee, it modified its title to 'Administrative Committee on Co-ordination' in 1948 at the instance of the Council in order to distinguish it from the Co-ordination Committee which the Council had begun to set up out of its own membership at each summer session.

5. Before the first meeting, this was informally agreed between Mr Trygve Lie and Mr Edward Phelan, the Director-General of ILO, who was anxious to foster between the specialized agencies and the United Nations relations similar to those that had existed between the International Labour Office and the Secretariat of the League of Nations.

6. Nor has a general revision of the Agreements been seriously considered since.

7. The headings included UNICEF; Relief for Palestine Refugees; child welfare; prevention of crime and treatment of offenders; housing and town

planning; the United Nations Scientific Conference on the conservation and utilization of resources; the World Economic Report; migration; manpower and refugees; transport and communications including the question of the respective functions of ICAO and ITU in the matter of radio communications for civil aviation and the relations between international aeronautics and meteorology; statistics; fellowships; public information and missions.

8. General Assembly Official Records: Fourth Session, Supplement 3 (A/972); p. 16.

9. Except for the Bank and the Fund, whose financial and hence administrative arrangements have always been separate and different from those of the United Nations and the other agencies.

10. On the question of Chinese representation, the USSR had suspended participation in the Security Council.

11. A/6001/Add.1.

12. See E/1991/Add. 1, a fifty-page annex to the ACC's report of May 1951 entitled 'Information on regional co-ordination of programmes of the United Nations and the Specialized Agencies'.

13. Similar arrangements were made in connection with the Economic Commission for Africa when the latter was established in 1958.

14. The years in which agencies' Agreements with the United Nations entered into force and their executive heads thus became members of ACC are as follows: ILO, FAO, UNESCO in 1946; ICAO, the World Bank (IBRD) and the International Monetary Fund (IMF) in 1947; UPU, WHO and IRO (liquidated in 1951) in 1948; ITU in 1949; WHO in 1951; IFC and IAEA (technically not a Specialized Agency but an 'agency under the aegis of the United Nations') in 1957; IMCO in 1959; IDA in 1961. The President of the IBRD is also President of IFC and IDA.

15. A notable further step in the direction of internal co-ordination within the United Nations Secretariat was taken in 1959 when the Technical Assistance Administration was merged with the Department of Economic and Social Affairs.

16. Excluding the IBRD and its affiliates, and the IMF.

17. Estimate.

18. E/3613.

19. The merger was approved by the General Assembly on 22 November 1965, and on 1 January 1966 the United Nations Development Programme came into being.

20. The spring meeting of 1961 was held in Rome, that of 1964 in Paris, and that of 1965 in Vienna.

21. Resolution 799 (XXX) of 1960.

22. Report on the meeting of the Council's officers and Chairman of the Co-ordination Committee with the Administrative Committee on Co-ordination, held on 20 July 1964 (E/3957).

23. Resolution 992 (XXXVI).

24. For example, FAO received through EPTA and the Special Fund a total of $8·3 million in 1959, while its regular budget amounted to $10·5 million. In 1964 the corresponding figures were $32·8 million and $19·5 million.

25. In 1964 IBRD decided to broaden its agricultural activities and began to finance development projects in the field of education; it concluded agreements with FAO and UNESCO for co-operation in this connection.

26. *Five-Year Perspective, 1959-64*, United Nations 1960.

27. The experiment tried in 1963 of dispensing with the autumn meeting in New York, which presents particular difficulties for some members, was unhappy and was not repeated in 1964 or 1965.

28. This observation applies not only to several of the members but also, for example, to the ILO representative on the Preparatory Committee, and the Director-General's alternate on ACC, who has occupied those positions since the first session in 1947; to the present representative of IMF on the Preparatory Committee who has held that position since 1947; to the senior official of the State Department who has been US representative on ECOSOC for co-ordination matters since 1946; and to the author of the present chapter.

29. *Five-Year Perspective, 1959-64*, United Nations 1960, p. 105.

30. E/3957.

31. There are, of course, important fields of co-ordination in which the Specialized Agencies are mainly concerned, e.g. work in respect of education and training, oceanography and co-operatives.

7 UNITED NATIONS PEACE FORCES

Evan Luard

Political institutions, as they develop, often take a form very different from that mapped out for them in theory. The peace-keeping forces established under UN control perfectly demonstrate such a case. The forces that have actually been created have borne little resemblance to the *ideas* about such forces commonly expressed beforehand. They have been closely conditioned by the particular types of situation that called them forth. Only certain kinds of situation have proved capable of bringing them into existence at all. That there has nevertheless been a fairly clear course of development, both in the kinds of force established and the principles under which they have operated, is partly a result of a consistent evolution in the types of situation that have arisen. But it is also the result of a gradual development and crystallization of thought about the nature and scope of such forces within the organization.

Already under the League of Nations there were provisions for international peace-keeping activity. Under Article 16 of the Covenant, the Council of the League (which corresponded to the post-war Security Council) had the power to recommend 'to the several governments concerned what effective military, naval or air forces the Members of the League shall severally contribute to the armed forces to be used to protect the Covenants of the League'. This provision envisaged the establishment, as each crisis arose, of an *ad hoc* force to subdue aggression. The League Council's 'recommendation' to join this force was, moreover, to be discretionary and not, like the corresponding 'decision' of the Security Council, mandatory: in 1923 a resolution was passed explicitly asserting the voluntary principle. The arrangement was indeed the embodiment of the classic theory of collective security: joint, but voluntary, action by the community to put down breaches of the peace by any of its members. Such a 'recommendation' to governments to provide an *ad hoc* force was never in fact made (any more than a corresponding 'decision' under Article 25 of the UN Charter has been made). And the much milder provision for sanctions against an aggressor was only once, and then very half-heartedly, put into practice.

An international force on a more permanent basis was proposed by the French Government during the Disarmament Conference of 1931-4. The main object of this however appeared to many rather to preserve the existing territorial settlement and balance of power against Germany than to preserve peace in a more general sense. And since other powers were not yet ready to contemplate such a drastic renunciation of sovereignty, for this or any other purpose, the proposal received little support elsewhere.

In practice, therefore, it was only where specific crises arose that serious consideration was given to creating an international force. International forces (other than allied, punitive or occupation forces) were established, or proposed, on three occasions in the inter-war period. For the dispute between Poland and Lithuania over Vilna in 1920 the League Council began to make arrangements for an international police force with contingents from ten European powers to control the city; but the plan finally broke down owing to objections from the main parties concerned. For the dispute between Peru and Colombia over Leticia, a League force, though composed in practice of Colombian soldiers wearing League armbands, served, under a League Commission, helping to administer Leticia for a year, pending the final settlement of the dispute. Finally, to police the plebiscite for the future of the Saar in 1935, an international force was set up under the authority of the League's Governing Commission for the Saar.[1]

The forces established during this period, therefore, were all for peace-keeping, rather than enforcement, purposes; only for situations, that is, where little or no fighting was to be expected. And at the end of the Second World War, the League's failure was widely attributed to the lack of 'teeth' for more effective enforcement. Thus when the UN was established it was hoped to establish international forces that could play a far more dominant role in preserving the peace. For this purpose only a permanent international force under the authority of the Security Council, it was felt, would be effective to deter or prevent breaches of the peace. Therefore the Security Council was empowered, in cases of 'threats to the peace, breaches of the peace or acts of aggression' to take steps 'to maintain or restore international peace and security', and, in the final resort, to 'take such action by air, sea or land forces as may be necessary. . .'. Members of the UN were 'to make available to the Security Council . . . armed forces, assistance, and facilities, including rights of passage, necessary for the purpose of maintaining international peace and security'. Special agreements would 'govern the numbers and types of forces, their degree of readiness and general location, and the nature of the facilities and assistance to be provided'. They would be negotiated between the Security Council and individual members or groups of members (such as the OAS) on the initiative of the Security Council. A military staff committee was established, from among the chiefs of staff of the permanent members, to advise and assist the Security Council and provide overall direction of the force.[2]

The negotiations to set up this force broke down on three main points. First, the Soviet Union wished to preserve the principle of exact equality in contributions to the force. The US, Britain, France and China, on the other hand, demanded that each country should be able to contribute according to their ability. Secondly, the US (though not her allies) wanted a considerably larger force than the Soviet Union; however, even the Soviet Union wanted a powerful force, having twelve divisions, about 600 bombers, five to six cruisers, and twenty-four destroyers. Thirdly, the Western powers wished the force to be stationed in bases outside the home country of each contingent; while the Soviet Union (presumably fearing a hostile alliance brought near to her borders) did not.[3]

It is arguable that even if the particular points on which differences arose could have been resolved (and probably today most of the Western powers would be ready to move nearer the Soviet position on each question) it was most unlikely that a force in the form proposed could have played a useful part in the situation actually confronted over the next fifteen years. For the force was to be founded, like the entire UN structure, on the premise of great power unity. The five permanent members were to join in controlling the force to keep the world in order. But the divisions in the world at that time were above all between the permanent members themselves. And there was no conflict in any part of the world that was not to some extent dominated by this division. Since the use of the force would have been governed by a veto, it is unlikely that there could ever have been an effective decision to bring it into action. In the event, when it did finally become possible to establish peace-keeping forces, the permanent members, far from dominating and controlling the force, had to be explicitly excluded from their membership, and deprived of their powers in directing the force by delegating sweeping authority to the Secretary-General.

But the negotiations may have served to make clear some of the more fundamental problems of raising an international force. There were always likely to be differences concerning the strength and powers of the force. There were always likely to be some nations who feared that in such a force they would be putting a weapon into the hands of their enemies. For this reason it was always likely to be the policy of any power in a minority in the UN that a UN peace force should remain under the strict and exclusive control of the Security Council where a veto on its use could be exercised.

As between the wars, therefore, the type of force originally envisaged never came into existence. Partly in consequence of the failure of the talks in the Military Staffs' Committee (this still exists and occasionally meets, though it does not actively function) less ambitious conceptions of the form that UN forces should take began to be aired.

Mr Trygve Lie, the Secretary-General, proposed in July 1948 the creation of 'a small UN guard force' of 1,000 to 5,000 men, 'which would be recruited by the Secretary-General and placed at the disposal of the Security Council and the General Assembly'.[4] This would not, like the proposed force under Chapter VII, be a striking force to resist an aggressor, but a peace-keeping force which might be used 'in the conduct of plebiscites' or 'the administration of truce terms, or as a constabulary under the Security Council or the trusteeship council in cities like Jerusalem and Trieste . . .'. It might 'also be called upon by the Security Council under Article 40 of the Charter, which provides for provisional measures to prevent the aggravation of a situation threatening the peace'. The proposal aroused some opposition in the Assembly because of the cost, the difficulties of organization, and, in the case of the Soviet countries, because they thought the proposal was designed to circumvent the Security Council. Probably the most influential reason was, as Mr Trygve Lie himself later suggested, his idea that the force should be internationally recruited. But the Assembly accepted a less ambitious proposal, also put forward by Mr Lie, for a UN Field Service of 300 communications technicians and guards, to be of assistance in the operation of UN field missions.[5] This force was established and has remained in existence, serving a number of UN activities in the field ever since. The same resolution also set up a panel of Field Observers containing the names of individuals nominated by governments to serve as observers in crisis spots, though this has rarely been used.

As under the League, it was specific crises that produced effective action. UN groups and missions were set up to help keep the peace in particular areas. A UN Truce Supervision Organization was established in Palestine, with several hundred men, to maintain the armistice there, and has remained ever since. Observer groups were set up in Indonesia. And in Kashmir the activities of a UN mediator were supplemented by UN observers on the ground. None of these were themselves peace forces. But the gradual accumulation of actions of this sort served to strengthen and consolidate the concept of international action to police troubled areas.

This remained the situation in 1950 at the time of the outbreak of the Korean War. Here was perhaps the first completely clear-cut case of external aggression since the foundation of the organization. It was also one that was particularly likely to stimulate combined action on behalf of the nation attacked, occurring at a moment when the US in particular, and many of its allies, had become most determined to resist communist expansion in any part of the world. It was made possible to invest such action with Security Council blessing in this case owing to the fact that the Soviet Union was absent from the Council in protest against the refusal to award the China seat to the communist government. And it came at a time when there was a known Western majority in the organization. The Security Council, under the leadership of the United States, called upon all members of the UN to 'furnish such assistance to the Republic of Korea as may be necessary to repel the armed attack'. Military forces for this purpose were afforded by sixteen member states, and non-military support by twenty-one other states. These forces, together with those of South Korea, were designated 'UN forces'. They flew the UN flag. But they retained national uniforms and other emblems of their national origin.

These two facts symbolized the ambivalent status of the force. Though nominally it was subject ultimately to the decisions of the General Assembly, the main collective directing organ was the committee of sixteen, representing the participating powers only, which met in Washington (not New York). And in practice the greater part of the major decisions were made by the US government itself, through direct orders to the 'UN Command' in Korea. This relationship was seen at its clearest in the dismissal of General MacArthur from command of the UN forces. For this dismissal President Truman, and not any UN body, bore both the risk and the credit. Thus the contingents taking part in the Korean War on behalf of the UN cannot be considered in any proper sense a UN peace force. It could be argued that the nations participating were mainly those that would have taken part in any case, on grounds of direct national interest, whether or not it had been possible to legitimize the force through investing it with UN authority.

But the Korean experience re-awakened attention to the problem of UN peace-keeping. On the one hand, the realization that under normal circumstances it would not have been possible to take action there under the UN colours brought a determination to find means of circumventing the Security Council where necessary. On the other, the lack of readily available UN forces that could be quickly brought into use in such emergencies revived the search to establish such forces once again. These two concerns were reflected in the Uniting for Peace Resolution, passed, largely at US instigation, on 3 November 1950.

The first concern was met by the best known provision of the resolution. This provided that, when a resolution to deal with a threat to the peace, a breach of the peace or an act of aggression fails in the Security Council because of the veto, an emergency session of the General Assembly may be called, on the affirmative vote of any seven members of the Council, at twenty-four hours notice. The second concern was met by another, less well-known, recommendation of the resolution, that:

> each member maintain within its national forces elements so trained, organized and equipped that they could be promptly made available in accordance with its constitutional processes [i.e. only with the member's consent], for service as a UN unit or units, upon recommendation by the Security Council or the General Assembly.[6]

In addition, the resolution established two other organs, a Collective Measures Committee, to study and report on measures which could be used collectively to maintain and strengthen international peace and security; and a Peace Observation Committee, with fourteen members, to be used by the General Assembly or Security Council to observe and report on the situation in any area of international tension.

Only the first of these four recommendations can be said to have exerted any significant change in UN practice. The procedure for referring a matter from the Security Council to the General Assembly in case of deadlock in the former has been used a number of times, including several of the most acute crises faced by the organization; for example, over Suez, Hungary and the Lebanon and Jordan crisis in 1958. It has been crucial in the development of peace-keeping operations, since only through it could the first UN force be established and maintained under the authority of the General Assembly.

The appeal to members to set aside part of their forces for international peace-keeping purposes on the other hand elicited virtually no response at all. Although the system now proposed was in fact far less ambitious than had been envisaged in the UN Charter itself (for the forces would no longer be made over to the Security Council, to be used entirely at the discretion of that body, but would be 'maintained' by individual governments), the proposal foundered on the resistances of national sovereignty (despite the fact that a majority had originally voted in its favour). The Collective Measures Committee approached all UN members asking them 'as a matter of urgency' what they intended to do to implement the resolution's recommendation to earmark forces. Only four, Denmark, Norway, Greece and Thailand, unequivocally offered forces, to a total of 6,000 men, mainly from Thailand. Uruguay offered two destroyers. The other answers (of those which answered at all) were either negative, non-committal, or so hedged about with conditions as to amount to refusals. Even the United States, which had sponsored the resolution, now became supremely cautious, indicating merely that the forces which it already maintained under the North Atlantic Treaty could, if necessary, 'participate in collective military measures to maintain or restore peace and security in the North Atlantic area in support of UN action'. And Mr Trygve Lie's alternative proposal of a 'UN legion', by which smaller nations could contribute troops to a UN force, won no more support than his earlier proposals, and partly for the same reason: namely, that it was suspected, despite Mr Lie's strenuous denials, that the real objective was the creation of a fully international force that would be largely independent of national control.[7]

A somewhat similar fate befell the Peace Observation Commission, designed to send teams of observers to situations of tension to supply the UN with accurate information. The Commission has remained in existence, with a largely unchanged membership, since that time. A Sub-Commission was used to report on the frontier areas of Greece between 1952 and 1954. But apart from this the Committee has not been used at all. This could scarcely be for lack of situations requiring observation. The Collective Measures Committee, which the resolution also established, met between 1951 and 1954. It considered a large number of different measures, political, economic, financial, as well as military, which could be used as sanctions against international breaches of the peace. The General Assembly took note of these reports. But it has never called for any of the proposals suggested to be put into effect in subsequent crisis situations.

During the second five years of the organization, therefore, one major UN force was established and undertook perhaps the only successful military action by an international organization to defeat aggression yet achieved. A major revision of the constitutional structure of the United Nations was put through (perhaps illegally), which alone made possible the accomplishment of some future peace-keeping operations. The first, however, was a type of success most unlikely to be repeated. The second, by sacrificing the goodwill of important members, carried dangers of its own. Hard experience of the type of peace-keeping operation that was normally to be possible had yet to be acquired.

This remained the situation in 1956, before the first of the three major peace-keeping operations of the organization began. The Suez crisis of 1956 had many of the ingredients best calculated to spur effective international action. Like the Korean invasion it was one of the few cases the organization had met in which there occurred a clear and flagrant case of external attack against the territory of a member. Next, it was a situation calculated to arouse the wide body of anti-colonial sentiment within the organization. Finally, it was not a case where any active fighting was likely to be required by the force set up. For by the time it was established all the three principal parties concerned, the Egyptians, the Israelis and the British and French, had expressed their readiness, however reluctantly, to a cease-fire. That this readiness existed was the result of factors wholly independent of the proposal for a peace force: the unexpected violence and unity of world reactions, the uncompromising position of the US, the severe financial crisis precipitated for some parties, and the gradual realization of the folly of believing that the capture of the

Canal would enable the three powers to dictate terms to Egypt (and the world) on the three quite separate issues on which they were in dispute with her.

The peace force therefore was not so much a military device as a diplomatic one, a face-saving procedure which might serve to soften the humiliation of withdrawal, and offer, to Israel, as much or more than to Egypt, some satisfaction of basic apprehensions. It was indeed the British delegate, not Mr Lester Pearson, who first proposed the force. And it could be successful mainly because to each of the parties it could be represented as securing some different, but important, purpose. To Egypt it might serve to evict the invading forces; to Israel it might restore security in the Gaza Strip; and to Britain and France it could, so at least they hoped, restore the Canal to international control and strengthen the bargaining position of the maritime powers in negotiating on the Canal's future. Without these conflicting concepts of the force's function it is perhaps unlikely that it could have been made acceptable to the four governments concerned and their public opinions at home.

These facts had a considerable bearing on the shape the force took and the principles adopted in its creation. Mr Pearson, in his first demand for the force, had called for one 'large enough to keep these borders at peace while a political settlement is being worked out',[8] so implying that the force would be used not only to shoo out the invading forces but to police the frontier after the withdrawal as well. The resolution passed by the Assembly on November 4 authorized the Security Council to submit a plan 'for the setting up, with the consent of the nations concerned, of an emergency international UN force to secure and supervise the cessation of hostilities'. But it also said that this was to be done 'in accordance with the terms of the resolution of November 2', which in turn had referred to the need to refrain from attacks from either side of the border. It was because of such ambiguous provisions that the proposal could be made acceptable to the invading powers, providing for them some promise of pacifying the border. Conversely, because of the unanimity of feeling in favour of an international force to secure withdrawal, not to speak of the need to distract attention from Hungary, the Soviet Union too, despite her strongly-held constitutional objections, was constrained to abstain both over the invocation of the Uniting for Peace procedure, and on the creation of the force by the Assembly rather than the Security Council (though she expressed reservations in explaining her votes).

As a result, a UN command was established under General Burns, the Chief of Staff of the UN Truce Supervision Organization in Palestine. The Secretary-General proposed that the stationing and operation of the force would be subject to the consent of the governments concerned. Troops would not be drawn from countries that were permanent members of the Security Council. Nations providing troops would be responsible for all costs for equipment and salaries, but all other costs would be borne by the UN from a special fund outside its normal budget. The force as established contained contingents from ten countries of the twenty-four that offered. The Secretary-General declared that he had refused no contributions but that practical considerations made necessary a selection in order to have a limited and balanced force. In this case UN berets were issued, establishing the contingent as an international UN force, as the armies in Korea had never been.

The first 600 men arrived by 20 November 1956, but the force did not reach its full strength of 6,000 till February 1957. By 22 December, all British and French troops had left Egypt. The Israeli government attempted to negotiate on the terms on which withdrawal from the Gaza Strip and the Gulf of Aqaba would be carried out. After long discussions, and a further resolution in the General Assembly, Israel finally withdrew all her forces by the end of March 1957, though she never allowed the UN force to operate on her own side of the border. The force has remained on the other side of the frontier line ever since. It has been slightly reduced in number to about 5,000 and the number of countries participating reduced to seven.

A number of key problems of peace-keeping were encountered for the first time by UNEF and certain principles of operation established. Some, but not all of these, have created precedents that have been maintained since.

The first of the problems was the extent to which the national sovereignty of the host country must be respected by a peace-keeping force. In this case there was some difficulty in persuading the host country to accept a force at all. Mr Hammarskjöld thus laid great emphasis on the principle that the UN force could not function without the full consent of, nor against the interests and wishes of, the host government. The second of the reports on the proposed force which he presented to the Assembly on November 6 declared that:

> while the General Assembly is enabled to *establish* the force with the consent of those parties which contribute units to the force, it could not request the force to be *stationed* or *operate* in the territory of a given country without the consent of the government of that country. . . . There is no intent in the establishment of the force to influence the military balance in the present conflict and, thereby, the political balance affecting efforts to settle the conflict.

This last was a particularly sensitive point because there existed here a political issue of the highest importance – the future control of the Suez Canal – which might have been influenced by the presence of an international force. Without such assurances, it is doubtful whether the Egyptian government would have accepted a force at all. Considerably greater deference than on subsequent occasions was paid also to Egyptian views about the composition of the force. Largely because of Egypt's objections, Pakistani and New Zealand troops were not accepted, and though she was not allowed to exclude Canadian troops altogether, she succeeded in ensuring that they served only in a supporting, and not in a front-line role.

Next, there arose the question of the nature and permanency of the responsibilities undertaken by the force. It was conceived originally as a temporary and *ad hoc* undertaking. The UN contingent was described, and remains, 'an emergency force'. The Secretary-General declared that the length of the assignment of the force would be 'determined by the needs arising out of the present conflict'. Few UN members could have believed that the force would still be in existence eight years after its formation.[9] Yet as we have seen, there were some who, from the start, expected the force to have wider functions than supervising the evacuation of the invading troops. The force was to 'secure and supervise the cessation of hostilities' . . . 'in accordance with all the terms of the General Assembly Resolution 997 of November 2nd, 1956'. The word 'all' is significant. That resolution had demanded not only a cease-fire, but had called on Egypt and Israel to 'withdraw all forces behind the armistice lines, to desist from raids across the armistice lines into neighbouring territory, and to observe scrupulously the provisions of the armistice agreements'. It is in fulfilment of the terms of this resolution therefore that the force has maintained its existence so long after the final withdrawal of all invading forces.

Next, there was the problem of control of the force. It was ultimately under the authority of the General Assembly which set it up. In the Secretary-General's words 'the basic political decisions of the Assembly constitute the fundamental law of this whole operation'.[10] But in practice a large measure of day-to-day authority was assigned to the Secretary-General himself. The Secretary-General suggested the Commander of the force, formulated the plan for UNEF and its operations, negotiated with individual governments concerning their contributions, determined at his own discretion which contributions should be accepted and which declined, negotiated with Egypt concerning the admission of the force and with Britain, France and Israel concerning the conditions of their withdrawal and determined very many other matters. Though an Advisory Committee was established 'to undertake the development of those aspects of the planning of the force and its operations not already dealt with by the General Assembly and which do not fall within the area of the direct responsibility of the Chief of Command', consultation with the Committee was largely a formality. Many of the most important decisions were undertaken by the Secretary-General, or his officers, on their own responsibility. In all these points, therefore, the control procedure was very far from that envisaged in the UN Charter, which had assigned all responsibility for the maintenance of international peace and security to the Security Council. The Security Council was the one organ of the organization not at all concerned in the operation of the UNEF. It was on these grounds that the Soviet Union rapidly became increasingly critical of the force. And, with France, she declined altogether to contribute to its cost, declaring that this should be undertaken by the countries whose forces had taken part in the invasion.

Next, principles had to be developed concerning the powers of the force, especially in relation to the host government. Mr Hammarskjöld's skill in ambiguity is well known, but it was perhaps never so useful to him as on this occasion. For example, the resolution of 2 November, which was to guide the operation of the force, had declared that 'upon the cease-fire being effective, steps be taken to re-open the Suez Canal and restore secure freedom of navigation'. This might have meant, as Britain and France demanded, that the force should be empowered to retain control of the Canal until Egypt had agreed satisfactory terms for its operation; or, as Israel demanded, that it should ensure the opening of the Canal to Israel's ships. In fact, Egypt demanded and received private assurances from Mr Hammarskjöld that the force would not be used for purposes of this kind. But there were many other uncertainties. The exact powers of the force only came to be defined closely as its operations proceeded. Representatives of the UN, including the Secretary-General himself, negotiated with the Egyptian government concerning the terms on which the force should operate. Eventually, in February 1957, an explicit agreement defining the status of UN forces, and arrangements over criminal and civil jurisdiction, privileges and immunities, was concluded. This agreement, more comprehensive than anything reached in subsequent operations, was embodied in an exchange of letters, and subsequently approved by the General Assembly.

There was the problem concerning the power to use armed force. In the beginning, largely to reassure Egypt about the force's possible political role, the Secretary-General stressed the fact that it was 'not a force with military objectives', and could not become a force 'temporarily controlling the territory in which it was stationed'. On the other hand it was to be 'more than an observers' corps', so the forces involved would in fact be armed soldiers. In policing the border especially, the need to use force might arise. When such policing became the main role of the force, General Burns specifically asked for the right to use force for this purpose if necessary. The Secretary-General, and the Advisory Committee, in replying, laid it down that shooting by the force would only be permissible 'in self-defence'.

Finally, there arose the crucial problem of whether the withdrawal by invading powers needed to be unconditional. Many UN members felt that there should be no discussion between the Secretary-General and Israel concerning the long-term future of the border until her own aggression had been 'vacated'. Mr Hammarskjöld himself maintained in his talks with Israel that the object of the force would be to restore the *status quo ante* (as defined in the Armistice Agreement of 1949) and could not be used to alter that situation (for example by denying Egyptian re-entry to the Gaza Strip or to the shore of the Gulf of Aqaba). But other members of the UN felt it was proper to provide some assurances for Israel. A resolution was passed in the Assembly on 2 February (before the Israeli withdrawal) which, while it called for a withdrawal 'without delay', also declared that after this the

> scrupulous maintenance of the Armistice Agreement requires the placing of the UNEF on the Egyptian–Israel armistice demarcation line and the implementation of other measures . . . with a view to assist in achieving situations conducive to the maintenance of peaceful conditions in the area.

This was no doubt of great importance in securing Israeli withdrawal; but it was held by some members to represent a concession to Israeli demands under duress and a violation of the principle that Israel should not be able to claim that she had extracted any advantage from her act of aggression.

Before the next use of a UN peace-keeping force in the Congo, there were other occasions on which a UN presence of a lesser kind was established or requested.

During the civil war in Lebanon in 1958, Lebanon complained to the Security Council of intervention in its internal affairs by the UAR. On Swedish initiative, the Security Council passed a resolution in which it was decided to 'dispatch urgently an observation group to proceed to Lebanon so as to ensure that there was no illegal infiltration of personnel, or supply of arms or other material across the Lebanese borders'.[11] The force as constituted consisted of two parts: the observation group 'composed of highly qualified and experienced men . . . selected from various corners of the globe'; and the group servicing these drawn from the UNTSO in Palestine. Mr Hammarskjöld made clear the group was not supposed to be a police force such as the UNEF in Sinai. There were about 600 observers, drawn from countries thought to be neutral, and not including the permanent members of the Security Council.

After the revolution in Iraq in July of that year, US and British troops were flown to Lebanon and Jordan respectively at the request of the governments of those countries. During the subsequent debates at the UN, first in the Security Council and subsequently in the General Assembly, there were demands from a number of countries for the despatch of a UN peace force to the two countries. The Secretary-General, who was perhaps reluctant that the UN should be placed in the position of sending forces to defend a government that might have lost the support of many of its people, declared this to be impossible without exceeding present instructions and violating the charter.

> In a police operation the participants would . . . need the right, if necessary, to take the initiative in the use of force. Such use of force would, however, have belonged to the sphere of Chapter VII of the Charter and could have been granted only by the Security Council itself.[12]

This contention is interesting and important in the light of the subsequent Congo operation.

The Secretary-General preferred proposals to strengthen the observer group. Subsequent proposals for the formation and despatch of a UN peace force, both to Lebanon and Jordan, were all rejected. A final settlement was reached, after stability had already returned to the two countries concerned, by the passing of a resolution, accepted by the US and Britain, calling for a withdrawal of all foreign troops. The Jordan government accepted the despatch of a special representative of the Secretary-General to Jordan, with adequate staff to 'assist in the implementation of the resolution, specifically with a view to help in upholding the principles and purposes of the Charter in relation to Jordan in the present circumstances'.

The despatch of a special representative was also the solution found in the case of the appeal by Laos for assistance against an alleged invasion from Vietnam in 1959. As a result of guerrilla activity in the northern provinces, the Laotian government appealed to the UN for the despatch of a UN emergency force 'to halt aggression and prevent it from spreading'. The Security Council decided to send a UN sub-committee to Laos to investigate the situation. The sub-committee reported that the evidence 'did not clearly establish whether there were crossings of the frontier by regular troops' from Vietnam, though there was some evidence of support from outside. Later Mr Hammarskjöld paid a visit to Laos to inform himself of the situation and finally, against the wishes of the Soviet delegate, appointed a special representative to the area, to review the economic assistance that might be required there and to act as a kind of personal observer on his behalf.

Over the civil war in the Yemen, a team of UN observers was despatched in April 1963, for a limited period in the first place but subsequently extended over a period of a year and a half. Here the main purpose was to bring about the disengagement of Saudi Arabia and Egypt, both of whom accused the other of intervening in the war. These two countries agreed themselves to bear the cost of the operation. The mission was, however, unable to achieve any effective degree of withdrawal, especially by Egypt, and it was finally withdrawn altogether. Finally, a UN force was set up temporarily in West Irian (again by the Assembly) for a period of nine months to supervise the change-over from Dutch to Indonesian administration, and to keep the peace during the interim period of UN control there.

Perhaps more important for the general development of peace-keeping forces was the 'summary study' which the Secretary-General drew up after the Levant crisis, comparing the UN operations in Suez, Lebanon and Jordan.[13] This might be regarded as a sort of progress report on UN peace-keeping operations to that time (though it was very shortly to be outdated by events elsewhere). The report set out a number of conditions that should be met in UN peace-keeping operations (as opposed to enforcement action). It underlined the need for specific agreements with the host government concerning the terms on which the force could operate (like the Status of Forces Agreement with Egypt). It maintained the principle of freedom of movement for UN forces in any area where they were engaged. It laid down that units from any of the permanent members of the Security Council, or from any state having an interest in the dispute, should be excluded from such forces. It made a clear distinction between enforcement action under Chapter VII and peace-keeping action under other headings. For all operations of the latter kind the consent of the host government was required. But even when this was obtainable, not all conflict situations were suitable for UN action. A police force had been suitable at Suez for dividing 'regular, national military forces which were subject to a cease-fire agreed to by the opposing parties'; and because it had a mandate which 'entirely detached it from involvement in any internal or local problems, and . . . enabled it to maintain its neutrality in relation to international political issues'. None of these conditions was met in the Lebanon and Jordan cases. Here the forces involved were not 'regular, national' forces, already divided and bound by a cease-fire agreement, but irregular rebel forces; the UN could not have been detached from 'internal or local problems'; nor would it necessarily have been able to maintain neutrality in relation to international political issues.

The Secretary-General could scarcely have been expected to foresee that in the next major operation in which peace-keeping forces were to be required the conditions to be met were precisely those defined by him as unsuitable for peace-keeping operations.

The circumstances that brought about the creation of a UN force in the Congo in 1960 had some similarities to those that had had a similar result at the time of Suez. The original object, here again, was to secure the ejection of foreign forces, the Belgian army units that were flown back to the Congo at the time of the mutiny of the Force Publique. Assistance was demanded by the newly independent Congo government 'to protect the national territory of the Congo against the present external aggression which is a threat to international peace'. The request was therefore able on the one hand to appeal to the very powerful strain of anti-imperialist sentiment within the UN; on the other, it could represent the threat as one of external, rather than, as it subsequently became, of internal aggression. A further factor encouraging international action, in both cases, was fear that without it there was risk of cold war rivalries being injected (at one point the Congo government was threatening that if no UN force was sent, they would 'regretfully' invite Soviet troops instead). As a result of these three elements in the situation, members of the UN, including the permanent members, were able to agree relatively quickly on the despatch of a force. They might have been less willing to do so if they could have foreseen the nature of the conflict they were in fact to be mainly concerned with.

The Congo Government, from the very start, may have hoped that the UN force would be of assistance in restoring internal law and order. The very insistence with which they asserted that 'the purpose of the aid is not to restore the internal situation in the Congo but rather to protect the national territory against an act of aggression by Belgian metropolitan troops' indicated how conscious they were that other motives might be attributed to them. The resolution setting up the force reflected this ambiguity. It authorized the Secretary-General to take necessary steps 'in consultation with the government of the Republic of the Congo, to provide the government with such military assistance as may be necessary until, through the efforts of the Congolese government with the technical assistance of the UN, the national security forces may be able, in the opinion of the government, fully to meet their task'.[14] This left wide latitude for interpretation.

The new operation therefore already followed the precedent of UNEF in placing primary responsibility on the Secretary-

General for the raising and day-to-day management of the force. This had the advantage of overcoming the possibility of veto action by permanent members over individual acts of policy in the Congo. It was for this reason that it commended itself to many members. And it was for the same reason that the Soviet Union, so soon as it became apparent that the Secretary-General was not to defer to Mr Lumumba on every point, turned from support to increasingly vociferous criticism.

It was proposed by the Secretary-General and accepted by members that, as before, the forces of permanent members should be excluded from membership of the force. And in general Mr Hammerskjöld sought at first to follow the principles he had laid down in his 1958 report. He specifically reaffirmed, among the most important of these, that:

> the authority granted to the UN Force cannot be exercised within the Congo either in competition with representatives of the host government or in co-operation with them in any joint operation.

It could not be used to enforce political solutions or influence the internal political balance. Similarly the Security Council in its resolution of 9 August affirmed that 'the UN Force in the Congo will not be a party to, or in any way intervene in or be used to influence, the outcome of any conflict, internal or otherwise'. Such an ambition, like others held in the early days, proved under later conditions totally impossible to fulfil.

A greater independence of action was obtained for the Congo force even at the start than had occurred for that in Sinai. The Secretary-General, through personal talks with the Congo cabinet, on 30 July 1960, reached an agreement laying down the basis on which the force would operate.[15] It was laid down, perhaps to forestall the type of difficulty that had occurred with Egypt, that the UN alone was to decide on the national composition of the military elements in the force, though 'with full consideration of the host country's views'. The principle of freedom of movement for the force, laid down by the Secretary-General in the 1958 memorandum, was reaffirmed in the agreement. The principle of the consent of the host country, on which such emphasis had been placed in the Suez operation, though not repudiated, was here significantly weakened. For example, in the 30 July Agreement, it was laid down that the UN 'is prepared to maintain the UN Force until such time as it deems that the latter's task has been fully accomplished'. The words 'it deems' (that is, the UN deems) marked a very significant departure from the insistence on the host government's consent maintained in relation to Egypt. Immediately after the agreement was reached, Mr Gizenga, the Deputy Premier, was complaining of the fact that some of the operations of the UN infringed the Congo's sovereign rights. The UN Force increasingly defied Mr Lumumba's express wishes. By occupying the radio station and the airfields it effectively intervened in a crucial sense in the civil war. And six months later there was a period when Mr Kasavubu, the acknowledged president of the country, was calling for the removal of the entire force, wholly unheeded by the UN.

In speed and efficiency of execution, the Congo operation compared extremely favourably with that in Sinai. While in Egypt it was three months before the full force of 6,000 men was in operation, in the Congo, by the end of July, barely a fortnight after the first Security Council resolution, a force of about 11,000, from seven different nations, was already deployed and Belgian evacuation had begun. Though the Secretary-General himself had at one time spoken of a force of African nations only, and though this was strongly demanded by certain African states and by the Soviet Union, in fact contributions from outside Africa were accepted. But in this case these were entirely non-aligned. Thus, while Canada, Denmark and Norway, all NATO nations, had been permitted to take part in the Egyptian operation, in the Congo the only non-African countries to send troops were Ireland, Sweden, India and Malaya.

After only a few weeks the character of the operation quickly changed. By mid-September, all but a handful of Belgian troops had been evacuated. By this time, however, various serious internal conflicts had developed. The government of Katanga had declared its independence and was refusing entry to central government forces. Soon afterwards, the central government was itself disputed between the President (Kasavubu) and his Prime Minister (Lumumba). Later, new secessionist movements grew up in other provinces. Increasingly the main threat to the Congo's peace came not from the Belgians, but from internal Congolese dissension. In consequence the UN Force was increasingly unable to avoid intervening in the internal affairs of the country.

This inevitably brought changes in the principles hitherto adopted for peace-keeping operations. The principle that the force should not intervene in domestic matters was repeatedly proclaimed, not only by members of the UN of all political persuasions – communist countries determined to maintain the principle that the UN had no right of political intervention, colonial and other Western governments anxious to preserve the letter of Article 2 (7), African nations apprehensive of the reintroduction of 'neo-colonialism' within a UN Trojan Horse – but by the Secretary-General, seeking to preserve the principles he himself had laid down for the conduct of such operations. There were attempts to interpret all UN action as directed at the eviction of white mercenaries. But in practice UN troops were obliged, increasingly, to take over control of airfields, broadcasting stations and other strategically vital points. The UN was forced to determine whether other forces, including those of the government itself, should have access to such facilities. And increasingly it had to determine whether itself to take action, in Katanga and other provinces, against the various secessionist forces there.

In fact, so long as UN intervention was only on behalf of the legitimate and internationally recognized government, that is, to preserve the existing situation of a unitary Congo state against the forces that threatened it, there seems little reason why UN intervention need have been thought impermissible. Dr Bunche, the Secretary-General's special representative in the Congo, declared that 'the principal purpose of the UN force in the Congo . . . is to assist the government in maintaining law and order'.[16] Even the initial resolution despatching the force had declared that the force would 'provide the government with such military assistance as may be necessary' pending the restoration of law and order.[17] The maintenance of law and order inevitably demanded, on occasion, action against armed forces hostile to the government. And action to subdue secessionist forces in Katanga was not different in kind from action against dissident and unruly forces in the countryside. Both of them were different in kind from the form of action undertaken in Egypt, designed to separate the forces of different national armies. But they were not necessarily illegal, especially as they remained under the ultimate control of the Security Council. And it may be that in practice the Secretary-General's reservations were based rather on considerations of expediency than of principle.

Similarly, it became more and more difficult to maintain the principle that UN forces could act only in self-defence. This demand became increasingly difficult to reconcile with the force's basic aims. Partly for these reasons, under the terms of the Security Council's resolution of 21 February 1961, a new mandate was given to the force. The new resolution called for the reorganization of the army to prevent its interference in the political life of the Congo, demanded the withdrawal of all mercenaries and other foreign advisers and urged that the UN 'take immediately all appropriate measures to prevent the recurrence of civil war in the Congo, including arrangements for cease-fires, the halting of all military operations, the prevention of clashes and the use of force, if necessary, in the last resort'.[18] This last phrase served to release the UN Force from the restriction which had been placed on it by the Secretary-General's earlier principles. The permissibility of force 'if necessary, in the last resort' meant that in practice (for who can determine what is 'necessary'?) there was no longer any insuperable restriction on what it could do. And when, later, Dr O'Brien led UN forces on a campaign of conquest in Katanga, his action was, in the light of this resolution, open to criticism rather on the grounds of exceeding the bounds of political prudence than of legal authority.

The nature of the Congo peace-keeping operation also made necessary rethinking on the question of financing. The Congo operation was far more extensive and far more costly than that in Egypt. The difficulties were temporarily eased by the device of issuing low interest bonds for this purpose, which were taken up by both member and non-member governments. There remained, however, the intensely controversial point of whether member states that had not approved, or themselves participated in, such undertakings were under an obligation, as members of the organization, to pay part of the costs. While the Congo operation was still taking place, the General Assembly requested an advisory opinion on this point from the International Court of Justice. A majority of the court ruled to the effect that such costs, while outside the normal budget of the organization, must be regarded as part of its general expenses (even when, as in Sinai, the action was authorized by the General Assembly rather than the Security Council); and therefore must be paid for under the formula for assessing all other costs of the organization. This advice, though accepted by the Assembly, was rejected by the Soviet Union, France and several other governments. As a result, these finally became so overdue with their total contributions, including those for the force, that they were liable to forfeit their right to vote in the General Assembly. Only the establishment of a committee deputed to consider the whole question of the authorization, control and financing of peace-keeping operations in February 1965, served to avert the crisis that ensued. In course of its discussions the defaulting nations were no longer threatened with the loss of their votes and the general principles governing peace-keeping operations were examined afresh.

The UN did eventually succeed in reconquering Katanga and in handing it back to the authority of the central government. Even by the time the force finally left, in June 1964, however, it had not been successful in securing the reintegration of other parts of the country, notably Orientale Province. Indeed, in that year, Lumumbist forces once again captured Stanleyville and increased their strength elsewhere. The ultimate irony came with the installation of Mr Tshombe as Prime Minister, leading the government's forces on behalf of a united Congo against secessionist forces in the provinces. This was a case therefore of a peace force whose task was not completed when it was disbanded. It was obliged to leave ultimately because members of the UN were no longer sufficiently convinced of the urgency of the situation to vote the funds necessary to maintain or extend its operations. During the four years of its existence it could however perhaps claim to have improved the internal security position of the country over the period when it arrived, and to have helped to build up an administrative and governmental structure considerably more competent than that which created for it so many difficulties when it first began operations.

Even the UN operation in the Congo, therefore, was increasingly directed towards internal disturbances. In Cyprus, where the third UN peace-keeping force was established, the conflict was, from the start, domestic. It is true that the close association of the Greek and Turkish governments with the dispute made it easy to find an international justification for UN action. But it was clearly recognized that, in practice, the force would be operating primarily to prevent civil war in Cyprus.

In this case the UN force had been preceded by a purely national, British peace-keeping force called in earlier for the same purpose. During 1963 there had been prolonged tension over the proposal of the Makarios government to amend the constitution agreed between Britain, Greece, Turkey and the two Cypriot communities under the Zurich Agreement of 1960. Bitter intercommunal fighting broke out at the end of December. After a visit to Cyprus by Mr Sandys, British Minister of Commonwealth Relations, it was agreed between Britain, the Cyprus government, Greece and Turkey that British troops should be sent to Cyprus to take responsibility for maintaining order. In January 1964, a conference opened in London between Britain, Greece, Turkey and the representatives of the two Cypriot communities, but failed to reach any agreement. An Anglo-American plan for a NATO Force to hold the ring in Cyprus was rejected by President Makarios. And on 15 February Britain and Cyprus both independently brought the matter before the Security Council. Both supported the establishment of an international force, though there were varying ideas about its exact functions. On 4 March, the Security Council recommended 'the creation, with the consent of the government of Cyprus, of a UN peace-keeping force in Cyprus'. The function of the force would be 'in the interests of preserving international peace and security to use its best efforts to prevent a recurrence of fighting, and, if necessary, to contribute to the maintenance and restoration of law and order and a return to normal conditions'. A UN mediator, to seek a final settlement, was also appointed. The force was to be stationed for a period of three months only in the first place, but this was prolonged by subsequent resolutions.

The limitation of the duration of the force was probably partly the result of previous difficulties over financing. These also had the effect that this time it was laid down that the costs were to be met, 'in a manner to be agreed upon', by the governments providing the contingents and by the government of Cyprus (the observer force in the Yemen had also been paid for by the parties to the dispute) though the Secretary-General might also accept voluntary contributions from other governments. In fact voluntary contributions of this kind, from the US, West Germany, Greece and some other countries, have covered a large part of the cost.

As in the Congo, it was the Security Council that authorized the force. But once again considerable powers were delegated to the Secretary-General. The composition and size of the force was to be 'established by the Secretary-General, in consultation with the governments of Cyprus, Greece, Turkey and the UK'. Thus the main responsibility of the Secretary-General for determining the force's composition was laid down from the start. In this case consultation was to include other governments than the host country, a new departure which the special circumstances in Cyprus could justify. But no exclusive right of the host country to determine these matters was acknowledged. The force established was made up of contingents from Austria, Canada, Finland, Ireland and Sweden.

Responsibility for the day-to-day running of the force was also accorded to the Secretary-General. Concern on this point was expressed in a new way. In the Congo, the Soviet Union, which became increasingly and violently critical of the authority wielded by the Secretary-General there, had been vulnerable to the reply that she herself had voted in favour of the force's formation. On this occasion, the Soviet Union, Czechoslovakia and France all voted in favour of the whole resolution with its varied recommendations. But they called for a separate vote on paragraph 4, containing the proposals for the creation and control of the force. On this they abstained (to vote against the paragraph would have brought the veto into effect). All three governments expressed objection to this further delegation of the power of the Council to the Secretary-General, but France objected on more general grounds to the entire principle of 'intervention by the UN in a military form'.

An agreement between the UN and the Cyprus government

on the status of the UN force was entered into and published. This provided among other things for freedom of movement for the force. It laid down that Cyprus security forces would assist the UN in maintaining order when requested to do so. But conversely, if the Cyprus security forces requested assistance, the UN force commander would decide whether he might meet the request within the framework of the Security Council resolution. Such provisions, which protected the United Nations to some extent from the demands met in the Congo that it should use its power on behalf of the government, were another indication of the powers and authority demanded by the UN in this case. In practice, the UN forces became involved in a number of incidents with both Greek and Turkish Cypriot irregulars. They were obliged on occasion to open fire, and in some cases its members were even taken prisoner for a few hours, though they did not, like those in the Congo, suffer any deaths through armed action.

Thus the force was from the start inevitably, like the Congo force, faced with the highly delicate political problems associated with peace-keeping in a civil war. Although Greece and Turkey were closely involved, and even had forces in the island (under the terms of the Zurich agreement) the disturbances that occurred were primarily between the Greek and Turkish Cypriots. In this case therefore there was no attempt even at the start to restrict the operation of the force by a principle of non-intervention. But some of the same problems that had occurred in the Congo re-emerged. The chief of these naturally concerned the extent to which the force could resist the demands and wishes of the legal government. Once again, that government put forward the claim that the purpose of the force was to assist it to enforce its authority on dissident subjects. And once again, the UN, officials and soldiers alike, refused to accept this interpretation. But while in the case of the Congo, the UN, though insistently denying the right, or power, of intervention, even on behalf of the government, in practice had increasingly become ready to do so (especially after the resolution of 22 February 1961), in Cyprus the reverse was the case: though the UN professed respect for the constitutional position in Cyprus and for the rights of the government to exert authority, in practice they would not assist it militarily to accomplish those ends, even when the Turkish Cypriots could claim no clear legal right on their behalf. The UN, for example, consistently refused to seek to remove the Turks from their positions along the Nicosia–Kyrenia road. They would not attempt to disarm Turkish Cypriots in isolation from similar attempts in relation to Greek Cypriots. In certain cases they refused access to Cyprus government officials or forces to parts of their own country, in case of the danger of conflict. Finally, they strongly resisted the right of Cyprus government officials and soldiers to restrict their own freedom of movement.

There was a certain justification for this attitude. First, the Turks in Cyprus could at least claim legally entrenched rights in Cyprus to the extent that they upheld the legality of the Zurich agreements, while President Makarios and his government never concealed their determination to overthrow them. In carrying out Mr Hammarskjöld's principle of not overturning the political balance, therefore, the UN could claim that they were obliged to protect the position of the Turks, in a way that they were not obliged to protect the status of Katanga. Secondly, from a practical political point of view, equally, it is undeniable that if the UN had been ready to undertake action on behalf of the Cyprus government to bring the Turks to submission, the chances of achieving a long term reconciliation would have been almost totally destroyed.

Problems concerning the powers of the force were also raised, more forcefully than in any previous operation, by the governments participating in it. Incidents in Cyprus involving British UN troops aroused intense controversy in Britain and a demand for stronger terms of reference for the UN Force. On 11 March, U Thant sent confidentially to the British and other interested governments a list of fourteen points and an *aide-memoire* sum-marizing his instructions to the commander of the force. When, later, Mr Sandys, in reply to criticism, declared that the question of getting clear and effective terms of reference for the force was 'under active discussion with the Secretary-General and other countries concerned', a UN spokesman denied this, and said that the terms of reference of the force could not be the subject of negotiations or discussions with individual member-governments, yet another striking assertion of autonomous UN powers. There was a strong demand in Britain for the publication of the terms of reference, though Mr Sandys said he himself recognized them to be reasonable. Eventually, Mr Butler, the Foreign Secretary, informed the House that, though the exact terms of reference and instructions to the UN Commander were still regarded as confidential by the Secretary-General, the Secretariat had made available an *aide-memoire* on the functions and operation of the force that could be made public. This maintained, *inter alia*, that the force would 'avoid any action designed to influence the political situation in Cyprus except through contributing to a restoration of quiet and through creating an improved climate in which political solutions may be sought'. The force would use its arms 'only for self-defence, should this become necessary in the discharge of its functions, in the interest of preserving inter-national peace, of seeking to prevent a recurrence of fighting and contributing to the maintenance and restoration of order'. The UN troops 'would not take the initiative in the use of armed force, which was permissible only in self-defence'. No action was to be taken by the UN troops which was likely to bring them into direct conflict with either community. Finally, the force would maintain 'close contact with the appropriate official in the government of Cyprus in connection with the performance of the force's functions'.

Though more independent than elsewhere, the effective power the force exercised in Cyprus thus derived, like that of a police force, rather from the moral authority it could claim, than from the exercise of physical armed force. This has mainly been true of the other peace forces that have been established elsewhere. As their name implies peace forces have been designed to maintain peace rather than to put down war. This is likely to remain true, except in a few exceptional cases, of most of the operations of such forces in the near future.

This history invites certain general conclusions concerning the factors affecting the development of peace-keeping forces by the UN.

First, efforts to create such forces as a deliberate and abstract initiative to alter the existing structure of international relationships have proved unsuccessful. In the early years of the United Nations, and even before, there was much discussion of the necessity for international forces. But in the absence of concrete, crisis situations that might serve as the impetus nothing could be agreed. Pre-war French proposals, the negotiations in 1946-8 for the establishment of a Security Council force, the proposals put forward by Mr Lie, and the requests of the Collective Measures Committee for national contributions to a stand-by force, all revealed the inadequacy of generalized discussions in promoting action, in the absence of the necessary specific stimulus. Each demanded a fairly dramatic alteration of the established structure of power and the traditions of disposing of armed force, without the corresponding consciousness of crisis required to induce this. It was the urgent need for rapid collective action, arising successively in Korea, Sinai, the Congo and Cyprus, which alone generated sufficient emotional dynamic to bring to fruition the complex and unaccustomed process of creating an international force. Again it was the acute crisis over the UN's finances in 1964-5 which alone could stimulate a general reconsideration of peace-keeping methods and principles through the Special Committee on Peace-keeping.

Secondly, precisely because of the difficult process of adjustment required, progress has been made rather by a series of slow and relatively limited steps, than by single decisions to embark on radically new departures. Habituation has played an important role in encouraging adjustment. Each step made easier the next pace after. It was easier to establish a peace force in 1960 than in 1956, and in 1964 than in 1960. It was certainly easier to induce host-powers to accept international forces. This gradual progression applied to individual operations too. The readiness of governments to respond was assisted in several cases by the sense that the forces were to be established for limited and immediate purposes, rather than for long-term and far-reaching ones. But once formed, the functions each force has performed have often been extended. At Suez, Mr Hammarskjöld needed considerable convincing of the wisdom of setting up a force at all. And it was partly because he insisted so strongly on the respect for national sovereignty to be shown by the force that he was able to assure a positive response from the members chiefly concerned. Similarly, in the Congo, the fact that the prolonged civil conflict to be faced could not be foreseen at the moment of its formation, made it far easier to bring agreement for the establishment of a peace force. But in both cases the forces' functions expanded.

The growth in the forces' role, the extension of their length of life, the widening of their encroachments on national sovereignty, are developments that have occurred not only slowly but only half perceived, and have thus proved easier for governments to accept. In particular, they have been far easier to stomach as *ad hoc* responses to the pressure of events than if governments had been asked to sign their approval in abstract terms. In this sense, the delegation of power to the Secretary-General, able to interpret his authority in relatively flexible terms, is, as the Soviet and other hostile governments are well aware, more likely to lead to the development of the Organization's powers than the rigid adherence to constitutional formulae which need to be agreed in explicit form. Gradualism has also been a condition for development in long-term constitutional arrangements for peace-keeping. Not only the arrangements under Chapter VII for a Security Council force, but the proposals for an internationally recruited UN brigade or for permanently earmarked forces were all too far from existing reality to be acceptable in practice. Only much more modest plans, for unilaterally earmarked forces without any explicit UN authority, have successfully brought about changes in the existing system.

Thirdly, although many of the developments that have taken place may be said to correspond with a fairly broad movement of opinion within the organization, the initiatives of individual governments have, in some cases at least, been important factors in influencing change. The action of the US government in demanding action in Korea and in bringing about the passage of the Uniting for Peace Resolution, the initiative of the Canadian government in demanding an emergency force in 1956, the unilateral action of the Scandinavian and other governments in earmarking parts of their forces for peace-keeping purposes if required, all these represent examples of actions by individual states that have exerted an important influence on the gradual growth of UN peace-keeping potentialities. Similar actions are likely to remain influential in the future.

Fourthly, the evolution that has taken place has similarly clearly been partly influenced by the actions of the Secretariat. The production of reports, such as that of Mr Hammarskjöld in 1958, or the inspiring of resolutions, can undoubtedly exert considerable influence on individual delegations and, equally important, on public opinion at large. The strengthening, by the Secretary-General on his own authority, of his military staff to assist in the management and direction of such operations has influenced general conceptions of the feasibility of international action. The character and methods of individual Secretary-Generals may be equally important. The somewhat ambitious and perhaps not always realistic character of Mr Trygve Lie's proposals undoubtedly detracted from the influence they might otherwise have enjoyed. On the other hand, the intense cautiousness of Mr Hammarskjöld (who was able to benefit from the lessons of Mr Lie's experience) served, together with the general respect in which he was held, to make his own proposals, even when they became more ambitious, more widely acceptable. U Thant, who has similarly been able to benefit from his predecessor's unhappy experience over the Congo, has been obliged, largely because of the dispute over financing, to retreat into caution again. And, though he benefits from his Afro-Asian background, he is perhaps less likely at present to be able or willing to launch imaginative new ventures in this field.

Fifthly, the evolution of the UN's peace-keeping capacities has been partly conditioned by the prevailing climate of world opinion on their value. Operations of this kind will always be limited by the readiness of nations to contribute, either militarily or financially, to operations in far-off places for purposes that may sometimes seem remote from their interests. This is the difficulty that has always confronted any collective security system: that of securing a conception of common interest in the defence of peace, even in distant areas, comparable to the conception of national interest that motivates the nations involved in conflict. When the peace-keeping operation is one that involves little risk of fighting this readiness may often be present, both among governments and publics. Where that risk does arise, willingness to contribute troops is often lacking: the decision of some nations to withdraw contingents from the UN force in the Congo when it became involved in fighting is some indication of this. On the other hand, the fact that, in that case, many nations were ready to continue to make their forces available for UN purposes, even though they might suffer considerable losses, suggests that national governments and national public opinion are now more ready to support operations of this kind than in the past. The maintenance of such support is likely to be crucially affected by the success or failure of further operations.

The development of peace-keeping functions has been even more crucially limited, however, by the differences of opinion arising over the authorization, control and financing of such activities. These at one stage reached a pitch which wiped out one Assembly session and, it seemed, might threaten the entire Organization's existence. Because they could affect the continued membership of important members, they inevitably influenced the readiness of the Organization as a whole to undertake further ventures of the same type. Such difficulties can only be overcome by the evolution of some consensus concerning the principles that should govern authorization and control. Difficulties over finance are only reflections of differences on these points. Some compromise, on both authorization and control, may be possible. There should be room for some half-way house between the letter of the Charter itself, conferring exclusive authority to the Security Council; and the subsequent practice of the Organization, according a larger authority to the Assembly and Secretary-General. The activities of the Special Committee on Peacekeeping may serve to accomplish such a compromise. For the rest, development in the immediate future is likely to take the form of the expansion and increasing co-ordination of earmarked forces; and the strengthening of the headquarters staff of the Secretary-General's military adviser.

It would be possible, without undue distortion, to point to a continuous line of evolution in the peace-keeping operations of the UN, for example in terms of their progressive limitations of national sovereignty. In the Suez operation, the greatest deference was paid to the rights of the host-state, both in relieving its apprehensions about the political functions of the force and in determining its composition and powers. In the Congo, the host-government was given little right to influence the composition and powers of the force, and there was an increasing readiness to play an active role in an essentially civil conflict. Here, however, such action was regarded as permissible only in support of the recognized government against rebel forces. In Cyprus, the host-government was allowed still less say in the composition and powers of the force, and intervention has been undertaken as readily against the forces of the government as on their behalf. To some extent this model is a misleading one, since it derives in part from the chance characteristics of the particular situations encountered. And it is by no means sure that one could expect a similar progression to continue in the future.

Yet there is no doubt that habituation to the practices adopted in previous cases has encouraged greater readiness to adopt them, even to extend them, on subsequent occasions. In this way expectations concerning the capacities and powers of peace-keeping operations have been gradually modified, among countries contributing forces and those receiving them alike. It is perhaps this change in expectations above everything else that has increased the UN's peace-keeping capacity over the last twenty years.

TEXT REFERENCES

1. For further details about international forces between the wars, see D. W. Bowett, *United Nations Forces*, London 1964, pp. 3-12.

2. UN Charter, Chapter VII, Articles 39-51.

3. For fuller accounts of these negotiations see Security Council, official records, second year, Special Supplement No. 1; L. N. Goodrich and A. P. Simons, *The UN and the Maintenance of International Peace and Security*, pp. 398-405; W. R. Frye, *A UN Peace Force*, pp. 175-84; and I. Claude, *Power and International Relations*, pp. 177-90.

4. General Assembly, official records, third session, Supplement No. 1.

5. General Assembly, official records, fourth session, Supplement No. 13.

6. General Assembly, official records, fifth session, Supplement No. 20, resolution 377.

7. See W. R. Frye, *A UN Peace Force*, London 1957.

8. General Assembly, official records, first emergency session 562.

9. The Swedish government in agreeing to send a contingent, explicitly informed the Secretary-General that it presumed that the resolution would not 'imply that the force should remain on watch duty in the area for an unspecified period of time, or pending the solution of the political questions affecting that area'. Finland accepted on similar terms. See G. Rosner, *The United Nations Emergency Force*, New York, 1963.

10. General Assembly, official records, first emergency session, 553 meeting.

11. Security Council, official records, S/4022.

12. Security Council, official records 8207, para. 64.

13. General Assembly, official records, thirteenth session.

14. Security Council, official records 4387, July 1960.

15. Ibid.

16. UN Official Records S/4389, 29 July 1960.

17. On 7 December the Secretary-General himself admitted that although the resolution of 14 July 'had not specifically stated that the force was to maintain law and order, it was clear from the context that that would be its essential function'.

18. Security Council official records S/4741, 21 February 1961.

BIBLIOGRAPHY

Bowett, D. W., *United Nations Forces*, London and New York, 1964.

Burns, A. R. and Heathcote, N., *Peace-keeping by United Nations Forces from Suez to the Congo*, New York, 1963.

Frye, W. R., *A United Nations Peace Force*, London, 1957.

Goodrich, L. N. and Simons, A. P., *The United Nations and the Maintenance of International Peace and Security*, Washington, 1955.

Rosner, G., *The United Nations Emergency Force*, New York, 1963.

8 THE INTERNATIONAL LABOUR ORGANIZATION

John McMahon

Something of the ideal location of the International Labour Organization, situated on the edge of the lake of Geneva, in a rather monastic and austere building, is reflected in the preamble to its Constitution, which is the usual compound of counsels of perfection, lofty aspirations and altogether a model of imprecision.

It affirms that, 'all human beings, irrespective of race, creed or sex, have the right to pursue both their material well-being and their spiritual development in conditions of freedom and dignity, of economic security and equal opportunity and that it is one of the responsibilities of the Organization to examine and consider all international economic and financial policies and measures in the light of this fundamental objective'. More specifically it refers to the need to further: full employment, the employment of workers in satisfying occupations, the provision of facilities for the training and transfer of labour, policies calculated to ensure a just share of the fruits of progress to all, the effective recognition of the right of collective bargaining, the extension of social security measures, adequate protection for the health of members, provision for child welfare and maternity protection, provision of adequate facilities for recreation and culture and the assurance of equality of educational and vocational opportunity.

Apart from this preamble (which strictly speaking is more of an epilogue than a prologue, as it is in the form of an Annex at the end of the Constitution, and was adopted rather late in the life of the Organization, in 1944 at Philadelphia), the Constitutive treaty itself, like all good Constitutions, is short and obscure. It contains merely forty Articles, the first thirteen of which are devoted principally to describing the composition and competence of the three Organs of the Organization; the General Conference, the Governing Body and the International Labour Office; the following twenty-one Articles deal with the procedure to be observed for the adoption of a Convention or Recommendation and the machinery for enforcement of any obligations which may have been assumed under a Convention; and the final Articles contain provisions regulating the amendment and interpretation of the Constitution, the legal status of the Organization and its privileges and immunities.

Apart from one radical amendment in 1946 at the Montreal Conference, to remove all reference to the League of Nations and to insert instead mention of the United Nations, and to increase the nature and extent of the obligations incumbent on states under Article 19, the formal structure of the Organization is much the same as it was in 1919. However, in practice, it has expanded and changed almost beyond recognition. It is for this reason that obscurity is a prerequisite for the successful functioning of the Constitution. If formal amendments to the Constitution are difficult to achieve and all the future conditions in which the Organization will have to operate are impossible to envisage, then the constitutive treaty must be given in practice a dynamic and teleological interpretation to fulfil the purpose of the Organization. Only in this manner will it be able to adapt itself and respond to new situations and needs, such as that presented by the influx of newly independent states.

Before the Versailles Peace Conference and the establishment of the International Labour Organization in 1918, international attempts to regulate labour problems had been meagre. A Conference was held at Berlin in 1890 to examine these matters, but, although it proved of value in focusing public opinion on the subject, it ended in failure. Continuous and vigorous efforts by the International Association for Labour Legislation were more successful, giving rise to the Berne Conventions of 1906, the only two general treaties purporting to regulate labour conditions before the war; one restricted the night work of women in industry and the other prohibited the use of white phosphorus in matches. A technical conference in 1905 preceded the adoption of these Conventions and a second technical conference was held in 1913 to prepare for the drafting of two more Conventions. However, the subsequent diplomatic conference was not held due to the commencement of the war. During the war, conditions facilitating and the impetus towards the international regulation of labour problems gathered momentum, as is manifest in the important resolutions adopted by the Leeds Conference of Trade Union representatives of the Allied Countries in 1916, the Berne International Trade Union Congress in 1917 and the Inter-Allied Labour and Socialist Conference in 1918, all concerning the desirability of the international regulation of labour problems.

At the Peace Conference itself, the Article which gave rise to most difficulty was Article 19, which concerned the powers of the Organization. Concerning the structure, there was more immediate agreement, establishing its tripartite nature and the composition of its three organs, the General Conference, the Governing Body and the International Labour Office.

The Conference, which meets every year (usually for three weeks during the month of June) is composed of four representatives of each of the Members, of whom two are Government delegates and two represent the employers and workers of the member state. The Governing Body consisted originally of forty persons (now increased to forty-eight), twenty of whom represented governments, ten the employers and ten the workers. Of the twenty persons who represented governments, ten were to be appointed by the Members of chief industrial importance and ten were to be appointed by the Members selected for that purpose by the government delegates to the Conference, excluding the delegates of the ten Members of chief industrial importance. Members are elected for three years and the Governing Body meets three or four times a year for two or three weeks at a time.

The International Labour Office is composed of the Director-General, who is appointed by the Governing Body and is subject to the instructions of the Governing Body, and the staff which is appointed by the Director-General under regulations approved by the Governing Body. The functions of the Labour Office, according to Article 10 of the Constitution, include the collection and distribution of information on all subjects relating to the international adjustment of conditions of industrial life and labour and particularly the examination of subjects which it is proposed to bring before the Conference with a view to the conclusion of international Conventions. The Office is also to prepare the documents on the various items of the agenda for the meetings of the Conference and to assist governments with the framing of laws and regulations on the basis of the decisions of the Conference.

The early history of the Organization, before the adoption of the Declaration of Philadelphia, indicates that the Constitution was interpreted in such a way as to extend the activities of the Organization. In a number of Advisory Opinions, given by the Permanent Court of International Justice, it was held that the competence of the Organization included the regulation of the conditions of employment of persons engaged in agriculture (and not merely in industry in the narrower sense of that term); that it was competent to propose labour legislation which, in order to protect workers, also incidentally regulated the same work when it was done by the employer himself and, finally, that there is no presumption concerning a labour convention that it must be interpreted as being restricted in its operation to manual workers unless a contrary intention appears.

The scope of the activities of the Organization, during the first twenty years, is reflected in the subjects chosen for formulation in international labour conventions. They include: Hours of Work in Industry (1919), Night Work of Women (1919), Night Work of Young Persons in Industry (1919), Rights of Association in Agriculture (1921), Workmen's Compensation in Agriculture (1921), White Lead Painting (1921), Medical Examination of Young Persons at Sea (1921), Seamen's Articles of Agreement (1926), Sickness Insurance in Industry (1927), Marking of Weights of Packages Transported by Vessels (1929), Forced Labour (1930), Old Age Insurance (1933), Sheet Glass Workers (1934), Unemployment Provisions (1934) and Safety Provisions concerning Buildings (1937).

After the war, there were a number of important conventions concerning, for example, Social Security of Seafarers (1946), Labour Inspection (1947), Contracts of Employment (1947), Freedom of Association and Protection of the Right to Organize (1948), Labour Clauses in Public Contracts (1949), Fee Charging Employment Agencies (1949), Right to Organize and Collective Bargaining (1949) and the Forced Labour Convention (1952).

Within the last ten years, however, the emphasis has changed from standard setting to technical assistance. Of course, conventions, recommendations and resolutions concerning labour standards are still proposed, discussed and adopted and a genuflection is frequently made, in the Report of the Director-General, or the speeches during the General Conference, to standard setting as a most important function of the Organization. However, even a cursory survey of the Conference debates, the annual Report of the Director-General and the budget of the Organization, substantiate the view that the activities of the Organization are increasingly concerned with technical assistance to the newly independent states, as well as establishing an international network of labour standards. In March 1963 it was decided to set up an International Centre for Advanced Technical and Vocational Training at Turin. Vocational training, in industry and agriculture, is also the objective in thirty-one of the forty-nine Special Fund projects within the competence of the ILO. A number of regional advisory missions have been established, so that experts may be more conveniently available to countries in a particular region to survey, advise and assist the implementation of projects. The activities covered by such missions include vocational training, manpower planning, labour statistics, labour administration, social security and occupational safety and health. In 1964, experts were sent to Burundi, Chile, Taiwan, Congo (Leopoldville), Iran and Uganda to assist their governments in the preparation or modification of labour legislation and regulations. In 1961 an International Institute for Labour Studies was established.

Concerning industrial problems, one might note the existence, since 1945, of the Industrial Committees. These are tripartite organs for the consideration of conditions in certain industries and their activities include such areas as labour–management relations, conditions of work, safety and health, the consequences of technological change, vocational training and regulation of employment.

Although the formal structure of the Organization (apart from the adoption of the Declaration of Philadelphia and the amendments at the Montreal Conference in 1946) remains substantially the same as it was in 1919 in practice its activities have changed extensively. As we have seen, in the early days, labour standards, covering a great variety of subjects, constituted its principal activity. Although such a function is still considered vital, attention and emphasis is now given to problems such as labour training, the development of manpower resources, industrialization and technical assistance to the newly independent states.

If these are the subjects of concern of the Organization, it may next be worth considering the legislative techniques which it employs in dealing with them.

When it was established in 1919, the International Labour Organization was in many ways a British creation, with much assistance from France and rather less assistance from the United States. As a British product it was a practical compromise between two schools of thought. First of all, the Italian school was eager for the Conference to possess direct legislative power so that a Convention which obtained a two-thirds majority in the Conference would be immediately binding on all states, and even those who had voted against it would be under an obligation to implement the Convention within one year. On the other hand, the United States, as a federal country, where the competence to legislate on labour matters was almost exclusively restricted to the individual states and not the Federal government, was anxious to restrict the element of legal obligation to a minimum. The solution agreed upon was that a Convention, when adopted, would give rise to certain legal obligations even for those states who had voted against its adoption. However, there would be no legal obligation to implement the Convention in municipal law unless a state had formally ratified a particular Convention. United States anxiety on this point is reflected in her meagre record concerning the ratification of Conventions. Out of 117 Conventions adopted by the International Labour Conference, the United States has ratified only 6. The practice of other federal states is almost equally significant on this point: Australia has ratified 24, Canada 18, India 27 and Switzerland 27.

As a stimulant for the future, however, and as a sedative to Italian sentiment, the Commission on International Labour Legislation, adopted a resolution in February 1919, expressing the hope 'that as soon as may be possible an agreement may be arrived at between the High Contracting Parties, with a view to endowing the International Labour Conference with power to take, under conditions to be determined, resolutions possessing the force of international law'. This hope has yet to materialize.

Under these circumstances the word 'techniques' would seem to be the most appropriate to characterize the powers possessed by the International Labour Conference. Article 19 of the Constitution provides that Conventions or Recommendations must be adopted by a two-thirds majority. They must then be signed by the President of the Conference and by the Director-General for the purposes of authentification. Conventions which have been ratified are registered with the United Nations in order to satisfy the requirements of Article 102 of the Charter concerning the registration of treaties.

So far the Conference has adopted 117 Conventions and 120 Recommendations. At present these Conventions have received approximately 4,477 ratifications (including the 1,500 declarations made on behalf of non-metropolitan countries). They thus represent a substantial international labour code which makes extensive inroads on the domestic jurisdiction of states. The subjects covered by these 117 Conventions are extremely varied, including hygiene, holidays with pay, social security, the night work of women and young persons, wages and hours of work, labour inspection, safety provisions, employment policy, benefits in the case of employment injury, and many other matters.

The Organization also acts to influence the policies of individual states through Recommendations. The principal distinction between a Convention and a Recommendation is that the former is intended to be ratified and so deals with subjects which give rise to precise legal obligations which are to be implemented in municipal law. Recommendations, on the other hand are not intended to give rise to formal, legal obligations, but are merely to provide states with a standard to which they are to aspire and to attempt to implement. However, one important attribute which they both share, is that once they have been adopted by the Conference, they immediately give rise to certain obligations for all states, even those who voted against their adoption.

States signing a Convention must submit the Convention within one year, or under exceptional circumstances 18 months, to the national authority competent to give effect to it and must inform the Director-General of these measures. If they then ratify a Convention, they must communicate the formal ratification of the Convention to the Director-General and take such action as may be necessary to make the Convention effective. They must submit an annual report to the International Labour Office on the measures taken to give effect to the Convention. Even if a state does not ratify a Convention, it must still report to the Director-General at appropriate intervals, as requested by the Governing Body, the position of its law and practice concerning the matters dealt with in the Convention, showing the extent to which effect has been given, or is proposed to be given, to any of the provisions of the Convention by legislation, administrative action, collective agreements, or otherwise, and stating the difficulties which prevent or delay ratification.

Thus, although the consent of a state is still required before it will be legally bound to implement the contents of a Convention, it is subjected to a good deal of direct, intensive and recurrent pressure to ratify. The Organization proceeds by a process of attrition, directed at wearing down the resistance of states. As with human beings, this policy is frequently successful.

Recommendations may be distinguished from Conventions on two grounds: the kind and extent of the legal obligations to which they give rise and the nature of the subject matter with which they deal. As Recommendations may not be ratified there is no legal obligation incumbent on member states to implement their provisions in Municipal law. However, as in the case of a Convention, a state is under an obligation to submit the Recommendation to the competent national authority within one year or 18 months, to inform the Director-General of the measures taken to discharge this obligation and to report, when requested, the position of the law and practice in its country in regard to the matters dealt with in the Recommendation. The 120 Recommendations adopted by the Conference cover a broad spectrum of subjects including benefits in the case of employment injury, employment policy, hygiene in commerce and offices, the guarding of machinery, the termination of employment at the initiative of the employer, prohibition of the sale, hire and use of inadequately guarded machinery, employment agencies, unemployment, public works, the prevention of industrial accidents, labour inspection and other matters.

These suggest that on the whole Recommendations have been used to serve four purposes. First, to embody general principles and objectives, many of which it would not be suitable to embody in the form of a Convention. Secondly, to act as a precursor to a Convention which will follow when conditions are more appropriate. Thirdly, to act as a Model Code. Finally, a Recommendation is frequently adopted at the same time as a Convention, the latter containing the underlying principles regulating a subject and the former the details concerning implementation.

One might also mention the increasingly important role played by the adoption of resolutions by the International Labour Conference. Such instruments do not give rise to any legal obligations, not even submission to any national organ. States are therefore much less reluctant and apprehensive about their adoption. They are frequently used to express views concerning the work and structure of the Organization, to deal with subjects which might ultimately be suitable for a Convention or Recommendation, to deal with matters which are primarily the concern of other international organizations and to express a view on a subject which would be wholly inappropriate for regulation by a Convention.

A number of interesting legal issues have arisen in connection with International Labour Conventions and Recommendations.

Concerning their interpretation, although a formal genuflection is made in the direction of the International Court of Justice in Article 37 of the Constitution, in practice they are usually interpreted by the International Labour Office itself. Secondly, reservations to Conventions are impermissible. This attitude is justified on three grounds. First of all, it is maintained that Conventions are to provide uniform standards and that reservations would be incompatible with this objective. Secondly, it is urged that to allow reservations by governments would constitute an undesirable departure from the tripartite procedure by which Conventions are adopted and enforced by the Conference. Thirdly, reference is made to the numerous flexibility clauses already built in to Conventions. This last point is particularly important in relation to the new states. Almost without exception, at the moment, the new states contend that many of the old Conventions are not relevant to their economic and social context, and that new Conventions are often insufficiently flexible to accommodate the widely divergent and disparate conditions in the developing states. It is for this reason that they often advocate the adoption of a Recommendation rather than a Convention. To circumvent this difficulty, the Labour Office is exercising all its ingenuity to mint as many flexibility clauses as possible, in order to encourage the new states and make it easier for them to ratify more Conventions. For example, a number of Conventions contain optional parts; or a new state may be allowed to ratify by stages; or it may be permitted to exclude certain areas from the application of the Convention or even in some cases to accept a standard lower than that embodied in the Convention.

These techniques for influencing the policies of member states have recently come to be applied by other international organizations. The International Labour Organization has played the role of a pioneer and its example has been followed by a number of the other Specialized Agencies. UNESCO, WHO, ICAO, and FAO all make provision for something comparable to

Conventions and Recommendations. As a result, even without anything that can properly be regarded as legislative powers, international organizations have nevertheless developed techniques to exert considerable influence on the policies applied by individual governments.

Next, in considering the development of the Organization it may be useful to examine its procedures for securing the observance of its Conventions and standards.

Of the forty articles contained in the Constitution of the Organization, more than one-quarter of them concern the establishment of machinery for the enforcement of Conventions and Recommendations. However, as is frequently the case with an international organization, the constitutional practice of the Organization as it has developed over the pasty forty-five years, has assumed far greater importance than the formal provisions elaborated by the Constitutive document.

Under Article 24 of the Constitution, an industrial association of employers or workers is empowered to make a representation to the Governing Body that a member state is not observing a Convention to which it is a party. In practice, however, this procedure has only been invoked on seven occasions.

Similarly, under Article 26 of the Constitution, any of the members has the right to file a complaint with the International Labour Office if it is not satisfied that any other member is securing the effective observance of any Convention which both have ratified in accordance with the foregoing articles. This complaint is then considered by the Governing Body, and if necessary referred to a Commission of Inquiry. The Governing Body may adopt the same procedure, either of its own motion or on receipt of a complaint from a delegate to the Conference. Articles 27-34 provide that in such cases all information will be placed at the disposal of the Commission, that the Commission will prepare a report embodying its findings and that either party may appeal to the International Court of Justice whose decision will be final. However, despite the existence of this elaborate and detailed machinery, it has only been invoked in two cases, both of them very recent. The first in 1962 concerned a complaint by Ghana against Portugal on a charge of non-observance of the Abolition of Forced Labour Convention 1952; and the second in 1963 concerned a complaint by Portugal against Liberia for violating the Forced Labour Convention of 1930.

This meagre number of cases indicates that the above machinery has proved unsatisfactory. It is altogether too cumbersome and politically unacceptable. What was required was some more flexible, informal, expeditious and continuous method of supervision and control. This has been developed by a vigorous and extensive interpretation of Articles 19 and 22 of the Constitution.

Article 19 provides that:

apart from bringing the Recommendation before the said competent authority or authorities, no further obligation shall rest upon the Members, except that they shall report to the Director-General of the International Labour Office, at appropriate intervals as requested by the Governing Body, the position of the law and practice in their country in regard to the matters dealt with in the Recommendation, showing the extent to which effect has been given, or is proposed to be given, to the provisions of the Recommendation and such modifications of these provisions as it has been found or may be found necessary to make in adopting or applying them.

Article 22 stipulates that:

Each of the Members agrees to make an annual report to the International Labour Office on the measures which it has taken to give effect to the provisions of Conventions to which it is a party. These reports shall be made in such form and shall contain such particulars as the Governing Body may request.

Last year, about 3,000 such reports, including both annual reports and special reports, were completed. Questions on each Convention are drawn up by the Governing Body and are devised to extract information not only concerning the law but also the practice. As a result, states are required to send texts of the relevant laws, Court decisions, statistics, the comments of organizations of workers and employers and to state what provision is made for inspection.

The reports are then examined and analysed by a Committee of Experts which was first set up in 1927. The members of this body are usually eminent jurists, nominated by the International Labour Office and chosen by the Governing Body. The experts then make observations on the reports or requests for further information and embody their findings in a report to a Committee of the General Conference of the Organization. This Committee, tripartite in composition, is chosen from the members attending the Conference and is called 'the Committee on the Application of Conventions and Recommendations'. This Committee then arraigns the representatives of defaulting governments before it (in 1964 sixty-three were summoned) and they are asked to justify or explain their conduct. In 1959 this Committee drew up a Black List for habitual offenders or some particularly outrageous violation of a Convention. The Committee then reports to the Conference itself and the offending states are exposed to public pressure and shame.

On the whole this system has worked reasonably well. It is one which is now employed by a number of the other Specialized Agencies, including WHO and more recently UNESCO. About 80 per cent of the questionnaire forms are returned, although of course a number of the returns are incomplete or imprecise or do not give full details concerning practical application. However, the machinery is quite effective and it was noted by the Committee that there had been seventy alleged violations of Conventions by States in 1963, which were rectified by 1964, as a result of the observations made by the Committee of Experts. A number of special Committees have been established to deal with the enforcement of particularly important or difficult

Conventions; for example, the Freedom of Association Committee, since it was established in 1950 has heard 250 complaints. By this system of reports the control exercised over the application of Conventions and Recommendations is recurrent and the criticism offered constructive. This blend of judicial and political machinery (the Committee of Experts and the Conference Committee) seems to succeed in securing impartiality tempered by political expediency.

What have been the main factors determining the changes in the practice of the Organization previously outlined?

One of the principal causes of changes in the practice of the ILO has been changes in the composition of its membership. At the present moment the Organization contains 113 member states; its original membership was twenty-nine, mainly European. Most of the states subsequently admitted are newly independent states. These have appreciably influenced the development of the Organization in several different ways.

First, if one examines a number of the recent amendments to the Constitution the influence of the new states emerges quite explicitly. The size of the Governing Body of the Organization has been increased from forty to forty-eight in order to permit a more equitable representation of the new states. Then Article 35, the so-called 'colonial clause', allowing a member to make a declaration of acceptance of a Convention on behalf of a non-metropolitan territory, has been expunged from the Constitution, although the substance of Article 35 has been reintroduced and incorporated in the Constitution under Article 19. Another recent amendment adopted in June 1964 after a most heated debate in June 1963, empowered the Organization at any session, on the agenda of which the subject had been included and by a vote concurred in by two-thirds of the delegates attending the session, including two-thirds of the government delegates present and voting, to expel from membership of the Organization any member which the United Nations has expelled therefrom, or suspend from the exercise of the rights and privileges of membership of the organization any member which the United Nations has suspended from the exercise of its rights and privileges of membership. The amendment also provided for suspension from participation in the International Labour Organization Conference any Member of the ILO found by the United Nations to be flagrantly and persistently pursuing by its legislation a declared policy of racial discrimination, such as apartheid. Of course, this amendment was directed particularly against South Africa, who had already declared her intention to withdraw from the Organization. However, under Article 1, Paragraph 5, of the Organization, withdrawal only becomes effective two years after the Director-General has been notified. South Africa therefore will continue to be a member of the Organization until 1966, and even after that date the obligations arising from the Conventions she has ratified will still continue.

Another important example of the impact of the new states on the Organization has been in the field of state succession and International Labour Conventions. At the first African Regional Conference in 1960 it was noted with great satisfaction that all the African states which had become Members of the ILO since 1950 had recognized that they were bound by the obligations of Conventions, the provision of which had previously been declared applicable to their respective territories by the countries which were responsible for their administration and international relations. The above doctrine was initially formulated in relation to Burma in 1937, and since that date every newly independent state within the Organization has acknowledged that it succeeded to obligations under International Labour Conventions accepted on its behalf. As there are now well over 1,000 such conventions, it is evident that the influence of the new states in this area has been beneficial and has enabled the Organization to preserve the integrity of its international network of labour standards.

The advent of so many new states has also given an added impetus and urgency to decentralizing a number of the activities of the Organization and to establishing a number of Regional Committees and Field Departments. So far an African and an Asian Advisory Committee have been set up and one has also been proposed for Latin America. The task of these Committees and Regional Conferences is to advise the Governing Body on regional matters, to assess the need for and efficacy of technical assistance in that particular area, to ensure that local interests and conditions are taken into account when a new Convention is being drafted and to assist in enforcing Conventions in that particular region.

The fourth manner in which the influence of the new states has manifested itself concerns the tripartite character of the Organization. The composition of the Conference and of the Governing Body is partly diplomatic and partly occupational. Each government nominates four persons, of whom two are the delegates of the government and the other two represent the employers and the workers, being chosen by the government in consultation with the most representative industrial Organizations. The Constitution explicitly provides in Article 4 that every delegate shall be entitled to vote individually upon every matter which comes before the Conference. As a result, the delegates of the employers and of the workers habitually act as groups which represent interests and which play a part in the proceedings of the Conference frequently not unlike that of parties in national legislatures. It was even suggested in 1918 that the Conference should be tri-cameral and that the three groups should only meet together when necessary; however, this suggestion was rejected. With the arrival of so many new states, the tripartite character of the Organization, perhaps its most dominant feature, has been subjected to severe strain. First of all, different regional, economic and political interests now complicate and cut across the traditional lines of division and it is no longer just a question of an employer viewpoint and a worker viewpoint; instead there is now a trend and tendency more towards the bloc politics of the United Nations General Assembly. Secondly, the Director-General of the Organization at the 1964 Conference suggested that the viability of the whole concept of tripartite representation was beginning to break down in the world outside the Organization, particularly in the new states, and that this breakdown must have repercussions on and be reflected within the Organization. As the Director-General said:

> The pluralistic concept of society – the concept of a variety of organizations pursuing their aims within the nation – this concept is weak in many parts of the world, weak because old and traditional forms of society are disintegrating, old social bonds are weakening, and the new groupings of people characteristic of modern societies have not yet succeeded in establishing themselves in the allegiance of people. And this weakness within the nations makes itself felt in the forums of the ILO.

Thirdly, a good deal of the work and the resources of the Organization are now devoted to giving technical assistance and establishing operational programmes for the newly independent states. Yet it is precisely these kind of activities which are least susceptible to tripartite control. The Governing Body and the Conference may formulate the underlying principles to regulate such programmes, but they cannot maintain very close control over them.

A fifth, fundamental and most important manner in which the impact of the new states has impressed itself on the Organization concerns the role of the Organization in providing technical assistance. The Declaration of Philadelphia, adopted by the Organization in 1944 adverts to the need 'to promote the economic and social advancement of the less developed regions of the world' and the Director-General of the Organization in 1952 observed that 'since taking office as Director-General, I have repeatedly laid stress on the importance of a new emphasis in the

activities of the ILO designed to promote an intensification and
expansion of the advisory and operational work of the Organization as a complement to its legislative functions'. During 1964
the provisional estimate of expenditure on all ILO Technical
Co-operation programmes amounted to $12·2 million as com-
pared with $11 million in 1963; an increase of about 11 per cent.
The ordinary budget of the Organization contributed $1,337
million to this total, the Expanded Programme of Technical
Assistance $5,414 million, the Special Fund $5,151 million and
Trust Funds $311 million. The distribution of the total ILO
operational programme expenditure by region for 1964 was as
follows; Africa 31·5 per cent; Latin America 23·2 per cent;
Asia 30·4 per cent; Europe 4·3 per cent; the Near and Middle
East 7·8 per cent; Inter-regional 2·8 per cent.

The distribution of the expenditure by reference to the five
major fields of activities was: manpower organization (including
vocational training) 49·2 per cent; productivity and management
development 16·7 per cent; co-operation, small scale industries
and handicrafts 12·6 per cent; social security 3·5 per cent; labour
conditions and administration 18·0 per cent. In other words,
over 70 per cent was devoted to the development of human
resources, due principally to the fact that recipient countries are
placing emphasis on industrialization, and adequately trained and
skilled manpower is essential for this. Analysis of the type of
assistance provided in 1964 indicates that 74·8 per cent was spent
on experts, 12·4 per cent on fellowships, 12·8 per cent on equipment and miscellaneous.

A second, though related, cause of change has been a reconsideration of basic purposes by officials and members. The
Organization has been intensely occupied during the past three
years, in reappraising its position and formulating a hierachy of
objectives. The Director-General in his report to the International Labour Conference in 1963 suggested that the priorities
to be implemented by the organization should be: first, the

development of human resources, secondly, the development of social institutions and, thirdly, concentration on living and working conditions. ILO action in the first field would be directed principally at unemployment and underemployment; the shortage of trained personnel; high rates of population growth; illiteracy and educational systems insufficiently geared to economic realities. The second objective required: the growth of workers' and employers' organizations which were genuinely representative and independent; ensuring that such representative organizations were given the opportunity to play an active and constructive part in the society to which they belonged; assisting governments in developing administrative machinery capable of dealing with complex problems of labour relations; enhancing the status of the worker, both within the undertaking and in society as a whole; educational action to provide additional training for the persons directly involved in labour relations at all levels.

The above objectives, together with the traditional activity of the Organization in endeavouring to improve the living and working conditions of workers, seem to have obtained the general approval of the Organization and now constitute the principal aims which the Organization will pursue, together with its activity in the field of international labour standards.

This change in objectives has brought some change in structure. The Labour Office itself has been reorganized and now contains a smaller number of larger units, Departments instead of Divisions, corresponding to the major emphases in the programme of the Organization. Secondly a small programme Committee has been established which will be served by a research department, with the task of reviewing the main needs for ILO action in the light of developing social and economic conditions.

The following tentative conclusions may now be advanced concerning the process of change in the ILO.

The real seat of power in the Organization, and the principal organ for initiating change in the structure and practice of the Organization, is the Governing Body. As a small, cohesive body, meeting regularly, and responsible for drawing up the agenda of the Conference, it is able to exercise a substantial measure of executive power and control.

The Conference on the other hand, although it is responsible for the final adoption of Conventions, Recommendations and Resolutions, and for their enforcement, and for modifications in the actual structure of the Organization, now consists of 452 members who only meet for three weeks in the year and most of that time is devoted to a discussion of the Report of the Director-General. It will be apparent that such an organ is far too cumbersome and amorphous, and its meetings too infrequent, to enable it to assume substantial power. Of course, it is able to exercise considerable pressure on the Governing Body and a number of the new states have agitated on several occasions for an increase in the powers of the Conference (where all the new states are represented and command a majority) and a curtailment of the powers of the Governing Body, which is principally dominated by the states of chief industrial importance.

The influence of the Director-General and of the secretariat is also considerable. The Annual Report of the Director-General forms the basis of the discussion of the Conference and is the instrument employed to put forward new ideas concerning the structure and activities of the Organization. In 1963, the Director-General presented a report of over 200 pages, for discussion by the Conference, stating that:

> it is intended to be an action document, the first step in the consideration of what precise tasks the ILO should address itself to now and in the years ahead, and what changes need to be made in ILO methods and organization to carry out these tasks with the greatest practical effect.

The secretariat, as a permanent body, responsible for a good deal of the preparatory work and administration, assumes the inscrutable but very real and important power of any civil service.

Much of the work of the Organization is discharged through Committees such as the Committee of Experts and the Conference Committee on the Application of Conventions and Recommendations, the Conference Drafting Committee, the Finance Committee, the Regional Committees and Industrial Committees. In many cases therefore, the essential decisions have been made before the report of the Committee reaches the Conference.

The tripartite character of the Organization, in the Governing Body, the General Conference and the Committees, is an important factor influencing the development and changes in the Organization. It ensures that individual workers' and employers' representatives have both a forum to express their views on labour problems and the power to adopt instruments which governments will be obliged to consider for legislation.

Of course the principal external factor, responsible for a radical transformation of the nature and purpose of the Organization, is the admission of the newly independent states. The manner in which they have affected the form and, more especially, the function of the Organization has already been described in detail.

In conclusion, one may note that the legislative techniques and enforcement machinery developed by the International Labour Organization are more advanced than in almost any of the other Specialized Agencies, and establish modest but important incursions on the concept of state sovereignty.

BIBLIOGRAPHY

The International Labour Code (1951, 2 volumes).

The International Labour Review.

Jenks, C. W., *The Common Law of Mankind*, 1958.

Jenks, C. W., *Human Rights and International Labour Standards*, 1960.

Jenks, C. W., *The International Protection of Trade Union Freedom*, 1957.

Jenks, C. W., 'The Significance for International Law of the Tripartite Character of the International Labour Organization', *Transactions of the Grotius Society*, Vol. XXII, 1936, p. 45.

Landy, E., 'The Effective Application of International Labour Standards', *International Labour Review*, No. 68, 1953, pp. 346-63.

The *Official Bulletin* of the International Labour Organization.

The Origins of the International Labour Organization (2 volumes, 1934, edited by Shotwell).

Price, W., Industrial Committees of the ILO, *International Labour Review*, No. 65, 1952, pp. 1-43.

Price, W., 'The International Labour Organization and Technical Assistance', *International Labour Review*, No. 66, 1952, pp. 391-418.

9 THE INTERNATIONAL MONETARY FUND

W. M. Scammell

The IMF is one of the Specialized Agencies of the United Nations existing primarily to assist member countries in dealing with short-term deficit sin their balances of payments. This it may do in several ways, but mainly by allowing deficit countries to draw for their temporary needs upon the pool of currencies and gold contributed by member states, which it administers. Its articles lay down conditions and limits for the supply of currencies and for ensuring that it holds an adequate amount of each currency. The Fund thus acts as a buffer between deficits in the balances of payments of members and their individual gold and currency reserves.

Apart from these specific tasks, however, the IMF stands at the centre of the system of world payments. The Bretton Woods Conference, which in July 1944 established the Fund, intended it to be the focal point of international co-operation in international finance and it established also the general principles for the ordering of exchange rates and international payments which we have come to call 'the Bretton Woods system'. Thus we must see the Fund not only as a functional agency but in a wider setting as the custodian of the principles of international monetary policy. In describing the development of its policies we shall consider both these aspects of its work and we shall touch briefly upon the various proposals for the reform of the Fund which have recently been made.

The Fund had its origin in the functional co-operation of the war years, when the enunciation of the principles of post-war planning in the Atlantic Charter of 1942, combined with the high degree of operational co-operation which the Allies achieved, provided a suitable climate in which to establish the framework of the post-war international economy. The immediate prime-mover was, however, the famous Article VII of the Mutual Aid Agreement of February 1942 under which Britain bound herself, in return for American Lend-Lease aid, to take part in 'agreed action . . . directed to the expansion, by appropriate international and domestic measures of production, employment and the exchange and consumption of goods.'[1] Originally, the actions contemplated under Article VII comprised a grandiose scheme for the ordering of the international economy – for international organizations to deal with exchange stability and investment, for international agreements on measures for full employment and the stabilizing of primary-commodity prices and for a progressive dismantling of tariff barriers after the war under the aegis of an international organization. Much of this subsequently perished[2] and in fact the Bretton Woods organizations were all that was to survive, but the scale of the general conception is a measure of the British and American desire to move away from the international anarchy of the thirties. Indeed, if there was a strong desire common to both the British and the Americans at this period it was for each to hold the other to the principle of co-operation in international economic affairs.

Work on the currency question began even before the Mutual Aid Agreement was signed and resulted in an exchange of plans in August 1942 – the British plan, prepared by Maynard Keynes, then attached to the British Treasury,[3] the American plan by Harry D. White,[4] of the American Treasury. Of these two, the Keynes Plan was at an early stage set aside in favour of the White Plan although important modifications were made to the latter at Britain's behest. It is fair to say that the final settlement was one dominated by American ideas but diluted by important concessions to the British viewpoint.

Nevertheless an adequate understanding of the Fund, still more of some of the controversies which now centre around its work, demands a brief examination of what was at issue between the Keynes and White Plans. Superficially, they were not dissimilar. Certainly both provided for an international agency to disburse aid for balance of payments disequilibria, both provided for supplementation of international liquidity and both placed powers of coercion in the hands of an international agency. But on many vital issues – the size of the pool of international liquidity, the freedom of access to it, the technical banking character of one and the inherently political character of the other, the conception in the mind of each man of what his agency would in fact become – on all these they differed fundamentally.

The Keynes Plan[5] was by far the more daring. It provided for supplementation of national reserves by drawing rights for member nations on an overdraft system. Countries suffering balance of payments deficits could then clear these deficits by transfer of units of overdraft from their accounts to the accounts of surplus countries. Each country would have a quota drawing right and the total of these ($35 billion) was the amount by which international liquidity was to be augmented. This system had two advantages: firstly, the Union could never become insolvent since the overdrafts of the deficit countries were compensated by the credit balances of the surplus countries; secondly, it was possible, since no actual contributions of gold or currency were demanded of members, to make the total a large one and if necessary to expand it as trade expanded or prices rose with the passage of time. The Union was not only to have benefits to confer: it was to have sanctions to enforce its will and opinions. Deficit countries were quickly to be disciplined by being required to adopt Union policies, if necessary even involving a revision of their exchange rate; but further, a new principle was invoked, in recognizing the equal responsibility for balance of payments adjustment of the surplus country which must quickly use its positive balance to import goods or lose it if a given period was allowed to pass. This Union, with its novel apparatus and sweeping powers, was to be governed by a body of bankers and technicians, dealing with the problems of finance as bankers, not as politicians.

What the White Plan[6] lacked in vision it made up in political realism. No American Congress would be prepared to accept from Keynes – the man who had thought the New Deal fainthearted – a scheme under which all the purchasing power of the mendicant nations of the world might be turned in one inflationary blast on the US. Any plan which was to be of use must be acceptable to Congress. More than ever here political economy became 'the art of the possible'. White bowed to this. The White Plan worked on a contributory basis, providing for a stabilization fund, based on quota subscriptions of gold and currencies, of $5 billion, from which deficit countries might purchase, on the approval of the Fund, currencies from the Fund in return for their own up to an absolute limit of 200 per cent of their quota subscription. In return for this they were to suffer only mild interference by the Fund in their economic policies. Control of the Fund was to be in the hands of a board of governors each of whom was to be appointed by a member government and voting power in the governing body was to be proportional to the size of quota. On the subject of exchange rates the White Plan was more militant than its British counterpart. These were to be fixed by the Fund and changed 'only when essential to a correction of a fundamental disequilibrium'.

The British were anxious that a part of the burden of balance of payments adjustment should be shared by the surplus country and that some form of sanction should be applied against such a country to force it to take corrective action. This principle was conceded by the Americans when the famous 'Scarce-currency clause' was, in a later draft, written into the White Plan. This provided that when the currency of a chronic surplus country became oversold in the Fund it would be declared 'scarce' and deficit countries would thereby be entitled to impose restrictions against imports from the surplus country. This was a very real concession. The fact that as the years have passed no currency has ever been so declared does not abrogate the principle. Surely since 1945 no nation has so demonstrated a sense of responsibility for its payments surplus and its actions in international finance as has the United States.

One element appeared in the White Plan which was to have much bearing on the Fund and on the whole financial history of the post-war period – the demand for non-discrimination and freedom from exchange control in international payments. Stemming partly from the doctrines of Cordell Hull and the old fight for the 'most-favoured nation' principle in pre-war days, partly from antipathy to the German methods of exchange control and economic warfare, the American demand for multi-lateral trade and convertible currencies ran like a thread through all their wartime and early postwar negotiations – in the discussions on the Atlantic Charter, on the Mutual Aid Agreement, on the Bretton Woods Agreement, on the Anglo-American Loan Agreement, in the frustrated negotiations for the establishment of an International Trade Organization and in their influences on the policies and views of the I M F. Here in the White Plan it took early definitive form. Member countries were to be pressed to abandon 'all restrictions and controls over foreign exchange transactions with other member countries'. This eventuated in the stipulation that the Fund was, during a post-war transition phase of five years, to operate on a restricted scale and that its resources should not during that period be heavily committed. The Fund was designed for a world of multilateral trade, unsullied by exchange controls or discriminatory trade practices. In this sense the whole *raison d'être* of the Fund was a grandiose programme for the restoration of multilateral trade; and the transition period was intended to produce a progressive elimination of these controls. This view, fundamental in the American approach to the Fund, was to have great influence upon it during its early years.

Perhaps the most interesting practical feature of the White Plan was the section which proposed a means of liquidating the blocked sterling balances which had accumulated during the war as a result of Britain's necessity to obtain primary commodities, equipment and services from certain countries for the war effort. In attempting to devise, at so early a stage, means of dealing with this problem White showed great appreciation of the sort of currency problems which would have to be met when the war ended. Had such a proposal been acted upon and applied to the IMF, it would not only have eased the burden of abnormal sterling balances which hung upon Britain until the fifties, but it would have brought the Fund into the centre of post-war currency discussion at a time when it was being relegated by events and its own policies to the holding of a watching brief.

In the negotiations that followed the exchange of the Keynes and White Plans the shape of the Bretton Woods arrangements emerged and the *Joint Statement by Experts on the Establishment of an International Monetary Fund*[7] which appeared in April 1944 saw the White Plan triumphant on the agenda for the conference at Bretton Woods. At the conference itself in July, the Bretton Woods Agreement established the Fund and Bank[8] as twin functional agencies and vested them with impressive trappings of legal definition, aims and powers.

Now, looking back upon the Bretton Woods Agreement and the negotiations which preceded it, it is apparent that, apart from the establishment of the Fund and Bank, the most interesting feature is that here were established certain basic principles in international finance, which have not since been abrogated and which have changed and are still changing the face of the international economy. First of these is the principle of international economic co-operation itself for, gloomy though international monetary affairs have often been since 1944, they have never displayed the naked self-interest or lack of concern for the consequences of national action which characterized the inter-war years. Second, the principle that the responsibility for a balance of payments disequilibrium rests equally on surplus and deficit countries has been accepted, by USA between 1945 and 1953 and by Western Germany during the fifties. Finally, the principle that multilateral trade maximizes the welfare derived from international commerce brought us, albeit belatedly, to a world of convertible currencies and freedom from direct control in December 1958. At first it seemed as if the establishment of these principles was to eclipse in importance the establishment of the Fund itself which might prove unequal to the task of administering them. Then, at a late hour the Bretton Woods system and the Fund had new life breathed into them and faith in them was renewed.

Although the Fund followed closely the principles of the White Plan described above it is necessary at this stage to give some brief account of its *modus operandi* before going on to assess its record.

The Fund consists of a pool of currencies and of gold contributed by member states according to a quota system – by far the largest quotas being those of the United States and Britain.[9] Upon this currency-pool members have specified drawing rights, being permitted to buy a currency which is, for the time being, scarce to them in exchange for their own. The Fund thus acts as a buffer between deficits in the balances of payments of members and their individual gold and currency reserves. Its articles lay down conditions and limits for the supply of currencies, and for ensuring that it holds an adequate amount of each currency. The pool has been augmented during the eighteen years of the Fund's life, (*a*) by the addition of new members' quotas, (*b*) by a revision of quotas in 1959 and (c) by the Fund's right under an agreement of 1961 to borrow up to a limit of $6 billion from the so-called Paris Club.[10] Member states are allowed virtually automatic access to the resources of the Fund up to the first 25 per cent of their quotas but beyond this so-called 'first tranche' the Fund has progressively the right to consult with a deficit country on the policies it is pursuing to correct the imbalance.

It is neither possible nor desirable to describe the Fund model in detail but three ideas are basic to the operational plan.

1. A satisfactory structure of world trade can only be built upon an ordered pattern of stable exchange rates.

2. Disequilibria in balances of payments are of short duration and are often self-correcting. They may be met by the deficit country drawing upon the resources of the Fund. Only if the disequilibrium is prolonged and would entail a heavy drain upon these resources is the Fund prepared to sanction a change in the member's exchange rate. Thus short-term disequilibrium of a member is met by drawings; 'fundamental disequilibrium' by a modification of the member's exchange rate.[11]

3. Only under conditions of multilateral trade and freedom from exchange control and discrimination can we derive the full benefits of international trade and preserve stability in international payments. A period of five years from the date of commencement of the Fund (1 March 1947) was appointed as a transition period during which restrictions and discrimination were deemed tolerable. Member states were to be progressively under pressure to make their currencies convertible and to end all restrictions on payments by March 1952.

Some comment on the implications of this model must be made. The Fund resembles the international gold standard in two respects: firstly, it provides for fixed exchange rates determined by agreed parities of all national monetary units with gold; and secondly, the concept of international equilibrium is basic to its operation. Thereafter resemblance ceases. The gold standard maintained the structure of exchange rates by movements of gold from country to country, these movements in their turn inducing upward or downward movements in the cost/price structures of the countries concerned. The process was automatic, disequilibrium in the balance of payments setting in train forces which served to correct it. Internal price stability was voluntarily sacrificed upon the altar of the fixed exchange rate. The Bretton Woods sytem has no such automatic corrective measure to restore equilibrium. The pursuit by virtually all countries of policies aimed at preserving full employment and economic growth precludes purposive deflations of the gold standard type. Deflation being politically impracticable and frequent exchange rate changes being contrary to the Fund model there is, under the Bretton Woods system, no real machinery of balance of payments adjustment. In default of such machinery the total volume of international liquidity (i.e. total reserves of gold, international currencies, accumulation facilities, etc.) in general and the Fund's contribution to it in particular becomes of crucial importance. We will recur to this matter when we come at a later stage to discuss the plans for reform of the Fund. Meanwhile, we must follow the logic of the argument and ask: if the Fund system lacks an adjustment mechanism to correct balances of payments and take the strain off national reserves can the model be altered to provide one? Can we, in short, circumvent the international liquidity problem?

An adjustment mechanism can only work via one or other of two variables: national price and income levels, or exchange rates. If, as seems politically and socially vital, we regard the former as relatively fixed at full employment levels allowing only the most minor 'rolling adjustments' we are driven back on exchange rate alterations. Is there a case for the Fund to provide for either a system of flexible exchange rates between agreed upper and lower limits or more frequent single changes of the fixed rates? Much might be said on this: much has already been said.[12] Alas, when all has been said the answer is no. Two great currencies, the pound and dollar, dominate the dozen or so international currencies whose exchange rates are significant for stability. Changes, frequent or infrequent, of the two giants, or of one of them, would affect all the others with who knows what ultimate consequences. If a rate change has to be made it must be made unilaterally and without warning. The Fund cannot negotiate it. It is impossible to negotiate exchange rate variations. A unilateral change by London or Washington would in most conceivable circumstances be a risk which is not worth taking. It would temporarily at least break up the system of trading and financial relations and we would have to hope that a new system would emerge. It appears preferable by far to recognize the short-comings of the Bretton Woods model in providing for adjustment and in default thereof provide instead adequate backing for international liquid reserves. The evolution of the IMF system has been determined by this recognition.

The first annual meeting of the Fund was held at Savannah, Georgia, in March 1946. It was at once apparent that the tone of the meeting was harsh and in contrast to the negotiations which had established the Fund. The main reason for this was the change which had taken place in the attitude of the Americans. Since 1944 all was changed. Roosevelt had been replaced by Truman; Morgenthau, at the Treasury, had been replaced by Vinson; Harry White had gone from the Treasury. Outstanding questions, set aside at Bretton Woods, had now to be settled – the location of the Fund, the powers and role of the executive directors. On these issues, indeed on the very conception of the Fund, the British and Americans clashed frontally. But the American delegation would brook no interference. They had a voting majority[13] and they used it to complete the Fund in their own image. It was to be in Washington, among the embassies and the political 'toing-and-froing'. It would have permanent, salaried executive directors, conscious of the scrutiny of their embassies around the corner. Keynes' conception of a small technocracy of central bankers perished. With this unwholesome show of force from its largest member the Fund turned to its task.

In dealing with the practical activities of the Fund it is convenient to divide these into:

(i) Its work of assisting in the establishment of a system of multilateral payments;

(ii) Provision of currencies, and

(iii) Its exchange rate policy.

We shall deal with these in turn.

(i) The Fund's task of re-establishing multilateral trade and of ending direct restrictions and discriminatory practices was a twofold one: to induce member nations progressively to remove the restrictions on transfer of their currencies and for the protection of their balances of payments which were the result of the war and its aftermath; and to induce member nations to discard the use of direct controls and devices such as multiple currency rates in normal usages of international trade.

The first of these tasks was a formidable one and early events were inauspicious for the success of the Fund's policy. Within the first six months of the Fund's operational life (i.e. from 1 March 1947) Britain had, under the impulse of the Anglo-American Loan Agreement, made her attempt to re-establish sterling as a currency convertible for external transactions; had failed and by August 1947 had regrouped and re-established the formidable protective screen of British exchange control. Of the international currencies, only the US dollar remained free of restrictions but the scarcity of that currency, resulting from the overwhelming surplus on the US balance of payments, forced all the leading trading countries to apply not only controls as between one another but strong discriminatory controls over their trade with the US. The prevailing condition of most of the

Fund's member countries in the later forties was one of acute external imbalance with an inability to export until reconstruction had been achieved and an immediate necessity to import on a large scale. In such conditions it would have been folly to have sought balance of payments equilibrium by depreciation. What use to stimulate demand for exports which did not exist? A very great measure of depreciation would have been required to limit imports and the fillip given to domestic inflation would, in many cases, have been great. It was far preferable to control imports selectively and quantitatively by direct controls and rely on foreign credits to meet the deficit of the balance of payments. The nature of the controls differed widely. In most European countries the necessity to conserve foreign exchange resulted in the extension and elaboration of wartime restrictions. In Eastern Europe exchange restrictions supplemented direct and comprehensive state intervention through state trading and barter arrangements. In Latin America a very high demand for imports brought exchange restrictions, mainly through multiple currency rates, in spite of high export earnings.

By the end of the transition period (March 1952) the tide was not receding although signs of an easement of the dollar problem and a strengthening of the West European economies gave more strength to the Fund's arguments. But in fact the initiative in this field had passed from the Fund. The renewed movement towards convertibility of sterling known as the Collective Approach and launched in 1954 was not a Fund initiative but the subject of direct negotiation between the British and American governments; while progressive dismantling of direct import controls among the Western European countries went forward during the fifties under the stimulus of OEEC.

During the later fifties hopes of general convertibility rose and fell with the fortunes of the British balance of payments but in the last few days of 1958 sterling and ten other European currencies were able to shed restrictions with the effect of securing general non-resident convertibility and the way was open for multilateral trade for the first time since the Second World War. This marked an important turning-point. It meant that the Bretton Woods system had weathered the transition phase and was now to operate at last in a world approximating to the original conception of 1944. This had a double significance: firstly, it came at a time when the IMF was, in other fields of its activity, quitting its role of docile detachment, and was thus able to advance, as it were, on a broad front; secondly, it brought virtually to an end a side of the Fund's activities which had earned it no love and scant respect and it enabled it to become, what Keynes had hoped it would become, a predominantly financial organization. It is too early yet to say whether this abandonment of control marks a climacteric in the international monetary system – a return to the multilateral trade world which had faded from view in 1939 – or whether it is a purely temporary experiment in more liberal trade and payments methods. To a great extent the answer to this question lies with the Fund. If it can provide over the years an adequate holding of international liquidity, appropriate to current prices and trade volumes, and available on reasonable terms to deficit countries, it may serve to prevent a condition in which controls and restrictions are relaxed when the economic weather is fine and reimposed when it is foul or threatening.

(ii) Table I gives a summarized account of the Fund's currency transactions from the beginning of its operations on 1 March 1947 to 31 October 1964.

The Fund's currency transactions fall naturally into three phases. The first phase, from the beginning of operations until 30 April 1949, was marked by a demand for dollars, then universally short. The heaviest dollar sales of this period were in the months from 1 July 1947 to 30 April 1948 – the period immediately preceding the European Recovery Programme and a time

Table I

Summary of Fund Transactions 1 March 1947 to 31 October 1964

$ million

Year	Total gross drawings	No. of currencies drawn
1947–49	777·3	3
1950	0	–
1951	34·6	2
1952	85·1	1
1953	229·5	3
1954	62·5	1
1955	27·5	1
1956	692·6	2
1957	977·1	1
1958	337·9	4
1959	179·8	4
1960	279·8	6
1961	2,478·5	11
1962	583·8	8
1963	333·2	10
1964 (to Oct. 31)	811·0	11

Source: *International Financial Statistics.*

of chronic dollar shortage for the European countries. It should be remembered, however, that the full brunt of Europe's demand for dollars did not, save for this brief period, fall upon the Fund, which was 'cushioned' in 1946–47 by the US and Canadian loans to Britain and American loans to other European countries and in 1949 by the European Recovery Programme. It is fortunate that the Fund's dollar holding was protected in this way for had demands been continued upon it at the rate of $600 million per annum, as from mid-1947 to mid-1948 its dollar resources would soon have been exhausted.

The second phase, from 1949 to late 1956, may be described as the 'phase of stagnation'. During this period the Fund purposely curtailed the use of its resources. It was recognized that during the years of post-war reconstruction many claims might be made upon the Fund's resources and that the Fund must not become the underwriter of relief and rehabilitation, still less of grandiose schemes of economic development. On the other hand it was realized that total withdrawal from the international monetary scene would entail a grave risk that the Fund would be regarded as devoid of use or initiative. It was, therefore, seeking a compromise by regarding applications for assistance on their merits. So far as dollars were concerned the Fund decided that the European Recovery Programme was the appropriate source of relief and that countries in receipt of aid from the programme were not entitled to apply to it for dollars.

In 1951 as the end of the stipulated transition period approached the Fund became more militant in its efforts to persuade members to remove restrictions on trade and payments and it informed its members that its resources would in future be available only on certain conditions, i.e. that countries should adopt anti-inflation programmes and should progressively relax trade restrictions. This heavy insistence on 'conditional' assistance was resented and, since its policy declarations were contemporary with and identical to United States' demands for anti-inflationary policies, it was regarded as further evidence of the Fund's pro-American proclivities. An important innovation in 1952 was the inauguration of 'stand-by arrangements'. These assured a member of drawings upon Fund resources up to specific limits and within an agreed period. Such stand-by arrangements were to be negotiable between the Fund and individual members but in the negotiations similar tests were to be applied as to requests for immediate drawings. The Fund was determined that, at least for the transition period, there should be no automatic recourse to its resources.

The Fund's phase of activity began in 1956 and coincided with the arrival of a new Managing Director, Mr Per Jacobsson.[14] It began with the granting of large stand-by facilities to France and the UK in December to meet the balance of payments difficulties created by the Suez escapade and from that time onwards a steady flow of transactions has taken place. 1961 brought the largest volume of transactions in the Fund's history. 1959 and 1960 were quiet years but this was due primarily to greater stability in international finance and not to any tendency for the Fund to return to its former policies of reticence. By 1958 it had become clear that the growth in the Fund's currency transactions was outrunning its resources and that its gold and currency holdings required to be expanded. At the annual meeting in 1959 it was agreed: (*a*) that there should be a general increase of quotas of 50 per cent; (*b*) that there should be special increases for Canada, Federal Germany and Japan because of their relatively high economic growth; and (*c*) that certain countries with small quotas should be allowed to increase their quotas by more than the general rise of 50 per cent. These increases more than doubled the currencies available for transactions and have allowed the more open-handed policy to continue although further increases in quotas are under consideration and the whole broad question of the adequacy of international liquidity and the Fund's contribution to it is in the forefront of discussion.

The years 1956-60 saw new life breathed into the Fund, which increased not only the volume of its business but its prestige and standing as an international organization. It was enabled thus to move to a central position in international finance once major currencies achieved convertibility in 1959. The failures and frustrations of its earlier history were in great part recouped.

(iii) The Fund's exchange rate policy, so far as it was defined in the Bretton Woods Agreement, rests on the conception that in short-term balance of payments deficits the Fund is prepared to assist member countries by supplementing their reserves and that only in the case of structural disequilibrium (i.e. a long-term disequilibrium of considerable duration) is a revision of exchange rate an acceptable policy. This doctrine of 'managed flexibility' has been exhaustively discussed elsewhere[15] and there is no need to refer to it here save to remind ourselves of its importance in shaping Fund policies.

The first exchange rate problem before the Fund was that of fixing initial parities in 1946. The inflations of the war years had realigned national price levels and rendered obsolete the exchange rates which had obtained in 1939. At the same time the task of establishing a structure of initial exchange parities to govern the trading of the post-war world was a daunting one. Moreover, the chaotic condition of world trade and finance in 1947 was such that any systematic structure of rates, even if successfully established for a short period, would soon have been superseded. It was also clear that, for some years at least, need and not cost (and therefore not exchange rates) would dictate the pattern of world trade. In the circumstances the Fund accepted in December 1946 the rates notified by its members, more than half of which were the same or higher than in September 1939. While this was probably wise and in the circumstances unavoidable it had two unfortunate effects: it made the Fund's attitude towards exchange rates appear passive, if not negative, from the very outset; and it implied that at some later stage an attempt would be made to establish a normative structure of rates appropriate to general payments equilibrium. This was, of course, never attempted. Inevitably the existing rate structure hardened and became the structure of the post-transition as well as of the transition period.

The sterling devaluation of 1949 and the realignment of parities which resulted from it were carried out with the passive approval of the Fund but without its aid. They were crisis adjustments and certainly did not constitute the systematic adjustment of parities to post-war conditions which the pursuit of an orderly exchange policy demanded. In 1948, in its Annual Report, the Fund had noted the restraints which exchange rates were having upon trade expansion but went no further. This was the time at which, if the Fund had pursued a positive policy and suggested to members a planned revision of parities, it would probably have been supported by its leading members. In default of a policy, it seems to have fallen back upon a series of maxims for good exchange behaviour by members. Of these the two most important have been its belief in an exact and unswerving application of the exchange rate rules of Bretton Woods and its abhorrence of fluctuating rates, multiple rates or any divergence from the system of managed flexibility.

It would be impossible in short compass to examine the full implications of the Fund's faith in managed flexibility. We will content ourselves with two comments. Firstly, it was almost inevitable that such a method, under which exchange rate changes were only made at long intervals to correct 'fundamental disequilibria' in balances of payments should lead to conditions in which rates become virtually fixed, except in extreme crisis when a rate cannot be maintained, or for a country so small or financially unimportant as to have the luxury of independent action. As time has passed it has become all too clear that rates can never be altered by negotiation. This of all national actions is one which must be taken unilaterally, without prior notice or leakage and without consultation. To avoid speculation against their currencies countries have avoided using rate changes, while the Fund has clearly shown that it regards exchange rate variations as undesirable and something to be avoided at almost any cost. This view is shared amongst the leading governments. The uneasy duality of the pound and dollar as the main international currencies, each with satellites, means that a rate change must have very wide repercussions. The events of December 1964 show how far the governments, the Fund and the central bankers are prepared to go to prevent the devaluation of a major currency, with the chain reaction which it would invoke. Indeed, it is no exaggeration to say that we have returned to a gold exchange standard under which exchange rate changes, at least for certain major countries, are virtually excluded both by the Fund and by established financial opinion.

Some of the above disadvantages of periodic adjustment of exchange rates might be avoided by a system under which rates of exchange were free to move over an agreed range above and below the Fund parity. This would short-circuit the problem of negotiating the change of rate with the Fund and would also provide the international economy with a mechanism for balance of payments adjustment which it at present lacks. It would also ease the strain upon international liquidity. On occasions some countries have either experimented[16] with it or been poised on the brink[17] of adopting a free rate for their currency but the balance of opinion, and certainly the Fund, is against it and there is little prospect of it being used in the foreseeable future.[18]

Two other aspects of the Fund's exchange rate policy must be mentioned very briefly: its efforts, in the early post-war period, to get rid of disorderly cross-rates[19] between currencies and its unrelenting war on multiple currency rates. Disorderly cross-rates occurred frequently during the immediate post-war period under exchange control and were used by some countries to achieve a concealed devaluation of their currency. Multiple currency rates,[20] often used by countries unable to institute an orderly or systematic exchange control and common for a period in Latin America, were the object of relentless Fund opposition. Since many schemes of multiple rates were used as protective devices for balances of payments, as well as for less worthy ends, the Fund had to tread warily, and with discernment. By formulating certain principles whereby countries might progressively dismantle systems of multiple rates it succeeded over a period of years in reducing these practices to an unimportant level.

It is twenty years since Bretton Woods, and reform of the international monetary system is in the air. The experiences of the post-war reconstruction period and the dollar problem revealed serious weaknesses in the system while more recently the weakening of the US balance of payments, the instability of sterling and the persistent surplus of Western Germany are features to be reckoned with.

The discussions of reform began in the late fifties when the new free-handed policy of the Fund gave rise to doubts of the adequacy of its resources. Since then discussion of the so-called 'international liquidity problem' has been continuous, its main effect having been to achieve a revision of Fund quotas in 1959, the probability of a second revision in the near future, and the Fund agreement of December 1961 to borrow from the Paris Club up to a limit of $6 billion. All these are useful increments to the Fund's original resources and it is clear that the Fund and others see the future with the Fund much in its present form, its resources being replenished when necessary by increases of quotas or extensions of its own borrowing rights. Even this simple view of the situation gives rise to some awkward problems. True the Fund's resources may grow by augmentation of quotas at a rate not very different (although probably lagging somewhat behind) the rise in the volume of world trade[21] but what about individual quotas? The size of national quotas decided at Bretton Woods was based upon pre-war trade levels and quota revisions, such as that of 1959, based on a general percentage increase, not only perpetuate the bias in the original quotas in favour of the large industrial powers, but accentuate it. If we compare the share of countries in world trade and their share in the total of Fund quotas we find Britain and the US with huge 'excess'[22] quotas while countries whose post-war economic growth has been rapid, e.g. W. Germany, Italy, Netherlands, France, Canada, Sweden and Japan have considerable quota 'deficiencies'. Moreover, the quotas of many underdeveloped countries are woefully inadequate in view of their import surpluses and development programmes. Consciousness of this problem of adjusting quotas not only to general Fund needs but to the needs of individual countries has produced delicate political problems each time a revision of quotas is mooted. Sooner or later selective additions to quotas will have to be made.

The simple international liquidity approach to reform of the international monetary system is minimal. A certain quantity of international liquidity (i.e. of means of external settlement of which gold, internationally accepted currencies and drawing rights on international organizations are the main items) is clearly needed to clear final deficits in balances of payments. It is generally taken that the greater the volume of international trade the greater the volume of international liquidity required for final clearing of balances. This is not entirely true for it is the size of disequilibrium in balances of payments and not the volume of trade which really determines the demand for liquidity. A glance at Table II will show that the ratio of total international liquidity to total world trade has differed widely over time and that in periods of stability in international finance it has fallen to very low levels. In gold standard days when the onus was on individual countries to adjust balance of payments disequilibrium by domestic monetary policy a very low level of total gold holdings appears to have been sufficient.

In fact, however, it is misleading to make time comparisons of the international liquidity ratio in this way. The high ratio of 1938 had to face huge potential demands in a world in which there was, as yet, little tradition of international economic co-operation. The relatively high ratio of 1948 did not prevent the American inventory recession of the following year from forcing a round of currency devaluations. Moreover, the fact that since the early fifties the flow of gold to the US has been reversed has created a far more favourable condition in international liquidity. A host of qualifications has therefore to be made to any comparison of international liquidity rates. The most that can be said on the desirable size of international liquidity is that the greater the volume of world trade the greater the *potential* demand for international liquidity. The real determinant of such demand is the size of balance of payments disequilibria.

Table II

Ratio of Reserves to Imports
(All countries except communist bloc.
Selected years 1913-57)

Year	Imports $ billion	Gold and exchange held by countries and International Organizations as percentage of imports
1913	21	21
1928	30·6	42
1938	23·6	117
1948	60·0	80
1950	59·3	82
1954	79·6	65
1957	107·0	51

Source: *International Reserves and Liquidity*.
IMF, 1958. Table 2, p. 18.

There are then two distinct facets of the problem of reform of the international monetary system: the question of imbalance and how this may be minimized and corrected; and the question of international liquidity, its nature, quantity and distribution. The optimum situation would be one in which countries were compelled to prevent or adjust balance of payments deficits while at the same time machinery existed whereby the volume of international liquidity could be expanded quickly if need be. It is not surprising, therefore, that a number of plans to reform the international monetary system and to incorporate both of these desirable features have been put forward in recent years – the Triffin Plan of 1958 with various qualifications of later date, the Bernstein Plan of the same year, the Franks Plan, the Stamp Plan and others.[23] All of these plans have been discussed exhaustively elsewhere and no useful purpose would be served by continuing the discussion here. It might, however, be profitable to consider briefly certain features which most of the plans have in common.

Firstly, the utility and standing of the Fund are recognized in that the arrangements advocated are adjustments or additions to the Fund's powers and functions. It is regarded as the established vehicle of international monetary co-operation and a natural starting point for further development.

Secondly, it has been suggested that the Fund should become the central repository of national gold and currency reserves. This would have the effect of placing with the Fund balances whose transfer would be the vehicle of final settlement and imparting to the Fund the role of an international central bank.

Thirdly, several of the plans seek to develop international monetary arrangements in the direction which domestic money has gone long since by adding to the existing stock by credit creation. At present international liquidity consists virtually of the aggregate cash holdings, viz. gold and internationally accepted currencies, of all countries and of the Fund. This is of course augmented by a large volume of international trade credit but this is a variable, its amount or nature cannot be anticipated accurately and it is not regarded as part of international liquidity proper. The essence of international liquidity is that its acceptability, quantity and nature are precisely known in advance. It is therefore limited at present to known cash assets of countries. It is this failure to get beyond the cash nature of international liquidity which makes it so inflexible. If, as with domestic banking systems, new liquidity could be created by international agreement, then we would be a great way towards solving the problem of shortage of liquidity. If, for example, the Fund were to be given powers of overdraft creation then the international monetary system would have a more modern look. As Robert Triffin has truly said, the international monetary system is now at about the same stage of development as was the British monetary system at the time of the Bullionist controversy.

Fourthly, a number of writers would seek to attack the imbalance problem by writing into the Fund Agreement provision for a more flexible exchange rate policy.

There is little doubt that in the next decade some of these proposals will be incorporated in the Fund. Whether they transform it into some new and powerful international entity which like Keynes' Clearing Union may be the embryo of 'the future economic government of the world', or whether they merely augment its powers and means to lend while keeping its present conservative character is a question still in the balance. The Fund has become a very different organization from the dreary, negative-sounding agency it was in the forties and early fifties. The reforms now being debated will complete its transformation. It is too soon to tell what will emerge when this is complete.

What have been the forces, in particular the non-economic forces, which have determined the development of the Fund? It is possible, indeed fairly easy, to enumerate these forces, but difficult to decide their interplay and relative strengths; and it is these which are the decisive factors determining the Fund's development. Even to highlight such forces may be of interest.

First among formative forces has been the influence of individuals – of economists and others not directly involved in the Fund's routine activities and of others within the Fund. The Fund was born of a marriage of British and American ideas on international finance. It was whipped by critics too numerous to mention during its years of inactivity, and when, in later years, its active use demonstrated its inadequacies new architects came forward to plan its extension and adaptation. Of the outside economists who have influenced the Fund the list is long: Keynes, White, D. H. Robertson, J. H. Williams, Mossé and Beyen at its inception; Mikesell, Samuelson and Lloyd Metzler, in the years which followed; Robert Triffin whose plan of 1958 was the first of a series; and, from first to last, E. M. Bernstein who, from his work at Bretton Woods itself on the technical clauses of the agreement to his plan of 1960 for international liquidity, has been the Fund's most discerning and constructive critic.

It is inevitable that in a field so technical and intricate as that in which the Fund operates the expert and technician should find themselves welcome and their opinions be attended to. Whether their advice is followed is, however, quite another matter. In the past the technicians have been indispensable: that is not to say they have been formative. In the great decisions which have moulded the Fund only one has been determined by the technicians. This was the decision to bring it into being. Without the assurances of Keynes, White and others that failure to meet the international currency problems of the post-war world would create monetary chaos and worse, and without a blueprint for the Fund, it would never have come into being.

From there onwards the experts have had to content themselves with being listened to. The more technical and, it would be argued by most economists, the more ingenious and far-seeing of the base plans was set aside in the interests of political expediency. The critics' calls for action on exchange rate policy and Fund action in the days of the dollar problem were ignored as the Fund itself gained strength, established its own views and reacted to the internal political pulls of its members. The decision to carry it into the arena in 1956 after its years of retirement was that of its newly arrived Managing Director, Per Jacobsson; while its views on the recently posed questions of international liquidity and its own reform are the creature of its own staff and their view of the path it must follow for its own survival. The position of independent experts is now different: at the Fund's birth they were inside, with full knowledge and the blessing of authority; now they are outside aiming their broadsides at a deeply entrenched, numerous and well-equipped force. It is possible that by weight of logic they will force a parley and exact terms: it is unlikely they will carry the day.

Then there is a majestic third force – which has come to power and influence in recent years. The central bankers, in disorganized retreat in 1944, still smarting from the defeats of the thirties, from which in the popular view they gained no credit, are back in favour. The old cry of gold standard days, 'central bank co-operation', has been raised again and has rallied several constructive actions in recent months. The new movement of central bank co-operation has shown results. The Basle Agreement, and the organized support for sterling in December 1964 have given new and great power to groups which in the Fund's earlier days were in eclipse. These will have their say in the Fund's future. It is unlikely, on the whole, that they will be on the side of the independent critics.

Second of the forces moulding the Fund has been the balance of forces within itself. In the period from 1947 to 1955 the dominance of the United States with its large voting power made the Fund a vehicle for the furtherance of American foreign economic policy. Throughout the period of the dollar problem (i.e. up to about 1954) the US was able through the Fund to press upon the dollar-hungry nations of Western Europe the policies by which, in the American view, they could move towards balance of payments equilibrium. It could also further through the Fund the general principle of multilateral trade, upon which it believed expanding international trade should be built. The

extinction in the early fifties of the American external surplus and
its conversion in the later decade to a deficit, together with the
establishment after 1959 of multilateral trade, fundamentally
changed the American position in the Fund. While still active
and sincere in its belief in Fund principles the US allowed Fund
policies in the later fifties to evolve under the aegis of the Fund
staff. As the nation with the largest voting power it saw itself not
as the main formative force in Fund policies and opinions but as
primus inter paries with other members.

Attitudes of other leading nations towards the Fund also
changed. In particular Britain and the Western Europeans who
in the period of stagnation had virtually 'written off' the Fund as
moribund and ineffectual came in the later fifties to see its worth
and thus to court its favour. The need for a 'Fund policy' was
tacitly acknowledged by the major members and by the early
sixties the main outlines of such policies were discernible. As
the international monetary debate on international liquidity and
the Fund's contribution to it developed the grouping became
clearer. For Britain, with her shaky balance of payments and the
task of running an international currency with a banking system
inadequately supplied with reserves and liberally encumbered
with quick liabilities, the task of expanding international liquidity
through a reformed Fund was attractive and towards this end
Britain was a prime mover. The US was slow to be converted
but by 1964 its conversion was complete. Left to themselves it is
probable that the US and Britain would, once they had reconciled
their own differences, which were of emphasis rather than
principle, have led the more monetarily conservative countries
(France, Holland, Germany, Belgium), who had stressed the need
for strict balance of payments disciplines, towards a compromise
settlement. Two things prevented this: the sharp sterling crisis of
November 1964 in which the main international currency was
wellnigh drained of reserves, and the emergence of France, led
by General de Gaulle, as monetary antagonist, on a broad front,

of the United States. The fact that the General had switched his vendetta with Washington to the currency field, imperilled the dispassionate consideration of the reform of the world monetary system. These events are still in process and the other group within the Fund, the underdeveloped countries, look on and cannot, let us admit, be inspired by what they see. A line-up more involved, more politically motivated and, in its potential effects, more dangerous than any the Fund has yet seen presents itself.

In spite of this there are grounds for optimism in the present position. Firstly, the Fund is firmly established and recognized as the venue through which international monetary reform must be made to work. Secondly, even the most conservative element in international finance, the central bankers, are now admitting that the gold exchange standard in its present form is unstable, outmoded and ripe for replacement. Thirdly, belief in national monetary sovereignty is (save in the Elysée) dying. The situation is one in which rapid progress towards a new international currency system is possible. And finally, if in this discussion an embattled France stands, with her High Constable, athwart the path of progress some consolation may be drawn from the fact that in few things so much as in international currency is it possible to stand alone. The French demand for a revived gold standard is such as to send all sorts of former antagonists scuttling to close their ranks against it. This sudden tactical intervention does not alter the long-term problem of developing a new international payments system around the Fund.

When Keynes spoke at the inaugural meeting of the Fund at Savannah in 1946 he spoke of the evil which would result if 'the Bretton Woods twins' should grow up politicians. Five years later it seemed as if his fears had been justified. Now as the twins approach maturity it seems that one has found its métier as a banker, shrewd and appropriately parsimonious; the other, after a brief and unfortunate excursion into the political field, is settling down to professional life as an economist.

TEXT REFERENCES

1. Agreement between the United States and the United Kingdom, 23 February 1942. Article VII, Cmd. 6391.

2. For an excellent account of the negotiations which resulted from the general directive of Article VII see R. N. Gardner, *Sterling Dollar Diplomacy*, Oxford, 1956.

3. *Proposal for an International Clearing Union*, Cmd. 6437 of 1943.

4. *A United States Proposal for a United and Associated Nations Stabilisation Fund*. US Treasury, 7 April 1943. Reprinted and republished in 1943 by HMSO.

5. An excellent critical account of the Keynes Plan is to be found in S. Horie, *The International Monetary Fund*, London, 1964, pp. 62-78.

6. Cf. S. Horie, op. cit., pp. 44-52.

7. Cmd. 6519 of 1944.

8. *United Nations Monetary and Financial Conference, Final Act*, Cmd. 6546 of 1944.

9. The US quota in the Fund as a percentage of total quotas is almost double its percentage of world trade.

10. 'The Paris Club' consists of Belgium, Britain, Canada, France, West Germany, Italy, Japan, Sweden, Switzerland, the Netherlands and USA.

11. This original conception has been considerably modified by the passage of time.

12. A very large literature has reviewed the case for free rates. See the following as specially germane to the problem discussed in the text. F. A. Lutz, 'The case for flexible exchange rates', *Banca Nazionale del Lavoro, Quarterly Review*, December 1954; W. M. Scammell, 'What sort of exchange rates?', *Westminster Bank Review*, August 1954; Sir D. MacDougall, 'Flexible exchange rates', *Westminster Bank Review*, August 1954; J. E. Meade, 'The case for variable exchange rates', *The Three Banks Review*, No. 27, September 1955; W. M. Scammell, *International Monetary Policy*, Second Edition 1961, pp. 92-99 and 198-204.

13. The Anglo-American Loan Agreement was not yet through Congress and Keynes hesitated to press the Americans too hard at Savannah lest he put it in jeopardy. Moreover, several other nations at Savannah which might have supported Britain were at this time applicants to the US for recovery loans.

14. Jacobsson was just the sort of monetary technician of whom Keynes would have approved. He had great expertise in international finance and

came to the Fund after years of experience as economic adviser to the Bank for International Settlements.

15. Cf. Scammell, op. cit., pp. 99-106.

16. Canada allowed her exchange rate to go unsupported from September 1950 to May 1962.

17. Britain seriously considered allowing the sterling rate to float in 1952. For an interesting account of Operation Robot under which this was to be done see 'The Treasury Under the Tories, 1951-64', Samuel Brittan, London, 1964.

18. This is difficult to foretell. Free rates, like beards, go in and out of fashion. By 1970 they may be 'in'; at present they are very much 'out'.

19. For example in 1948 when the French devaluation had the effect of producing disorderly cross-rates.

20. Multiple currency rates may be used to curtail luxury imports. For example a government may decree that foreign currency to import necessities may be purchased at a low official rate, and currency to import luxuries must be purchased in a free market at a high rate. Even Britain had two currency rates for a time in the fifties: the official rate of $2·80= £1 within the exchange control and the free rate in certain centres such as Zurich and New York in which sterling was generally at a slight discount.

21. Whether due to a volume increase, a price increase, or both.

22. The word 'excess' here is ambiguous. Clearly the British quota is not excessive relative to British balance of payments difficulties; that of the US is excessive since the US has very adequate national reserves and it is a matter of policy not to use Fund resources.

23. The original sources for these various international currency plans are as follows:

Triffin Plan: *Banca Nazionale del Lavoro, Quarterly Review*, March and June 1958.
Gold and the Dollar Crisis, Yale U.P., 1960.
Stamp Plan: 'The Fund and the Future', *Lloyd's Bank Review*, October 1958.
Franks Plan: *Lloyd's Bank Annual Statement*, 1958.
Bernstein Plan: *International Effects of US Economic Policy*, Study Paper, No. 16. January 1960, presented to Joint Committee of US Congress.
T. Balogh: 'International Reserves and Liquidity', *Economic Journal*, June 1960.
Alan Day: Evidence to Radcliffe Committee, Minutes of Evidence, Questions 9891-9977.

BIBLIOGRAPHY

Annual Reports of IMF, Washington, 1947-64.

Bernstein, E. M., 'Scarce Currencies and the IMF', *Journal of Political Economy*, March 1945.

Gardner, R. N., *Sterling Dollar Diplomacy*, Oxford, 1956.

Gowda, K. V., *International Currency Plans and Expansion of World Trade*, New York, 1964.

Harrod, R. F., *The Life of John Maynard Keynes*, London, 1951.

Horie, S., *The International Monetary Fund*, London, 1964.

International Financial Statistics, Washington.

Mikesell, R. F., *Foreign Exchange in the Postwar World*, New York, 1954.

Penrose, E. F., *Economic Planning for the Peace*, Princeton, 1953.

Postwar Monetary Plans, 3rd edition, New York, 1947.

Scammell, W. M., *International Monetary Policy*, 2nd Edition, London, 1961.

Tew, B., *International Monetary Co-operation 1945-56*, 3rd Edition, London, 1956.

Triffin, R., *Gold and the Dollar Crisis*, Yale, 1960.

10 THE WORLD BANK

Andrew Shonfield

The recent history of the World Bank demonstrates a capacity, unusual among international institutions, to break loose from a well established ideological framework. By the mid-1960s the Bank was lending money for projects that it would have rejected out of hand only a few years before, and doing so on terms which it would have regarded as quixotically generous.[1]

The old ideology had been taken very seriously. It was the badge of respectability, which was designed to make what might otherwise seem to be an eccentric enterprise acceptable to a suspicious banking community. The World Bank, its spokesmen during the 1950s appeared to be insisting on all possible occasions, is a straightforward honest-to-goodness banker with a portfolio and a lending policy which any Wall Street house might take over with benefit to its stock holders. Borrowers were carefully selected after a rigorous examination of their likely creditworthiness over the period during which a loan from the Bank would be current. And the particular projects for which a loan was made had to be shown to add fairly quickly to the earning power of the borrower a measurable amount of foreign exchange, sufficient to meet its obligations. The Bank's business was not merely profitable; it was almost riskless.

It had, of course, not always been so. The experience of the early years of the Bank immediately after its establishment in 1946 no doubt contributed to the later mood of over-caution and anxiety. During this period capital was short and lending

231

hazardous. The Bank's first $500 million of business were hurried loans for European reconstruction, handed over to the borrower without any serious vetting of either of the particular purposes for which the money was required or of the borrower's likely capacity to repay his debt. Once the Marshall Plan was in operation, the Bank was able to avoid further involvement in transactions of this kind. But its main shareholders, outside the United States, were very slow to provide it with the wherewithal for extending its operations. Its ability to finance development depended almost entirely on its standing in Wall Street as a sound and conservative lender. As late as 1954 the Bank had at its disposal for lending less than $150 million of non-US currencies out of the subscriptions due to it from member countries.[2] Meanwhile it relied largely on the American government's paid-up subscription ($635 million) and the capital put up by American private investors (some $500 million at this stage) to stay in business.

The change in subsequent years was gradual: it took some time before European governments regained sufficient confidence in their balance of payments not only to make their official subscriptions freely available for World Bank loans but also to allow the Bank to raise money from private investors in their capital markets. In the mid-1950s many of the West European countries still saw themselves essentially as borrowers of international capital, rather than as lenders. Indeed, at this time the Bank was still finding a lot of customers for its loans in Europe. Over the first decade of its operations 36 per cent of all its loans went to European countries, compared with 29 per cent to Asia and Africa combined. By now the European figure has come down to 20 per cent and the combined total for Asia and Africa has risen to 50 per cent.[3] At the same time the balance of bank borrowing between the United States and Europe has been reversed; today the European countries provide most of the new money used in World Bank lending. Indeed the Bank has since 1963 made it a point of policy not to go to the New York market for any fresh funds[4] – the object being to avoid any possible embarrassment to the American balance of payments. But even before this, the available evidence showed that a large proportion of capital subscribed to dollar loans issued by the Bank in the United States actually came from European investors.

The Bank's notions of the purpose of its loans have, since its foundation, also undergone some interesting changes. In its early days it was firm doctrine that the only kind of project which the Bank would even look at was a specific piece of fixed capital investment showing a measurable rate of return. Furthermore, it believed that there were certain types of projects which were appropriate for loans to governments or publicly owned corporations, and other projects which were clearly not. The Bank was especially loth to put up any money to develop a nationalized manufacturing industry. Manufacturing was deemed to be a proper task for private enterprise. Thus it was characteristic that the finance which it provided for the expansion of the Indian steel industry, amounting in all to the considerable sum of $158 million, went exclusively to two private firms, the Indian Iron and Steel Company and Tata, while the nationalized sector of the industry, which the Indian planners had cast for the leading role in the enlargement of the country's steel capacity, received nothing. The Indian government was in practice faced with the alternative of providing its guarantee for the loans made by these private sector firms – a guarantee which the Bank needs before it is able to lend money to a private firm – or going without any World Bank money at all for the steel industry.

Naturally, such a policy as this placed severe limits on World Bank lending for the expansion of manufacturing industry in the underdeveloped world. For in very many countries governments have decided, either on political grounds or simply because private capital and business management is deemed to be inadequate for the purpose, to take over the ownership of large-scale enterprise in new industries. Moreover the Bank's prejudice against nationalized undertakings was not reserved solely for manufacturing industry; it extended to the state, acting as a financial intermediary in an industrial investment bank. There were, of course, and still are, good reasons for trying to guard against the employment of such investment funds for political purposes. But in Latin America, for example, there are several countries in which there is no alternative to a public investment bank. Unless the political risk is accepted, this particular method of financing industrial investment, by harnessing international money to local business initiative, has to be forgone.

The same general point applies even more powerfully to agricultural investment. In its early years the Bank provided small sums of money to help in launching agricultural credit institutions; but it was not prepared to accept either the increased risks or the need for the detailed supervision of its loans, which would inevitably accompany any major expansion of its activities in the field of agriculture. The result of these inhibitions was that the World Bank's lending to underdeveloped countries until the early 1960s was almost entirely confined to individual large-scale projects in the sphere of transport, electric power and other public utilities. Mr George Woods, who was appointed president of the Bank in 1963, made it clear almost at once that he intended to break out of this restrictive framework. In his first address to the annual meeting of the governors of the Bank in September 1963[5] he said:

> The time has come when the Bank will have to add new dimensions to both its lending and technical assistance activities. We will have to be prepared, on the one hand, to give more help earlier in the development process and, on the other, to follow development into its more advanced stages and to use new techniques for that purpose.

The Bank thus asserted its right to go beyond the task of providing merely the infrastructure for other people's investment, and staked a claim for a more active role in setting the direction of development itself.

It could be argued that the wonder is not that there was a change of policy in the early 1960s, but that it took so long before the old régime was shaken. There is something in this. In fact, the aggressively conventional banker's attitude was sustained for so long largely as a result of the personal predilections of Mr Eugene Black, the President from 1949 until 1963. He had been very successful in building up the borrowing power of the Bank during the 1950s; indeed, by the end of the decade he had made it so popular with investors that it commanded far more money than it could lend, on commercial terms, to the underdeveloped world. And he not only established the Bank as an attractive investment proposition but also managed gradually to create a relationship of trust with a body of clients unfamiliar with international banking – the governments of the newly independent underdeveloped countries. But Black's very success then became an impediment to further progress. He continued to take the line that if the Bank was to perform its task of providing a channel for private investment funds into the underdeveloped world, it must hold fast to the stringent lending rules which it had initially set itself. There was no one to say no to him. In the context of the history of modern international institutions, the incident serves to illustrate the extent to which the accidents of personality in the official at the head may determine policy. That it was a matter of personal dominance in the Bank is indicated by the speed and ease with which new policies were introduced from 1963 onwards, after Black had retired. The change could not have been compassed so rapidly, if the senior staff of the Bank had not thought out a large part of the new programme well in advance.

That is not to say that they had fixed on particular measures, and were merely waiting for the opportunity to drop them into their appropriate slots. The personal contribution of Woods, the new President, was, once again, decisive. But he moved into an organization where many of the ideas which were eventually embodied in his new policies were already familiar. A visitor from outside can often detect the mood in such cases more readily than an insider. I was left in no doubt that by the early 1960s the Bank was ready for a change.

Some of this indeed emerges from the official report of the Bank for the year 1963-64, the first full year during which Woods was in charge. It had been, he said, 'an introspective year'. He struck the same note when he addressed the United Nations Conference on Trade and Development in March 1964, telling the delegates that the Bank had 'embarked on a programme of critical self-analysis'. Here again it is worth noting that the Bank is unusual among international institutions of the United Nations family in being confident enough to refer openly to its own sense of inadequacy. There is no doubt that the feeling was genuine. It was reflected most clearly in the decision about the employment of the Bank's profits in 1964. This was a dramatic reversal of its previous, rather tight-fisted Wall Street posture. The Bank had been especially proud of its big reserve of accumulated profits, to which it added generously each year. The existence of this fund enhanced its standing among investors. But among non-investors, the accumulation of this great wealth by an international institution which seemed to find difficulty in deploying the money already at its disposal in the service of the underdeveloped world had begun to cause resentment.

The 1964 decision was to hand over $50 million of the annual profit, equal to nearly 40 per cent of the total, to the Bank's poor relation, the International Development Association. IDA, which was set up in 1960 specifically in order to provide loans on easy terms to countries which could not meet the Bank's strict criterion of 'creditworthiness', fairly quickly ran through most of the not very large sum of money with which it had initially been endowed.[6] Unlike the World Bank, it could neither rely on the repayment of earlier loans to replenish its funds—since it normally makes fifty-year loans, interest free, with a ten-year period of grace – nor could it attract money from private investors. When IDA's funds were almost exhausted in 1964, the donor countries agreed to give it a fresh subvention designed to support a higher rate of lending ($250 million per annum) for another three years; and the World Bank's $50 million annual contribution has now been added to this. No formal promise was made that it would henceforth be a regular annual subscription; but that was clearly understood to be the Bank's intention, so long as its profits remained adequate.

Thus the Bank deliberately broke with the convention that it employs its money only in strictly 'bankable' projects. This was in fact a convenient and philanthropic method of giving away part of the annual addition to the Bank's reserve, which was becoming scandalously large.[7] Formally, however, the act of generosity was covered by the fiction that the $50 million was the equivalent of the dividend payable to the shareholders of the Bank, i.e. the countries which had put up its funds, and that this dividend was being transferred, instead, to IDA. Under the Black régime, the greatest care was taken to avoid any taint to the Bank's strictly commercial operation that might come from contact with the 'soft loan' activities of IDA. There is evidently no longer the same anxiety on this score. Instead, the Bank's own approach appears to have acquired some of the 'softness' characteristic of IDA.

Perhaps it was inevitable that this would happen once the Bank's staff began seriously to explore the extensive twilight area which exists between the strict commercial loan to an under-developed country and the straight gift. Once policy frees itself from the orthodoxies of banking doctrine on the one hand and from the conventions of the give-away on the other, the range of possible variations is very wide. They have only recently begun to be discovered. By 1964, when IDA's capital was enlarged, the annual total of its new loan commitments came to about half as much as the World Bank's lending to underdeveloped countries – $283 million against $588 million.[8] The actual disbursements of money by the IDA on the credits granted were at this stage still small by comparison with the Bank. But the proportion was bound to grow. The spending of money on the typical development project builds up only gradually; and the Bank having been in business very much longer had many more projects which had reached the heavy spending stage. The flow of IDA money into development schemes did not begin in earnest until 1963-64. By the middle of 1964 its loans had reached a total of $778 million, of which it had disbursed only $193 million. In addition to the amount already in the pipeline, money for new lending by IDA will be coming forward at a rate of some $300 million a year during the period 1964-67.[9]

Perhaps the most radical expression so far of Mr Woods's declared policy of taking 'development into its more advanced stages' is the long-term credit to India in 1964 for the purchase of industrial materials and components abroad for a variety of engineering industries. This was for all practical purposes indistinguishable from a general loan to help pay for a part of India's normal import bill. The $90 million made available did not finance any new fixed capital investment. In fact the money did something much more useful. It allowed Indian industry to make full use of existing manufacturing capacity, which would otherwise have been underemployed because of a shortage of imported materials and spare parts. But in order to do so a major doctrinal barrier between the principles of orthodox bank lending and common sense had to be surmounted. All the Bank's policies up to this point had been founded on the sharpest possible distinction between 'capital' and 'current' costs. Of course the distinction is in practice far from precise. When a factory increases its stocks, it is in fact making a capital investment; but at the moment when it buys the extra raw materials, the transaction is indistinguishable from any other current expense.

Admittedly the Indian credit was financed by IDA, not by the World Bank itself. But since it was laid down as a matter of Bank doctrine, when IDA was founded, that its loans should in the main be of the same type as those financed by the Bank itself,[10] the Indian loan may be regarded as a significant precedent. The other end of Woods's policy, 'to give more help earlier in the development process', has emerged most clearly so far in the search by the Bank for education projects in which to invest its money. Again, IDA has made the running; but the 1963-64 annual report announced that 'the Bank also is prepared, in appropriate circumstances, to enter the field (of education).[11] Perhaps even more remarkable, in view of the World Bank's past attitude towards the other Specialized Agencies of the United Nations, it has embarked on a joint project with UNESCO to identify particular schemes of secondary and technical education in the underdeveloped countries which promise to further economic development.

A comparable arrangement was made with the Food and Agriculture Organization of the United Nations in 1964. The Bank is keenly aware of the inadequacy of its contribution in the field of agriculture – leaving aside the big water and flood control projects, its investment in other forms of agricultural development have to date absorbed less than 3 per cent of its loans – and is looking for ways in which it can improve its performance. The stated intention of the Bank, moreover, is to administer any projects for agricultural investment which may emerge from this new venture in partnership with the FAO. In the 1950s, when one visited the World Bank headquarters on H Street in Washington, one had the impression that they regarded the people in the big UN building up in New York, and even more so those scattered about in the Specialized Agencies of the United Nations in remote European cities, as a volatile, spendthrift and not wholly trustworthy bunch. The attitude was unfortunate because several of the UN agencies would, in the course of their technical assistance work in the underdeveloped countries, have been able to bring forward the very investment projects for which the Bank was looking. This was indeed the purpose which the UN Special Fund deliberately set itself to fulfil when it got into its stride in the early 1960s. The ingenious method used by Mr Paul Hoffman, the first managing director of the UN Special Fund, to bring the point home to the World Bank was to employ it as the Fund's paid agent in conducting certain technical aid projects for which the Bank had particular expertise. The Bank for these purposes was treated on the same footing as any one of the other Specialized Agencies of the United Nations. The difference was that having become interested in the technical work of one of the Fund's 'pre-investment' schemes, it would be in a position to take matters further and put up the money for a full-blown investment project, if the preliminary studies looked promising. It would, in fact, in the successful cases, be preparing the blueprints for its own ultimate use.

That is what has now happened in a number of instances. The Bank's more recent employment of the FAO and UNESCO to act in the role of consultants and joint managers on certain investment projects is a logical extension of the 'pre-investment' work of the UN Special Fund. There is no doubt that the whole complex of UN institutions in the field of economic development will be greatly strengthened once the Bank is established in an integral relationship with the rest of the group.

Meanwhile the balance of effort within the World Bank family of institutions (which includes the International Finance Corporation as well as the IDA) has undergone a significant change. Originally when Black agreed to the establishment of IDA, the intention was that it should act as an auxiliary mechanism in the World Bank system, draining off those transactions which were not properly bankable, because the client's credit was inadequate to support them – thus leaving the World Bank itself in a better position to insist on the full commercial treatment for its own loans. Black's instincts were by no means favourable to the IDA principle, when it was first suggested in the late 1950s. In the end it was accepted chiefly as a means of helping to secure the continuance of the Bank's own commercial lending operations. But Black wanted it to be small, and he tried to ensure that it would not strike out on any initiatives of its own by insisting that it should be run entirely by the Bank's staff.[12] Now it is growing rather big, in relation to the Bank's own lending to the underdeveloped world; and more important, the management of the Bank appears to have been infected by IDA's spirit.

Having pressed the donor countries to be more generous in their lending terms, so that the credit of the underdeveloped countries would not be destroyed by an excessive burden of debt-servicing commitments, the Bank itself decided in 1964 that it would be right to set an example of making longer loans and allowing more generous periods of grace, in order 'to lighten the service burden where this is appropriate to the project and to the debt position of the country'.[13] Presumably what is meant by the latter condition is that countries which have already borrowed up to, or almost up to, the hilt will have a claim for special treatment. A policy of prizes for the *non*-creditworthy is a novel doctrine for the Bank. So is the recent ruling which makes some of the better off of the Bank's clients – the countries, like Japan and Australia, whose business is especially valuable and easy to handle – pay a higher rate of interest (at present $6\frac{1}{2}$ per cent) than the poorer and less creditworthy countries (who are now being charged $5\frac{1}{2}$ per cent). This two-tier system of lending, working on a principle which is the precise opposite of that which would be adopted by a normal banker, is justified on the ground that the countries whose credit is good could after all go and borrow the money that they need in the ordinary international capital market. If they have the advantage of using the World Bank, they ought to pay something to subsidize loans to other countries which are in no position to borrow on commercial terms.

Some of the forces responsible for the changes in the World Bank's approach to its task are obvious and personal. Others are more deeply embedded in a historical process. Eugene Black belonged to the first phase of the evolution of post-war policies towards the underdeveloped world, which lasted until the end of the 1950s. He played a large and creative part in establishing international development lending as a respectable form of finance for investors and as politically acceptable to the borrowers. But at the time when the World Bank established its own set of working procedures there was hardly any systematic information about the new economic problems of contemporary under-developed socieites. The phenomenon of the population explosion and its decisive consequences for the living standards of these societies were only beginning to be recognized. The model which the Bank used to guide its own thinking was an older one: it was essentially that of the growth of Western capitalism, with perhaps a little extra room for the odd bit of public enterprise. Until the Second Indian Five-Year Plan (1956-61) there was virtually no 'talk back' from the underdeveloped world. The Indian case was indeed the first serious effort to plan long-term economic growth in an underdeveloped country; and the experience soon began to show how little the process was really understood.

The World Bank's ethos was deeply affected by its involvement in the Indian experiment. The process was gradual; but by the late 1950s India had become much the biggest borrower of the Bank's funds, and the Bank's thinking about the proper relation-ship between a rich international institution and a very poor client, which was unlikely to be solvent for many years to come, had to be sorted out afresh from this base. The Bank then found itself compelled to take a much closer interest in what other providers of aid were doing, to urge them to examine their contributions in terms of the recipient's own long-range objectives, and finally to take the lead in an effort to co-ordinate the activities of all donor countries and institutions in a more systematic fashion. The first international consortium of countries financing Indian development was organized in 1958. The Pakistan aid consortium, again with the Bank in the lead, followed. This has now become a standard technique. In the course of the annual encounters between an organized group of donor countries and the planners of the recipient country, the Bank discovered that conventional doctrines on a variety of economic and financial issues affecting the relationship between lender and borrower were challenged by hitherto unknown facts about the process of development outside the Western capitalist world.

India, Pakistan, and later still the experience of dealing with the states of newly independent Africa, brought home two points. First of all it became clear that the need for external assistance to the poor countries which contain a majority of the population of the world was going to last over a period of several decades, and secondly that the share of strictly bankable loans of a traditional kind going into the process was likely to be a diminishing one. The IDA was the first response to this recognition; and the experience of actually working the more flexible machinery of IDA in the early 1960s helped to induce the Bank to think again about the use of new techniques in the management of its more conventional banking business.

Finally, there was the competitive urge. It was borne in on the Bank that as the volume of aid and development lending from a variety of other sources increased – as it did markedly during the late 1950s and early '60s – traditional policies would have to be modified if the Bank's contribution was not to be swamped. Even now after the changes, the World Bank family of institutions, including the IDA and IFC, is still responsible for only a very modest share of the total volume of development aid. The latest comprehensive calculation by the OECD of the flow of capital to the underdeveloped countries shows that this group of institutions provided a *net* amount of $310 million (*net* of capital repayments and subscriptions by these countries to the World Bank) in 1963, out of a total of $9,280 million.[14] The size of this contribution will certainly increase during the years immediately ahead, as the IDA credits already arranged become effective. But it is also clear that the Bank will have to go on experimenting vigorously with new forms of development lending, if it is to have a substantial impact on the needs of the underdeveloped world during the 1970s and beyond.

TEXT REFERENCES

1. The record for any IBRD loan to date is a total of thirty-five years for repayment, including an eight-year initial period of grace during which no capital payments have to be made.

2. 18 per cent of each country's original subscription was in its own currency, and 2 per cent in gold or dollars. The remaining 80 per cent was in the form of a guarantee to the Bank. When the Bank's capital was doubled in 1959, the increase was financed entirely by raising member country's subscriptions in the form of guarantees to the tune of some $10,000 million. The latter now account for 90 per cent of the subscribed capital.

3. Mid-1964 figures.

4. See IBRD Report, 1963-64.

5. World Bank press release, 30 September 1963.

6. Some $700 million in convertible currencies.

7. The total reserve at the end of 1964 amounted to $894 million.

8. Annual Report, 1963-64, p. 6. The figure for the World Bank excludes loans made during the year to Japan, New Zealand and other developed countries in Western Europe.

9. Including a $50 million annual transfer from the World Bank profits, following the 1963-64 precedent.

10. See 'Report of the Executive Directors on the Articles of Agreement of the International Development Association', IBRD, 26 January 1960 (para. 14). The only exceptions envisaged at this stage were certain public utilities, 'water supply, sanitation, pilot housing and the like', which were to be eligible for IDA financing even though they were not 'revenue-producing or directly productive' as World Bank loans are supposed to be.

11. Op. cit., p. 8.

12. See A. Shonfield, *The Attack on World Poverty*, London, 1960, Chapter 10, for an account of the World Bank's relations with IDA at this time.

13. Annual Report, p. 8.

14. See *The Flow of Financial Resources to Less Developed Countries, 1956-63*, OECD, Paris, 1964. Table V-5.

BIBLIOGRAPHY

Annual Reports, IBRD and IFC.

Black, E. R., *The Diplomacy of Economic Development*, Harvard, 1960.

Cairncross, A., 'The International Bank for Reconstruction and Development', in *Essays in International Finance*, Princeton, 1959.

The Flow of Financial Resources to Less Developed Countries, 1956-1963, OECD, Paris, 1964.

Morris, J., *The World Bank*, London, 1963; issued as *The Road to Huddersfield*, New York, 1963.

Scammell, W. M., *International Monetary Policy*, London, 1957.

Shonfield, A., *The Attack on World Poverty*, London and New York, 1960.

The World Bank: Policies and Operations, IBRD, Washington, 1957.

11 THE ECONOMIC ORGANS OF THE UNITED NATIONS

Ralph Townley

It often helps when reviewing the background to the evolution of international organizations to compare international with national experience. More than a hundred years ago, Benjamin Disraeli – then a young radical – wrote of the two nations in England: the rich and the poor; and the great task which awaited men of good will to make these two nations one. In England the process went through three stages.

In the nineteenth century, great hammer blows of remedial legislation were struck to correct the more glaring abuses of the industrial revolution. These were essentially protective measures. In the early years of this century, drawing on German experience, Liberal legislation involved the machinery of government in promoting measures directed towards the people's welfare. The climate of opinion had changed: in the words of Professor Titmuss poverty was no longer regarded as waywardness. The third phase began in the depression and gathered momentum after the Second World War, with the deepening involvement of government in directing and stimulating economic growth with a widening of the public sector. Government by then had become purposive rather than permissive.

It should perhaps be borne in mind, at this juncture, that these great developments were not without their moments of agony, indecision, failure and periods of adjustment, nor without first having to look elsewhere to find out how the other chap did it.

International experience has followed a similar, if somewhat more leisurely, pattern. The first expression of the concern of the international community for the need to introduce protective measures can be found in the guarantees of religious toleration in the Treaty of Westphalia of 1648. Following the Congress of Vienna in 1815, the Great Powers intervened vigorously in Central and Eastern Europe, and in Africa, to protect ethnic and religious minorities from capricious treatment and occasional massacre, as well as to suppress piracy and abolish the slave trade. The motives of governments then – as indeed they always are – were mixed and, on occasion, the measures taken precipitated just what they had been designed to prevent.

International preventive legislation had to wait until the present century to be effective. In 1906, at a conference in Berne, the first international labour conventions were opened for signature. One of these prohibited the use of white phosphorus in the making of matches, which caused workers to be exposed to the mutilation of 'phossy jaw'. Thus began international legislation directed towards safeguarding the worker, a responsibility heretofore the exclusive preserve of national governments.

The work undertaken in this field from 1920 by the International Labour Organization is the subject of Chapter 8. Mr Walters, in Chapter 2 on the League of Nations, has also described how, in a more cautious way, the League joined with ILO in the adoption of protective measures: indeed it extended the role of the international community to assume a collective responsibility for protecting refugees, minorities and, under the Mandates System, of peoples in the former German and Ottoman dependencies. Only one Article of the Covenant refers to international economic co-operation. Yet modest though the League's activities were in these matters, economic work came to absorb half of the budget. But it was not until the establishment of the United Nations that the world community began to be aware of Disraeli's two nations on a world plane and the tremendous responsibilities that awaited the Organization in making them one.

In 1944, at Dumbarton Oaks, the Great Powers met to prepare their blueprint for an international organization. Only the American hosts, it would seem, were wholly convinced by the proposals of the League of Nations' Bruce Committee which, in making recommendations for the improvement of the League's machinery, had proposed that an economic and social council be established so that special attention could be given by such a body to international economic and social co-operation.

Little is still known about the discussions that took place at Dumbarton Oaks. But it would seem that neither the British nor the Russians attached importance, as the Americans did, to the creation of a special body of the kind the Bruce Committee proposed for the League. While the British recognized the importance of the *problems*, they considered for two reasons that the Security Council should have general responsibility for such matters. They believed – mistakenly – that as there was a close relationship between problems of peace and security and economic and social questions, they should not be artificially separated. Also, and here the British had a point, if the Security Council were restricted to dealing with international disputes, its functions would be exercised in an arid and negative atmosphere. Lacking constructive purpose, it would not have the opportunity the League Council had, with its broad frame of reference, of being a positive instrument of international co-operation.

It is not surprising that the USSR, with a casualty list approaching the twenty million mark, should have been preoccupied with security provisions in the new Organization. The Russians did not want these obfuscated by the discussion of ancillary responsibilities such as the furthering of international economic and social co-operation about which, in any case, they held rather special views. The proposed economic and social council, therefore, did not feature as a Principal Organ in the proposals formulated by the Great Powers, which were to provide the basis for discussion at the San Francisco Conference.

At San Francisco, the small powers vigorously attacked the draft presented to them and succeeded in introducing a number of modifications which illumined the otherwise drab draft of the Great Powers. As a result, the Charter of the United Nations, placing increased emphasis on economic and political development, added an Economic and Social Council with broad functions, together with the Trusteeship Council, as principal organs along with the General Assembly, the Security Council, the Secretariat and the International Court of Justice.

Under the Charter, the Economic and Social Council was given formidable substantive responsibilities. These were to promote higher standards of living, full employment, and conditions of economic and social progress and development; solutions of international economic, social, health and related problems, and international cultural and educational co-operation; and universal respect for and observance of human rights and fundamental freedoms for all without distinction as to race, language, or religion. In addition, the Council was assigned the function of co-ordinating the activities of the many specialized agencies then joining the older technical agencies such as ITU and UPU, as well as ILO, as international agencies.

The Economic and Social Council is, then, the centre of the United Nations constellation of organs and agencies concerned with economic and social co-operation. It remains a relatively small body. Until 1966, eighteen members of the United Nations served on the Council, one-third of which was elected by the General Assembly each year for a three-year term. Its membership in 1966 was enlarged to twenty-seven by an amendment to the Charter, which entered into force in 1965. Each member has one vote and voting is by simple majority. As is the case in the General Assembly, the President is elected for a one-year term.

The Council has generally followed a cycle of meetings by which the Spring Session is held at United Nations Headquarters in New York and the more important Summer Session in Geneva.

It is not necessary to dwell at any length on the co-ordination function of the Council, which is the subject of an annual debate and intensive discussion in committee. A good deal is said on the subject in Mr Hill's chapter on the ACC.

The British and United States officials responsible for setting up the post-war machinery of international economic co-operation were bemused by the concept of 'functionalism'. Just as Pascal had postulated three orders, the political, the scientific and the religious, each serving different purposes and subject to different disciplines, so the negotiators at San Francisco, Bretton Woods, Hot Springs and elsewhere saw the United Nations principally (but not exclusively) as a political body. International technical and economic co-operation, however, would be insulated from the harsher political pressures of international life and carried forward by specialized agencies. Thus, the World Health Organization would deal with international health problems; the World Meteorological Organization would further co-operation in climatology; and so on.

The supporters of this concept were reinforced in their views by the actual course of events. President Roosevelt, possibly recalling the disaster experienced by President Wilson after the First World War, was not anxious to wait until after the war to set up the machinery of international co-operation. By the time the United Nations was created, several agencies, such as the International Monetary Fund, and the International Bank for Reconstruction and Development, had appeared on the scene to join with the older agencies, such as the UPU, ITU and ILO, whose terms of reference had been enlarged by the Philadelphia Conference. In addition, the preparatory work to establish UNESCO was well advanced.

So, instead of the relatively centralized machinery of the

League, the United Nations found itself at the centre of a decentralized – even dispersed – system with the Council saddled with the tasks of entering into agreements with the specialized agencies and then of co-ordinating their activities. How the Council, after an initial attempt to carry out its functions in these respects, came to delegate them to the Secretary-General and, how through the apparatus of the Administrative Committee on Co-ordination a systematic approach was made to this work is recounted by Mr Hill in Chapter 6.

Compared with its provisions on co-ordination, the Charter is almost laconic when it comes to describing the Council's approach to its own activities. It is empowered by the Charter to make or initiate studies on international economic, social and related matters and may make recommendations on any such matters to the General Assembly. The Council may also prepare draft conventions for submission to the General Assembly, and convene international conferences on matters within the Council's competence.

As is the case with some other Principal Organs, the Council's role has not been enhanced by the lack of precision concerning the responsibilities of the General Assembly. The Charter requires that the Council shall perform such functions within its competence in carrying out the recommendations of the General Assembly. It may, with the Assembly's approval, perform services at the request of the Members of the United Nations and at the request of the specialized agencies. It shall also perform other functions as are specified in the Charter or as may be assigned to it by the Assembly.

The General Assembly established two committees, one to deal with economic and financial, and the other with social and humanitarian items. As the membership of the General Assembly came to include an increasing number of economically under-developed countries who use the Assembly as a forum for making their needs known, the Council, with a membership which has kept a modicum of balance between the developed and the under-developed, has been frequently overshadowed by the Assembly whose debates have been characterized by a greater sense of urgency.

Churchill, in a characteristic outburst, is reported to have said of the British war effort that it was overrun with committees like the Australia was with rabbits. But as an old parliamentarian, he would have been the first to admit that any organization calling for collective decision-making requires a committee structure. The Economic and Social Council in its initial formative period erected such a structure and perhaps overdid it. For in addition to its own committees (economic, social, co-ordination, etc.), it embarked upon not only a functional decentralization, but a regional one as well. Each one, in turn became a centre of initiative in promoting activities.

FUNCTIONAL COMMISSIONS
Beginning with the Economic, Employment and Development Commission and its subcommissions, the Council increased the number by creating functional commissions for statistics, population, social matters, human rights, the status of women, narcotic drugs, fiscal questions, transport and communications and, in 1954, for international commodity trade. These bodies, which initially met annually, were composed of government representatives. Their tasks generally were to consider those matters within their broad competence and to advise the Council on what action it should recommend concerning them.

For various reasons some of the functional economic commissions did not fully serve the purposes of the Council. The range of subjects covered by a commission often exceeded the competence of representatives however well qualified. In other bodies, the discussions too often mirrored the debates in the Council proper. As part of a vigorous streamlining exercise, several of the economic functional commissions were discontinued. The Transport and Communications Commission, for example, had continued much valuable work originated in the League. But it was difficult for a representative to bring special competence to bear on such a wide range as, say, the transportation of dangerous goods, the pollution of sea water by oil, and ocean freight rates and road signs and signals. Also the Economic Commission for Europe retained much responsibility for inland transport matters and, with the establishment of the Inter-Governmental Maritime Consultative Organization (IMCO), maritime matters were transferred to the new specialized agency.

After the initial experience of the functional commissions, emphasis began to be placed on the convening of *ad hoc* committees of experts for specific purposes. Where expert opinion was required, the Secretary-General would be asked to bring together a group of experts, acting in their individual capacity, as in the case of the group whose report in 1949, *National and International Measures for Full Employment*, provided the mainspring for much of the Council's activity in this area. This pattern of work has overlaid that of the functional commissions, although those that have been maintained provide valuable support, particularly now that their meetings are normally held biennially and a longer period is given to the Secretariat to prepare for them.

REGIONAL COMMISSIONS

The regional economic commissions have attracted a great deal more attention, and have been found by the majority of the members of the United Nations to be a much more satisfying forum for discussion of their economic problems, than any of the Council's other subsidiary bodies.

In 1947, with Mr Gunnar Myrdal as its first Executive Secretary, the Economic Commission for Europe (ECE) was established with its staff housed in the Palais des Nations in Geneva. The Economic and Social Council created this Commission to facilitate the reconstruction of Europe, to raise the level of economic activity of European countries and to strengthen their economic relations. The Marshall Plan followed soon afterwards, leaving the Commission in its wake with only residual reconstruction responsibilities. Through its main committees and a host of working parties and technical groups, however, the Commission has worked constantly towards a Europe-wide pooling of economic and technical experience, a sharing of common problems and a centre where European co-operation in practically every economic sector could be furthered, even in the harshest days of European political differences.

The Economic Commission for Asia and the Far East (ECAFE) was established by the Council in the same year with its staff based eventually in Bangkok. Under the auspices of the Commission, which like that of ECE meets annually, economic experience has been shared and useful technical work accomplished, for instance through its Bureau of Flood Control. As an outgrowth of the activities of the latter, the massive effort to develop the resources of the lower Mekong River with large scale bilateral and international financial and technical support has been a landmark of ECAFE's activities. The Asian Development Bank, with its head office in Manila, opening its doors for business in 1966, will come into being as a result of initiatives taken by the Commission.

In the following year, the Economic Commission for Latin America, based on Santiago, Chile, was established. Meeting biennially, the Commission has emerged as the main centre of economic competence and experience in South and Central America. It has provided advanced training for Latin American economists and, through its trade committees and working parties, has formulated the concept of a Latin American common market and has fostered its development, as well as the economic integration of the Central American republics.

In 1958, the Economic Commission for Africa held its first

session in Addis Ababa, where it is now based. Serving a continent where most countries have only recently become independent, the Commission provides a forum for examination of common problems and the sharing of experience. Its work is directed towards providing the new countries with the services, assistance and training in economic development planning and related matters, of which African Members find themselves in such urgent need. The African Development Bank, established in 1965, is the most recent achievement of the Commission.

The regional commissions, served by secretariats, whose members, to a large extent, are recruited from the regions they serve, have developed strong regional ties. Recent representations in the Economic and Social Council and the General Assembly have forced increased recognition of these centrifugal tendencies to a point where decentralization of development programmes has had to take place requiring some major administrative adjustments in the Headquarters Department of Economic and Social Affairs of which the regional secretariats form a part.

NON-GOVERNMENTAL ORGANIZATIONS

The relationships of the Council extend to private groups termed by the Charter 'non-governmental organizations'. For the most part they are international associations such as the International Chamber of Commerce, the international trades unions federations, religious bodies and smaller, national groups with special interests and competence. The Charter foresees a two-way system of consultations between the Council and the NGOs but the Council has seldom availed itself of the opportunity.

The setting in which the Council and its related bodies have evolved is different from and considerably more complex than that envisaged by the Charter. As we have seen, the language of the Charter and the preparatory activities leading to its adoption clearly established economic and social co-operation as one of the main components in the global strategy to establish peace and security in the post-war world. Those responsible for drafting the Charter accepted, almost without discussion, the theory that war had economic causes and that their elimination was a prerequisite to peace. Fortunately, this argument is now purely academic. It has become academic as a result of other interrelated forces at work in the world at large which have caused the United Nations to give great prominence to economic and social co-operation, particularly to assistance in the development of the economically developing countries. The forces responsible have been clearly expressed in the debates in the United Nations and the conferences of specialized agencies and, over the years, have been brought into sharp focus when these bodies have settled to the task of formulating international development programmes.

Of greatest significance is the persistence of the economically developing countries in forcing recognition by the developed countries of their responsibilities to assist in the process of economic development and to enable the less developed to participate in world trade on something more approaching equitable terms. To a large extent these countries, which now comprise an overwhelming majority of the United Nations membership, have been by-passed by the industrial revolution and their economic condition, in spite of their own efforts and reinforced though they have been with external support, has not to any marked degree improved. The witnessing of the widening gap between economic growth rates in the developed countries and more modest rates of growth, or even the relative stagnation, of the economies of many of the underdeveloped countries, has resulted in a groundswell of informed opinion whose voice now dominates the proceedings, not only of the economic organs of the United Nations, but of many of its other bodies as well.

Just as social change in the nineteenth century was dominated by an interplay between the forces unleashed by the industrial revolution and the forces of nationalism generated by the American and French revolutions, in the twentieth century the development of the economically underdeveloped countries is inextricably bound up with the movement towards the emancipation of colonial and other dependent peoples. Political equality and independence cannot be pursued in isolation from considerations of economic viability.

To accelerate the process of involvement of the richer nations, there have been socialist allegations that governments and commercial interests of the 'free enterprise economies' deliberately maintain the primary producing countries in a condition of economic tutelage. This gadfly applied to the necks of the developed countries has been an irritant, but it has acted as a spur to the rich countries to respond more readily to the condition of the poor. Partly as a result of these pressures in the economically advanced countries of Western Europe and North America, there has developed a lively sense of collective responsibility for furthering the welfare of the underdeveloped, particularly those who are new arrivals on the international scene. But domestic pressures have also made themselves felt. Here, as elsewhere, motives may be mixed: self-interest, both political and economic, a strong sense of moral responsibility, possibly a desire to keep up with the international-aid-giving-Joneses as well as colonial relationships transmuted on independence into ties of a different nature, all play their domestic part in changing the climate of opinion.

Finally, in the organs of the United Nations, in keeping with the spirit of the Charter, there has been a deliberate movement, fostered by the Secretariat, directed towards the acceptance of the concept of a world economy and with it, too, a systematic effort to establish a sense of common responsibility for its well-being and development.

These forces, sometimes clamorous in their expression, permeate debate and deliberation, not only in the economic organs of the United Nations, but in practically every meeting of the Organization, whatever the subject, whether it be on disarmament or on human rights. They provide the background against which economic bodies of the United Nations have evolved.

The work of the Economic and Social Council and, with appropriate variations, that of its functional, regional and other subsidiary bodies, falls into four main categories. The cycle of work begins with the collection and analysis of basic information about the world economy. Statistical and demographic year books provide a continuing flow of basic data. The highly professional *World Economic Survey* and the regional economic studies provide the basic economic analyses.

These and other reports enable the economic organs to identify the basic problems of the world economy and make, with an increasing measure of success, concerted attempts to overcome them. Problems of the world economy, such as how to stimulate the international flow of private capital, how to adopt effective measures relating to land reform or increasing agricultural productivity – the world's economic laggard – the need to increase international liquidity, to bring about a degree of stability in the prices of primary commodities entering the international trade, or to mitigate the effects of the downwards trend with compensatory measures, are a few examples.

This process involves what has come to be termed the 'confrontation technique' which involves the periodic examination of government economic policies. This makes it possible to identify the secular trends in the world economy and the need to harmonize national policies in the long-term interests of the world community.

This process strengthens national awareness of the world economy and of a common responsibility for it. On the basis of this awareness, international agreements, action programmes and other common measures can be devised, fostered or encouraged.

This elaborate and sophisticated pattern of enquiry, deliberation and action in the economic organs of the United Nations did not spring fully grown from the ear of Zeus. As with national experience, international economic co-operation in the United Nations has been the product of trial and error, patience and hard work.

In the early years the economic bodies passed through what might be termed the platonic period. During these years the Secretariat, at the behest of the Council, collected information from governments through such devices as – in the spirit of the times – the Full Employment Questionnaire. The economic studies, which were based upon them, were presented as a setting for discussion. This may not seem to represent any marked achievement in itself. But it is unlikely that in the inter-war period governments would have been prepared to report to an international body in detail on their national economic condition and the policies they intended to follow: least of all is it likely that they would have been prepared to participate in their public scrutiny in international debate. Today, such reporting is routine.

In this period also, the functional commissions and the *ad hoc* groups of experts, such as the one that in 1951 produced the report *Measures for the Economic Development of Under-Developed Countries*, helped to identify the basic problems of the world economy and laid down the strategy of attack on them, in anticipation of the day when action could be taken. (We know today something of the problems: but yesterday, if we wished to read a book on, say, the industrialization of the underdeveloped countries, we would first have had to write one.)

In these ways the substratum of knowledge and awareness of the problems and what to do about them was built up. Also, and this was an almost imperceptible process, through the debates, tedious and time-consuming though they may have seemed, there developed a growing awareness on the part of national representatives of a concept of an international economy and of a common international responsibility for it. Today, this is axiomatic. But if we consider the economic, commercial and fiscal policies of the inter-war period where economic problems were exported on to the backs of weaker countries, competitive tariff and other protective measures and jockeying for position on the world's exchange rates were commonplace, we can see how much we have moderated our international behaviour in favour of the world's interest.

TECHNICAL ASSISTANCE

In 1948, the first breakthrough to an action programme took place with the Economic and Social Council and the General Assembly approving a first tentative step to provide technical assistance to the economically developing countries. The times could have hardly seemed less conducive to starting international action programmes with the Berlin airlift and other crises demanding attention. But in that year $350,000 was voted to provide for a United Nations Technical Assistance Programme.

In voting this small amount to start a modest programme, the General Assembly provided some general guidance on how the programme was to be administered. Assistance could be made available only at the request of governments themselves to meet urgent needs. It should be provided completely free of political considerations. Governments of countries receiving assistance would be expected to contribute to the solution of the problems concerning which international assistance had been requested. As international programmes evolved, these original criteria became embodied as basic requirements.

The debates and discussions from which the early programmes emerged were probably concerned with the short-term transitional problems of India and Pakistan and other countries which had just become independent. The size of the problems of the underdeveloped countries and the need to mobilize massive international support to assist these countries in overcoming them, was not fully comprehended: this was to come later. In 1949, the Economic and Social Council established the Expanded Programme of Technical Assistance, in which the whole United Nations family would participate, drawing on extra-budgetary funds contributed voluntarily by governments which were members of the United Nations or of the specialized agencies.

The climate of opinion changed almost overnight with the speech made by President Truman in 1950, in which he enunciated under 'Point IV' of that statement the need to provide large-scale assistance to the underdeveloped countries and the role of the United Nations in channelling much of that assistance. The discussion was immediately raised to a higher level of significance.

'EPTA', as it came to be known, was designed to bring the technical competence of the United Nations and the specialized agencies to bear in a co-operative programme of assistance to be placed at the disposal of the economically underdeveloped countries. In this way, a major programme could be launched in an attack upon poverty, disease, ignorance and social backwardness. Assistance could be provided in every sector of the economy as a result of the presence of the rapidly accumulating experience in the United Nations and the family of specialized agencies. Planning in economic development and the organization of public services; vocational and management training and trades union activities; agriculture, fishery, forestry and animal husbandry; education; public health and disease control; and the development of transport and communication, including civil aviation, all were considered areas in which support could be provided.

The forms in which such support was made available were aimed at the transfer of skills from the developed to the underdeveloped. This called for the services of highly qualified experts and the ability to work alongside their opposite numbers in the developing countries and transferring the skills to them. Fellowships were also made available so that advanced training could be provided abroad to limited numbers of counterparts so that they could, on their return, take over from the international expert. Contributions in usable currencies were voluntarily pledged on an annual basis at a Pledging Conference held every year, usually during the period of the General Assembly. Table I lists the amounts of these pledges from the inception of the Expanded Programme.

TABLE I

*Pledges to the United Nations Expanded Programme of
Technical Assistance and the Special Fund*
(figures quoted in US dollars)

FOR	EPTA	SPECIAL FUND
1950–51	$20,036,170	
1952	18,797,232	
1953	22,320,725	
1954	24,994,556	
1955	27,618,707	
1956	28,829,955	
1957	30,813,370	
1958	31,048,358	
1959	29,419,980	$25,800,218
1960	33,992,734	38,641,008
1961	41,785,237	47,577,315
1962	45,371,253	60,240,071
1963	50,052,739	72,850,063
1964	51,289,710	85,715,497
1965	54,015,373	91,581,000

UNITED NATIONS DEVELOPMENT PROGRAMME

1966	$153,000,000

The Economic and Social Council set up the Technical Assistance Committee (TAC) as a standing body to oversee the new programme. The central co-ordinating body was the Technical Assistance Board (TAB), comprising the administrative heads of the technical assistance programmes of the United Nations Technical Assistance Administration and the specialized agencies and presided over by the representative of the Secretary-General. Mr David Owen, who, as one of the first members of the Secretariat, had come from the Foreign Office to be the Assistant Secretary-General for the Department of Economic Affairs, acted as Chairman. In 1952, he became, full-time, the Executive Chairman of the Technical Assistance Board. This position he held until 1966 when he became Co-Administrator of the United Nations Development Programme.

Such was the machinery established to administer the new programme, which began operations in 1950.

To facilitate the handling of requests for assistance and the co-ordination and supervision of the support provided to governments, many of the agencies in countries where they had larger programmes appointed their own country programme heads. With the increasing impact of the Expanded Programme, Resident Representatives of the Technical Assistance Board were appointed by the Executive Chairman to provide overall co-ordination on the spot.

Within this framework, the Expanded Programme increased in utility and grew in size, drawing on the voluntary contributions of many more governments and extending the programmes to practically all the economically underdeveloped countries. As Table I shows, the enlargement of the Programme was not an even progression. In 1953, there was a loss of momentum as demands for assistance outstripped the resources available. This period of belt-tightening served as an opportunity to review and improve the techniques and administration of technical assistance. In 1956, country programming techniques were adopted by which the requirements of each country were projected and on the basis of which the total programme was shared between the United Nations and each of the specialized agencies participating in EPTA. A Contingency Fund was set up to be administered by the Executive Chairman to meet requests for assistance which were not foreseen when the country programmes were formulated. Eventually, biennial programming was adopted and the role of the Resident Representative strengthened. Thus, a degree of stability was introduced together with some much needed flexibility in meeting the needs of developing countries, particularly those that were becoming independent in increasing numbers.

OPEX

Under the lee of the Expanded Programme, a new and still small programme designed to transfer senior administrators to the service of the developing countries had its beginnings. In a world where nationalism was not so virulent, there was nothing odd about a national of one country serving the government of another. Hugo Grotius, it will be recalled, though himself Dutch, served as the Ambassador of Sweden to France. Earlier, Marco Polo was the governor of a Chinese province. Today, this would scarcely be possible. But the experience of the Expanded Programme had pointed up the urgent need for governments to strengthen their administrations, particularly as in the underdeveloped countries, as elsewhere in the world, government functions have broadened and the public sector widened.

In 1958, drawing initially on regular technical assistance funds and subsequently also on EPTA, an experimental programme was approved by the Economic and Social Council called Operational Administrative and Executive Personnel (OPEX). The United Nations was able to provide senior administrators to the civil services of the developing countries as a short-term measure to strengthen their administration in key areas, particularly that of economic planning and execution. Such civil servants received local salaries but their additional emoluments and travel costs were met from out of technical assistance funds.

SUNFED

In the identification of the world economic problems in the debates of the Economic and Social Council and in the Economic and Financial Committee of the General Assembly, the financing of economic development rapidly became the central issue. The international flow of private capital had shrunk to a trickle compared with, say, capital movements in the period before 1914. Lending by the International Bank for Reconstruction and Development, however, had extended to the economically developing countries and had steadily increased in volume. But this was lending at commercial rates and by the early 1960s the external debt burden of many countries had reached a point where further international borrowing did not seem feasible. In the 1950s, in any case, this kind of financing did not reach down in sufficient quantities to the economic infrastructure of the underdeveloped countries.

Normally, the financing of the capital costs of basic services, such as schools, hospitals and communications, is undertaken by the government from tax resources or local financing through the bond market. In most of the underdeveloped countries, because income per head is so low, the marginal propensity to consume is high and there are little or no savings for investment. As a partial measure to fill this void, in 1952 a committee of nine experts, appointed by the Secretary-General, recommended the establishment of a Special United Nations Fund for Economic Development (SUNFED) which would provide grants-in-aid and long-term, low interest loans for the financing of the economic and social infrastructure of the underdeveloped countries. An initial capital of 250 million dollars was called for.

Supported by most of the underdeveloped countries and some of the developed (notably the Netherlands), the proposal was poposed by most of the economically developed. The opposition stemmed from the concern of the potentially major contributors over the high levels of taxation prevailing in their countries, the burden of maintaining a high level of armaments and the need to find additional support for well-tried and successful programmes, such as those of technical assistance. Perhaps underlying these objections was the apprehension of the developed countries at the prospect of placing large funds at the disposal of the United Nations where, while they would remain a minority in the General Assembly, the underdeveloped countries might exercise their majority vote to control a fund to which they were only ever likely to be marginal contributors.

The 'SUNFED debate' permeated practically all the economic organs of the United Nations throughout the 1950s. The establishment by IBRD of two affiliates, the International Finance Corporation (IFC) in 1956 and the International Development Association (IDA) in 1962 – the latter with many of the characteristics of the ill-fated SUNFED – did little to reduce the intensity with which the proposal for a United Nations capital development fund was pursued. The debate continues in a broader context, made possible by the accumulating experience of United Nations economic organs in development programmes and in the light of the changing needs of the developing countries themselves.

The continuing debate on the financing of economic development has assisted in identifying many of the problems acting as obstacles to increasing the international flow of private capital. It has played its part in bringing into being IFC and IDA and the prospects for the establishment of a United Nations Capital Development Fund are now visibly brighter. But the debate's most tangible contribution, as far as the United Nations is directly concerned, was in the establishment, in 1958, of the Special Fund.

THE UNITED NATIONS SPECIAL FUND

Beginning its operations in 1959, the United Nations Special Fund represented the first major departure, since the establishment of the Expanded Programme, along the road to the creation within the United Nations framework of development assistance on a large scale. Due mainly to the initiative of the Secretariat acting on behalf of the Secretary-General and in consultation with delegations with special interest or responsibility in economic development programmes, the General Assembly in 1957 called for the creation of a special fund which, while it would not finance capital expenditures, would through pre-investment surveys, research schemes and training programmes make a significant impact on the development process.

In 1957, the General Assembly, therefore, appointed a preparatory committee to define the basic needs for assistance and the operational machinery required and to ask governments what they would be prepared to contribute. The General Assembly added a thumb-nail sketch of a fund that would be multilateral in character and devoted to assisting the underdeveloped countries. Control would be vested in a governing body reflecting in its membership a parity between donors and recipients. The fund would have an executive head. A link with the proposed SUNFED was preserved through the provision that, when the resources prospectively available were of the order of magnitude of $100 million, the status of the fund would be reviewed. A deadline of 1 January 1959 was set for commencing operations.

The preparatory committee, using as its principal conference paper the recommendations of the Secretary-General concerning the new fund, reported to the Economic and Social Council which, in turn, forwarded the committee's proposals to the Thirteenth General Assembly together with a draft resolution for adoption. The enabling resolution of the General Assembly, unanimously adopted in 1958, has only two operative paragraphs of twenty-two words. It contains a second part that lays down at some length the guiding principles and general criteria for a United Nations Special Fund.

In the words of the resolution, the Special Fund was designed:

> 'To provide systematic and sustained assistance in fields essential to the integrated technical, economic and social development of the less developed countries.'

The Special Fund was to enlarge the scope of technical assistance and to concentrate on relatively large projects of high priority likely to lead to earliest results. These projects might be supported over a period of several years and should be integrated with national and other international development programmes. Regional as well as national projects would fall within this scope. There should be no interference in the domestic affairs of recipients, and assistance should be so provided as to enable an early transfer of responsibilities to the countries concerned. Over a period, an even geographical spread of assistance should be maintained.

More specifically, the Special Fund should assist in the development of all economic sectors. Project support would take the form of surveys, research and training, including pilot and demonstration schemes. Special Fund support could involve expert services, equipment, supplies and services, and a limited number of fellowships for training abroad counterpart staff as an integral part of the project. Governments would be expected to contribute towards the cost of such schemes and participate actively in them.

The structure of the Special Fund was to include a Governing Council of eighteen members elected by the Economic and Social Council with a balanced participation required by the 1957 resolution. Voting would be by a two-thirds majority. Amongst its responsibilities was the approval of programmes recommended by the Managing Director.

The somewhat elaborate provisions concerning the appointment of the Managing Director were indicative of the significance attached by the General Assembly to his role. His appointment by the Secretary-General was to be made after consultation with the Governing Council and confirmation by the General Assembly. In the Managing Director was vested the sole authority for deciding what projects should be included in the programmes recommended for approval by the Governing Council.

Assisted by a small staff recruited on the basis of their special competence, the Managing Director was also chairman of a small Consultative Board comprising the Secretary-General of the United Nations, the President of IBRD and the Executive Chairman of the Technical Assistance Board.

Although there were some conspicuous gaps in the resolution (including how such a major development effort was effectively to be carried out), it was the most impressive act of the General Assembly in economic matters to date. Some differences and hesitations had been revealed in the negotiations. The underdeveloped countries were not satisfied with the tenuous link with the proposed SUNFED. They would have preferred elections to the Governing Council to take place not in the Economic and Social Council but in the General Assembly where their influence was greater. Most of all, they criticized the 'qualified' voting arrangements whereby a two-thirds majority was required in a body half of which was composed of developed countries. Many of the specialized agencies, accustomed to the spirit of collegiality that prevailed in the Technical Assistance Board, were critical at being excluded from membership (although not necessarily from participation) in the Consultative Board.

The apprehensions that gave rise to those criticisms were, for the most part, misplaced. Except on one occasion – and then a procedural matter was involved – the Governing Council of the Special Fund never voted but carried out its business by arriving always at a consensus. The United Nations and its family of agencies came to have exclusive responsibility for carrying out Special Fund supported projects and their technical evaluation was always sought before decisions were taken by the Managing Director.

Many of the features of the Special Fund represent a refinement of the techniques and approaches originated in the Expanded Programme. Support is not made available for country programmes, with the United Nations and the participating agencies assuming percentage shares of the total programme, but on a project by project basis. Assistance can be projected over a number of years so that forward planning both by the Governments and the Special Fund can take place without being subject to the annual pledge of funds. Government applications, as with the Expanded Programme, are submitted through a single channel designated by the Government – usually the Ministry of Planning – and not by individual ministries. Increased emphasis is placed on the primary role of the developing countries themselves, the assistance provided by the Special Fund serving to underpin and meet part of the foreign exchange component in the development effort. Finally, support is made available according to certain criteria laid down by the Managing Director.

The appointment of Mr Paul G. Hoffman, the former Chief Administrator of the Marshall Plan, as Managing Director and, for the initial formative period, Professor (now Sir) Arthur Lewis as his deputy, resulted in an aggressive management and high standards of administrative efficiency that became a continuing feature of the direction of the Special Fund. Their bracing effect was not limited to those who worked in the Special Fund. The new approaches to development assistance called for a major tooling up throughout the United Nations family of agencies and some psychological adjustment, not only on the part of the agencies but also of government authorities responsible for obtaining international assistance.

Nevertheless, the Special Fund followed the pattern of work

elaborated under the Expanded Programme. Funds were pledged by members of the United Nations or of the specialized agencies each year at the same Conference where technical assistance funds were pledged. Joint administrative arrangements were established for both programmes. The Resident Representatives of the Technical Assistance Board also became Special Fund agents and their field offices were strengthened for this purpose. Close working relationships were maintained throughout, particularly in the field where technical assistance experts came to play a significant role in helping governments to identify projects suitable for Special Fund support and assisting in their formulation, evaluation and, in many cases, their eventual implementation.

As a general framework for the provision of assistance a Basic Agreement is signed by the Special Fund with the government interested in receiving assistance. A government submits its application to the Managing Director through the Resident Representative. The project has to be of a pre-investment character. If the request is within the terms of reference of the Special Fund it will be evaluated by the staff in consultation with the United Nations, TAB, IBRD and other specialized agencies concerned. If necessary, the submission is reformulated jointly with the government, possibly drawing on the services of consultants specially trained for this purpose.

The Special Fund aims at supporting projects that are designed to attract or underpin investment, or to raise productivity. It will not normally support schemes which call for a Special Fund involvement of less than $250,000 (the Expanded Programme usually dealing with requests up to this amount). Nor can it participate in capital financing, i.e. it can assist in the feasibility surveys of a dam site – is it did for the Kainji Dam in Nigeria – but it is not permitted to participate in financing its construction. Governments are expected to contribute to the scheme and on an average 60 per cent of the total costs are met by them although there is no fixed percentage, burden sharing being determined by the requirements of each project. The Special Fund, however, will not meet expenditures in local currency or provide services or equipment locally obtainable.

By early 1966, the Special Fund had approved 604 projects of which 70 had been completed. As with the Expanded Programme, the availability of funds had not kept pace with the demands of the underdeveloped countries. Commitments totalling $583,115,400 have been made and recipient governments themselves have contributed $823,429,500 to this partnership in development.

The proof of the pudding is not in the eating, as we are often led to believe, but in the digestion. The impact of seven years of Special Fund effort has yet to be measured. To evaluate the significance of any work in progress is always difficult. In the case of the Special Fund anything other than an interim evaluation will inevitably have to wait; particularly as most Special Fund supported projects have a duration of five years.

THE UNITED NATIONS DEVELOPMENT PROGRAMME

The merger of the Expanded Programme and the Special Fund in 1966 into the United Nations Development Programme was a natural outcome of the earlier experience of both programmes. It provides for an integrated attack instead of a co-operative one on development problems. The Technical Assistance Committee of the Economic and Social Council is merged with the Governing Council of the Special Fund to make a UNDP Governing Council of thirty-seven members. The Technical Assistance Board and the Consultative Board have been replaced by the Inter-Agency Consultative Board with an increased membership, as its title implies. The staffs have been blended with the Managing Director appointed as Administrator and the Executive Chairman as Co-Administrator of the Development Programme. Thus concentrated, the economic organs and the secretariat serving them have evolved along lines similar to those that have resulted in the establishment, in the United Kingdom, under one Minister of the Ministry of Overseas Development and, in the United States, of the U.S. AID.

THE HAVANA CHARTER AND GATT

Of the many specialized agencies projected in the post-war period, one failed to come into being: The International Trade Organization. The attempts to implement piecemeal the provisions of the Havana Charter, which provided for this Organization, were a continuing feature of the work of the United Nations' economic organs concerned with world trade until 1964 when the United Nations Conference on Trade and Development enlivened – indeed revolutionized – the whole approach of the United Nations to international trade problems.

When planning for the post-war world, those concerned (including the economists of the League Secretariat, who continued their work at Princeton during the war), were naturally conditioned in their thinking by the breakdown in world trading relations that had been a feature of the inter-war period. To prevent a recurrence and in order to re-establish multilateral trade, the Economic and Social Council began, almost from its inception, to prepare for the United Nations Conference on Trade and Employment which, in 1947 and 1948, met in Havana. The Charter there adopted was the blueprint for the International Trade Organization. Of the fifty-two countries that adopted it, only two, Australia and Liberia, ever deposited their instruments of ratification.

The Havana Charter represented the highest common denominator between diverse and often contradictory interests. It laid down a régime for international trade which included full employment, economic development, commercial policy, tariffs, customs practices, primary products and restrictive business practices. The Organization failed to come into existence mainly because the major trading and commercial countries turned their backs on ITO, as they had failed to establish for themselves voting rights similar to those obtained at Bretton Woods. Also, few countries, on reflection, were prepared to accept wholly the doctrine of multilateralism propounded in the Charter at a time when quantitative and other restrictions were being increasingly imposed.

The Havana Charter itself remained a dead letter, but its concepts and concerns permeated the thinking of all United Nations economic organs where trade problems were given an airing. In the Economic and Social Council and elsewhere, attempts were made piecemeal to refine and implement the provisions of the ill-fated Charter. Economic development, as we have seen, came to be the main concern of the Economic and Social Council. Although it occasioned much debate and the attention of several expert bodies, measures concerning restrictive business practices did not command the necessary broad degree of support amongst the major trading partners in the Council. Greater success was achieved in the lowering of tariffs and in the stabilization of the prices of selected commodities entering international trade.

In 1947, as part of the preparatory negotiations for the Havana Conference, a multilateral contract, the General Agreement on Tariffs and Trade (GATT), was adopted embodying the tariff concessions negotiated amidst the preparatory discussions for the Havana Conference. Neither an agency, nor, strictly speaking, a part of the United Nations, GATT remained a series of agreements serviced by an Executive Secretary, and a small staff who have maintained administrative links with the United Nations. GATT has made a modest contribution to the freeing of international trade from quotas and tariffs. Through the annual meetings of the Contracting Parties in Geneva, it has established a code of good international conduct by limiting the use of quantitative restrictions. It has also served as a useful forum for international trade consultations as well as for trade disputes for which a Panel of Complaints was established.

Of greatest significance has been the 'binding' of tariffs. As a result of a series of marathon trade negotiations in Geneva in 1947, Annecy in 1949, Torquay in 1957, and subsequently at Geneva, thousands of agreements, initially negotiated on a bilateral basis, were adopted, reducing duties on individual items and 'binding' other duties against the increase. Moreover, GATT extended these reciprocal concessions to almost all the Contracting Parties. By the 1960s such arrangements affected half of total world trade in value.

Many loopholes necessarily existed in these arrangements and, in many instances, there was a reluctance, particularly on the part of European countries, to enter into trade agreements that might disturb domestic recovery measures. Waivers were so frequently granted that, in several cases, they substantially reduced the effectiveness of the agreements themselves. The emergence of regional free trade areas posed special problems for the Contracting Parties. But its chief weakness was the absence from GATT of most of the economically underdeveloped countries, who suffered most from this piecemeal implementation of the Havana Charter. They saw only marginal advantage in participating in tariff agreements without the accompanying provisions regarding commercial policy, economic development and commodity price stabilization.

COMMODITY TRADE

The most intractable world trade problem is undoubtedly the stabilization of international prices of primary commodities entering international trade. Not only are they subject to violent cyclical oscillation, but the secular trend of the prices of many of them is due to varying demand conditions on the part of the manufacturing countries who are their traditional importers. The experience of the primary producing countries, in many cases, had led them to the conclusion that their participation in international trade was not one based on the classical concept of comparative advantage, but rather of 'absolute disadvantage'.

International commodity agreements have remained the province of the United Nations for which the Interim Co-ordinating Committee for International Commodity Arrangements (known for having the longest title and the smallest membership of any United Nations body) and eventually the Committee on International Commodity Trade, were established. International agreements were concluded and periodically renewed, under Unted Nations auspices, for wheat, tin, sugar, coffee and olive oil. For other commodities, such as cocoa, lead and zinc, working parties, composed of both producers and consumers, have met to consult on the adoption of stabilization measures. For yet others, United Nations and FAO studies on commodity problems have provided information and analysis on current problems and prospects. Proposals for more broadly based compensatory financing schemes for a whole range of commodities entering international trade are now attracting attention in the economic organs of the United Nations and have recently provided the basis for an International Monetary Fund 'facility' in this field.

UNCTAD

The turbulent debates of the United Nations Conference on Trade and Development held in 1964 focused attention sharply on world trade problems, particularly those affecting the economically underdeveloped countries, many of whom were entering the world community as independent states for the first time.

The setting for the Conference was one in which the majority of the governments there represented were of economically underdeveloped countries. They saw a world economy in which trade was increasing substantially, but their share in the increase was proceeding at an appreciably lower rate than that of the developed countries. Between 1950 and 1962, the underdeveloped countries' share of world trade had declined from one-third to one-fifth. Moreover, the terms of trade were becoming increasingly unfavourable to them. The trade surpluses they had enjoyed in 1950 had vanished and, by 1962, their total trade deficit amounted to some $2,300 million. In addition, their payments, in 1960, for dividends and interest on foreign investments and loans, as well as for invisible items, amounted to $3,300 million.

Faced with this situation, with every indication that the 'trade gap' would widen still further, the Conference called for new and vigorous measures to stimulate the developing countries' trade, to stabilize international commodity prices and to take other related measures.

The machinery, devised subsequently by the General Assembly on the recommendation of the Economic and Social Council, was to make the Conference an organ of the United Nations. It is to meet triennially and is to be composed of members of the United Nations or of its specialized agencies. Its permanent organ is the Trade and Development Board composed of 55 members. A new feature in the development of economic organs has been the arrangement by which members are elected from among different groups. At present, Group A comprises 22 Afro-Asian countries (and Yugoslavia); Group B, 18 Western free-market economies; Group C, 9 Latin American, and Group D, 6 Socialist countries. It has four subsidiary committees dealing with invisibles and financing, relating to trade, commodities, manufacturing and shipping.

The Secretariat is headed by a Secretary-General, Dr Paul Prebisch, (a former Executive-Secretary of the Economic Commission for Latin-America). At the end of 1965, after a period of uncertainty, it was decided to establish UNCTAD's headquarters in Geneva.

The method of work follows the pattern of addressing recommendations on trade and related matters to members. This is followed by enquiry and public report on the action taken to implement these recommendations. Already, steps have been taken to implement the findings on the 1964 Conference and, in 1965, the Conference on Transit Trade of Land-Locked Countries adopted a convention that has already been signed by 29 countries on the trading rights of land-locked countries. In 1965, the international tin agreement was the first of such international agreements to be renegotiated under the auspices of UNCTAD.

FOOD SURPLUSES AND DEVELOPMENT

Perhaps one of the most successful aid programmes of the United States has been that of food surplus disposal permitted by Public Law 480. The massive farm surpluses, maintained at an increasing cost to the taxpayer, have been drawn down and shipped to feed the hungry of other lands. Other countries, such as Canada, followed suit and, today, bilateral food aid programmes have an average annual total of some $2,000 million.

After a period of debate and consultation in the United Nations and FAO, the General Assembly and the FAO Conference jointly established, in 1962, for an experimental period of three years beginning in 1963, a World Food Programme. Under the direction of its governing body, the Intergovernmental Committee, and vigorous administration by Dr A. H. Boefma, its Executive Director, the World Food Programme at the end of 1965 was placed on a continuing basis.

The Programme, in effect, is PL 480 internationalized with global participation. Its resources for the initial period were nearly $100 million in commodities, cash and services pledged voluntarily by some seventy governments.

As long as they do not disturb normal patterns of trade or price stability, commodities may be shipped at the request of the recipient governments. Much assistance has been devoted to emergency food needs. Faced with natural disasters such as earthquakes, hurricanes, floods and droughts, 25 countries have received surplus foods. Much assistance has gone to countries acting as hosts to refugees. Uganda, for example, is housing refugees from three neighbouring countries and is receiving regular shipments of food surpluses.

While food aid is made available in such emergencies, as well as for school and special feeding programmes, the World Food Programme has, as its major aim, not relief as such but development. In large-scale resettlement schemes the introduction of commodity surpluses can lighten the burden of cost to the government and relieve the newly-settled farmer of anxiety over his early harvests. Where labour is diverted to industrial development or major construction schemes, food may be used as a partial substitute for wages in cash; 116 such development programmes have received an underpinning wedge of food aid during the three-year trial period.

The problems of administering an international commodity surplus programme, on a global scale, in the interest of the economically developing countries are considerable. The application of counterpart funds accumulated from the sale locally of food surpluses may pose special problems if food aid is applied on a massive scale. Fortunately, the Programme has been administered with a flexibility rare in international administration, with considerable freedom of action given to the Executive Director who is permitted by his governing body to allocate up to $100,000 of surpluses without prior authorization. On the basis of the initial three-year experience, both the United Nations and FAO agreed at the end of 1965 to put the programme on a continuing basis. At the Pledging Conference held at the same time, forty-four governments made commitments for 1966 totalling more than $208 million.

Both the United Nations and FAO recognize that as experience is accumulated careful study of the role of food aid in the development process should be undertaken. At present both bilateral and international programmes of this kind are needed in the face of the relative failure – in spite of great efforts – of the agricultural sector in the developing countries. In the long run such countries have no alternative but to increase their domestic food supply. In such cases food aid can serve as a timely diversion, enabling countries to determine their development policies free from the pressures of recurrent food deficit. Others, such as India, are unlikely to be able to feed themselves entirely from their own resources at least in this century. For them food shipments should be programmed on a long-term basis.

It may be useful to take stock of the development that has taken place in the UN's economic organs and the factors influencing it.

One of the purposes of the United Nations, as stated in Chapter I of the Charter, is to achieve international co-operation in solving international economic problems and to serve as a centre for harmonizing the actions of nations in the attainment of these common ends. The aspirations of the governments meeting in San Francisco in 1945 have not yet become a universal reality. But remarkable progress has been made in spite of (and possibly, in certain situations, because of) the fact that the political climate of the postwar world, until recently, has not been conducive to international co-operation or the harmonization of economic policies.

From the labyrinth of economic organs created by ECOSOC, and regardless of the uncertainty of the Council's role *vis-à-vis* the General Assembly, great strides have been made. In the first place, governments have come to accept the concept of a world economy and, with it, there has emerged a sense of collective responsibility for its well-being and development. Considerations of short-term economic interest have come to be influenced by the beginnings of a sense of international responsibility, as a result of the deliberations of the General Assembly and the economic organs of the United Nations.

The emergence of what might be termed a new sense of international economic solidarity was facilitated, then fostered, by the United Nations. A start was made with the identification of world economic problems and opportunities. Beginning with the modest technical assistance programme, experience was rapidly accumulated in the techniques of international action on a global scale. The success of EPTA paved the way for more ambitious and far-reaching programmes, such as those of the Special Fund. That the economic organs were not condemned to endless debate without any tangible outcome acted as a spur to fresh efforts as confidence in the capacity of the United Nations to administer large-scale programmes, regardless of political differences among its members, grew. The building of the United Nations Development Programme on the experience of EPTA and the Special Fund, with the possibility of its being enlarged to embrace further responsibilities, including, in the minds of many members, that of a capital development fund, opens up a new series of opportunities for international economic co-operation.

The earlier experience of attempting to implement piecemeal the provisions of the Havana Charter and the lack of balance in existing trade agreements, has been overtaken by the impressive show of unity of purpose on the part of the underdeveloped countries in creating UNCTAD. Teething troubles are inevitable but, in the midst of them, the new body has built up an offensive against secular trends in world trade and has created the beginnings of a new economic framework for world trade and payments.

As economic agencies have evolved, two trends have become apparent. The proliferation of new agencies enjoying an independence and functional autonomy, co-operating with the United Nations within the framework of agreements negotiated on a basis of equality with the Economic and Social Council, would now seem to have ended. Instead, the trend is towards the establishment of new bodies within the United Nations proper, within the framework of which they enjoy a degree of administrative autonomy. Their staffs are part of the United Nations Secretariat and their governing committees are appointed by the Economic and Social Council or the General Assembly under terms of reference laid down by those Principal Organs. The process began with the Special Fund, developed with the establishment of UNCTAD and the Centre for Industrialization. The World Food Programme was created as a joint venture of the United Nations and FAO.

There is nothing new about these institutional trends. Emergency agencies and bodies to promote and administer special programmes have always been a characteristic of the Organization. The United Nations Korean Reconstruction Agency (UNKRA), the United Nations High Commissioner for Refugees (UNHCR), the United Nations Relief and Works Agency for Palestine Refugees in the Near East (UNRWA) and the United Nations Children's Fund (UNICEF) have shown over the years how such diverse programmes have been administered successfully from within the same house. In 1965, UNICEF was a recipient of the Nobel Peace Prize. The award of this highest international honour gives striking recognition to the achievements that can result from the work of a body of this kind.

The other, and related, trend has been the shift in relationships between the United Nations and the specialized agencies. Their early co-operation gave place in the late 1950s to concerted action in a number of operational programmes. With the creation of the Special Fund, leadership was provided in the UN for most of the international complex of agencies and a degree of control was exercised centrally over the work they undertook as executing agencies for the Special Fund assisted projects. The United Nations Development Programme, inaugurated in 1966, presents fresh opportunities for the adoption of a new strategy of development assistance, with each agency playing an appointed part.

Problems, however, are legion. The 1960s have been designated by the United Nations as the Development Decade. A target has been set up for a 5 per cent annual growth rate for the underdeveloped countries and the diversion of 1 per cent of the national income of the developed countries to the development needs of the underdeveloped. At mid-point the United Nations has been taking stock in debates of unprecedented frankness.

The results of the Development Decade are not heartening. The growth rate has not been near the target rate and increases in population in many countries nullify much of the growth that has taken place. Furthermore, there has been no net increase in the volume of development assistance. Development programming and the ways in which external aid can be most effective are considerably more complex than was thought. Pivotal scarcities in the agricultural sector are difficult to overcome. The acceleration of industrialization in the underdeveloped countries, by drawing on the 'pool of technology' of the developed countries, presents unforeseen difficulties.

These problems are probably better understood in United Nations' organs than anywhere else, but international programmes, on which they could have a direct impact, comprise only a fraction of total aid. (For example, less than 1 per cent of total aid to India comes from international sources.) Also, the complexity of the problems and the long-term nature of their solution discourage national legislators, whose immediate interests in any case are elsewhere, from devoting time and attention to these matters.

In spite of the immensity of the tasks which are now becoming apparent if the purposes of the Charter are to be fulfilled, within the United Nations organs themselves there are encouraging signs. The tools of analysis of world economic problems have improved. There is a rapidly accumulating body of international experience and competence in development matters. The techniques of confrontation by which national policies can be harmonized in the international interest have been refined. As a recognition of this process, governments are prepared to embark upon such discussions with increasing confidence. New bodies, such as the Advisory Committee on the Application of Science and Technology to Development, for instance, are drawing together experienced scientists and administrators with international reputations, to consider how the main development obstacles can be overcome.

The impact of the debates and deliberations in the economic organs are felt not only by governments, but also by international and regional bodies, both within and without the United Nations family. New institutional forms, administrative practices, techniques of approach and, perhaps of greatest importance, habits of mind, developed in the economic organs are now increasingly introduced elsewhere. The resilience and experience – as well as the scars – acquired on the long hard road from San Francisco have given the economic organs of the United Nations a primary but, of course, not exclusive position in furthering the integration of the international community.

BIBLIOGRAPHY

Asher, R. E. and others, *The United Nations and the Promotion of the General Welfare*, Washington, 1957.
Goodwin, G. L., *Britain and the United Nations*, New York, 1957.
Hadwen, J. G. and Kaufmann, J. *How United Nations' Decisions are Made*, Leyden, 1960.
Little, I. M. D. and Clifford, S., *International Aid*, London, 1966.
Shonfield, A., *The Attack on World Poverty*, New York, 1960.
Townley, R., *Developing International Institutions*, New York, 1966.
United Nations Publications, *The United Nations Development Decade: Proposals for Action*, New York, 1962; *The United Nations Development Decade at Mid-Point: An Appraisal by the Secretary-General*, New York, 1965; *Everyman's United Nations*, 7th edition, New York, 1964.

12 THE EUROPEAN ECONOMIC COMMUNITY

John Pinder

The European Economic Community differs from the League of Nations or the United Nations and its specialized agencies, which are the subject of the other chapters in this book, in being a supranational organization. Its institutions have been irrevocably given power by the member states to take decisions in certain matters of considerable political moment, such as tariffs and import controls; the member governments can no longer take unilateral decisions in these matters; and it is not legally necessary to secure the agreement of each government to such decisions, although in practice physical power (armed forces, police) remains with the member states, which could not therefore be coerced.

Although the Community has federal characteristics, it does not fit the traditional definition of a federation. It is therefore worthwhile, before considering the course of its evolution, to examine the precise nature of the supranationality that distinguishes it from the world organizations. This is to be found in a combination of characteristics that together enable the Community institutions to take important decisions that were formerly the preserve of the member governments.

The factor most often picked out by commentators on the Community as the main cause of its success is the existence of its independent Commission of nine members, charged with performing their duties 'in the general interest of the Community with complete independence',[1] who direct an international civil service of some two and a half thousand people. It is certain that without the Commission and its civil service, little would have been achieved. For the subject-matter of modern administration is so complex that it would not be possible to formulate or execute a policy without a competent administrative apparatus. In default of this, no amount of good intentions would have enabled policies representing the general interest to hold their own against the policies representing national interests and worked out by the powerful bureaucracies of member states.

It is not so much the existence of the Commission, however, that has distinguished the Community from the United Nations. The UN has, after all, an able and independent Secretary-General with a competent staff.[2] It is, rather, the role that the Commission, given the ability of its members and the competence of their staff, is empowered by the Rome Treaty and has been allowed by the member governments to play (at least up to 1965, when the Gaullist challenge to the role of the Commission became the centre of the Community's crisis). This is a political role: the Commission has not only to ensure the application of the Treaty and of the rules laid down by the Council (composed of a representative of each member state), but also to 'formulate recommendations or opinions in matters which are the subject of this Treaty, where the latter expressly so provides or where the Commission considers it necessary', and 'under the conditions laid down in this Treaty dispose of a power of decision of its own and participate in the preparation of acts of the Council and of the Assembly'.[3] The latter point is an essential one; in many important questions the Council can take a decision only on a proposal from the Commission, which gives the Commission an essential power of initiative. The Commission has, indeed, powers of the kind that Mr Hammarskjöld found he needed to deal with the Congo crisis, but which the Secretary-General of the UN has not in fact been allowed to exercise.

The provision for majority voting to take binding decisions on major issues in the Council of Ministers is another factor that distinguishes the Community from the United Nations. This provision has been used very infrequently; indeed, the Rome Treaty allowed but little scope for the use of the majority vote until the third stage of the Community's transitional period, starting in 1966; and even then it is not likely to be used for a long time against the wishes of a powerful member, and certainly not against France while de Gaulle is President. In the early years of the Community's development, the majority vote is to be regarded more as an earnest of the intention of the member states to modify their concepts of national interest sufficiently to enable agreement to be reached – which, until de Gaulle's explicit opposition to the Community method, they have by and large done. Even if the majority vote has so far been more a symbol of the will to agree than a working instrument, however, it is not the less important for that, as is witnessed by the fact that the Community has made greater progress in forming effective common policies on thorny issues such as agriculture, energy or cartels, than other international organizations have been able to do on similarly explosive political questions.

The third main cause of the Community's ability to act independently of the initiative of the member governments is what has sometimes been called the backbone of the Treaty: the precise and detailed agreements for the dismantling of internal barriers to trade and the erection of the common external tarriff, due to be completed by regular changes in the national tariffs and import quotas over a period of twelve to fifteen years from the establishment of the Community. The Commission is empowered to assure the implementation of this most radical tariff policy, negotiated as a part of the Treaty itself, and this has provided a momentum that consolidated the Community and carried it along in tackling the other, less quantifiable, issues of economic policy that constitute the concept of economic union.

These three factors – the Commission's power to take political initiatives, the provision for majority voting in the Council as an earnest of the member states' desire to reach decisions, and the 'backbone' of precise and detailed agreement on the formation of the customs union – all apply in relation to matters of real political importance, which were hitherto the jealously-guarded prerogative of national governments. There are several other factors that contribute to the Community's supranationality – the power of its institutions to act directly on legal persons as well as on member governments; the European Parliament with its limited but real power to dismiss the Commission – but these suffice to show that, even if it is not federal under the traditional definition, the Community can act independently of national governments in relation to politically controversial issues to a far greater extent than can the United Nations.

Many people consider that, if the members of the United Nations and its organs could be persuaded to endow it with similar supranational powers, it would be better able to discharge its tasks of ensuring world security and contributing to the good management of the world economy. Indeed, the proposals for complete and universal disarmament combined with the creation of a world peace force[4] imply such a development, as do some of the proposals for improving the world's monetary system by strengthening the International Monetary Fund.[5] There can be little doubt that, with the advance of technology in relation to weapons, transport and industrial development, the view that supranational world institutions are necessary will become increasingly widespread, and that this will often be reflected in proposals for solving world problems. It is therefore of value to try to assess under what conditions national governments are likely to agree to supranational solutions, and the experience of the European Community may be illuminating in this respect.

The analysis of the Community that follows deals, therefore, with the conditions that have made it possible for the Six to establish and operate a supranational organization, and with the reasons why difficulties in its operation have recently arisen, rather than giving a blow-by-blow account of the Community's evolution since it was established. This is, indeed, appropriate in terms of the Community's own development: the important act was the constitutional act of drawing up and agreeing upon the Treaty, which itself provided in considerable detail for the greater part of the progress that has since taken place. It is doubly appropriate when the Community is considered in relation to organizations at world level. The detailed problems of evolution of supranational bodies may seem of little direct relevance to the world organizations, for they have not yet reached that stage of development. But sooner or later they may do so; and it is to be hoped that the lessons learned in establishing the European Community will be of use in assessing when this may become possible, how such opportunities may be created and, once they exist, what are the most fruitful ways to proceed.

Perhaps the most important fact in relation to the establishment of the Community has already emerged in the last paragraph: that it obtained its supranational powers as a result of a deliberate constitutional act – or rather two constitutional acts. The EEC, established under the Rome Treaty (signed and ratified in 1957), was preceded by the European Coal and Steel Community, established under the Paris Treaty (signed and ratified in 1951), and it may be doubted whether the EEC would have materialized if its less ambitious forerunner, providing for a common market of the products of only the coal and steel industries, had not already been operating successfully.

It is conceivable that a supranational organization could develop from an inter-governmental one by a process of organic growth and without a deliberate constitutional act. But where matters of political importance are concerned, it seems unlikely that governments will relinquish their control without a treaty or, in the case of the United Nations, without amendment of the Charter; they are likely to wish to define precisely the conditions under which the supranational powers are to be exercised, and a constitutional act is the most convenient instrument for this. Such a view is borne out by the experience not only of the European Community, but also of all other occasions known to the writer on which substantial powers have passed from hitherto independent governments to a supranational or federal authority.

Another significant aspect of the establishment of the EEC reinforces the view that organic growth is not likely to be sufficient. The general movement for European union had already resulted in the creation, in 1949, of two bodies of which the majority of West European countries were members: the Council of Europe and the Organization for European Economic Co-operation. But the member states of those two bodies were divided between the Six, in which there was a strong desire to move towards a European federation, and the others, which were satisfied with inter-governmental co-operation. The Six soon realized, after proposals for converting the Council of Europe into a supranational body by 'the creation of a political authority with limited functions but real powers'[6] had failed to find favour in the other countries, that they would be unable to carry the others with them in developing the existing organizations in a supranational direction.

The French government, which, with German power at a post-war ebb, was the natural leader of the Six, therefore concluded that it would be necessary to establish a new organization, and that acceptance of the supranational principle would be a prior condition for joining in the negotiations to set it up. There were crucial problems at that time relating to the future of German steel production. M. Schuman, the French Minister for Foreign Affairs, therefore proposed on behalf of the French government an organization to pool the coal and steel production of at least France and Germany; it would be 'open to the participation of the other countries of Europe'; but it would be supranational:

> By pooling the basic production and by setting up a new High
> Authority, whose decisions will be binding on France, Germany and
> other member countries, this proposal will build the first concrete
> foundation of a European federation which is indispensable to the
> preservation of peace.[7]

The governments of Belgium, Italy, Luxemburg and the Netherlands agreed to join the French and Germans in the negotiations,
but the British and other European states rejected the supranational condition.

It seems inherently probable that some states will be readier at
any given time than others to accept the supranational principle.
Four out of the seventeen American states refused at first to accept
the United States constitution and, as has been seen, only six
European states were ready for the Community experiment at
the time of M. Schuman's declaration. It may, therefore, be
necessary at some stage in the evolution of world organizations
to choose between supranationality and universality, although if
the states willing to accept the supranational condition were
geographically or racially too limited, there would clearly be a
danger that the supranational body would never be able to achieve
a universal membership.

It is pertinent to ask what it is that makes some countries so
eager to take the radical step of transferring certain powers of
government to supranational institutions. In the case of the
European Community, there was a widespread loss of confidence
in the traditional institutions of the nation-state, which had failed
to prevent two world wars or, in the second one, to avert defeat
for each of the six countries. It is significant that in Britain, where
national self-confidence was at a high level in 1945, it was not
until the sixties, when the post-war change in British power and
the recurrent economic difficulties had become evident, that membership of the Community became a serious political proposition.

Given this dissatisfaction with national institutions, why did the Six look towards a supranational or federal union to solve their problems? First there was the desire to make quite sure that the dreadful experience of the two world wars would never be repeated, at least through conflict between France and Germany. The Schuman declaration made this clear:

> The gathering of the nations of Europe requires the elimination of the age-old opposition of France and Germany . . . The solidarity in production thus established will make it plain that any war between France and Germany becomes not merely unthinkable, but materially impossible.[8]

There was an emotional commitment to union, and an intellectual conviction that only a supranational form of union would be sufficiently effective. Secondly there was the consciousness that, from their position in 1913 at the centre of world politics, the nations of Western Europe had come to be overshadowed by America and Russia with their much greater populations. It seemed to follow that, in order to avoid dependence on the one and to resist being swallowed up by the other, the West Europeans would have to assemble a population of similar size under one government. Thirdly it was widely believed that, in order to emulate the wealth and prosperity of the United States in an age in which modern technology demands production on an increasingly large scale, it would be necessary to establish a market with a similar number of consumers. For all these reasons, the finger seemed to many people in the Six to point towards a federation of Europe.

In short, the belief was prevalent in the Six that only by joining their forces in an effective, and hence a federal, union would the European nations have enough power to achieve their aims of prosperity, independence and a restoration of their influence in the world. Although the force of these arguments was vaguely felt in all sections of society, and there was therefore general acceptance among the mass of the people for the policies of union, the driving force came from the *élites* rather than the masses. Perhaps a union of different nations is too remote and abstract a concept ever to excite the people as a whole; the political emotions of most people, where international affairs are concerned, tend to crystallize around the tribal gods. Perhaps the idea of assembling the necessary power to achieve certain aims is one that will appeal first to those who will be fairly close to the exercise of that power. But whatever the reason, the movement for European union was led by a few outstanding statesmen – Monnet, Schuman, Spaak, Adenauer, de Gasperi – and relied on the support of those who were active in the centre parties, the non-communist trade unions, business and professional people, and of federalist movements numbering not more than a few thousand members in each country. It was essentially a middle-class movement, but, apart from the communists and the nationalists (whose combined weight was of critical importance only in France), the bulk of the middle classes were supporters of the idea.

It might be thought that many members of national political parties and bureaucracies would resist the transfer of power to supranational institutions because, even if their country might gain influence as a result, they themselves would certainly lose it. The structure of the Communities, however, with the transfer of powers in limited sectors of political life, the close involvement and important policy-making role of national governments through the Council of Ministers, and the presence of national members of parliament in the European Parliament, was such that this fear seems not to have been important until de Gaulle became President of France.

The swing in the balance of power away from Europe during the first half of the twentieth century has been mentioned as a major motive for the desire of the Six to unite, so that they would regain some of their lost influence. The balance of power among the Six themselves is also a vital factor from which important lessons can be learned. If a union is to be of a democratic nature or, to put it another way, if none of its members is to be deprived of influence by entering it, it is necessary that no one member should be powerful enough to dominate the rest. The Six were certainly unwilling to repeat the pattern of the First German Empire, in which Prussia was by far the strongest member and which consequently fell under Prussian hegemony. It was therefore essential that there should be at least two members of the largest size. With France and Germany this was indeed the case. Italy, though similar in population, was much weaker in economic resources, and this explains the strength of the French position in negotiating the establishment of the EEC. For Germany the Community was the essential way back to international respectability and influence; the Community could conceivably have been created without Italy, or, alternatively, without one or more of the Benelux countries; but without France to counterbalance Germany, the Community would have been dominated by one country, and this was unacceptable to the others. France was indispensable and hence in a powerful negotiating position.

While the need for a balance of power between at least the two largest members of a supranational community is evident, the difficulties that arise from having only two members of the largest size are not quite so obvious. Yet John Stuart Mill pointed them out in 1861: 'if there be two [members much more powerful than the rest], they will be irresistible when they agree; and whenever they differ everything will be decided by a struggle for ascendancy between the rivals.'[9] Experience in the EEC has tended to bear out what Mill said: when France and Germany have differed progress has been held up; when, at the time of the Franco-German Treaty, they announced a special effort to maintain agreement, the others were immediately afraid of domination by a 'Franco-German axis'.

It is in fact clearly essential, if a union is to have two members much stronger than the rest, that they should have an understanding at least to the extent of being in agreement more often than not. The quotations taken from the Schuman declaration have already shown how the Community was based on a Franco-German alliance, and the crisis of 1965 arose after this alliance had ceased to function. This indicates that it would, as Mill suggested, be better to have at least three member states of the largest size, so that the union could work effectively even when they were not unanimous. In the European Community, this role could be played either by Britain if it became a member or by Italy when its economic strength has increased enough and has become reflected in its political influence. In organizations at world level, an understanding between Russia and America is in present circumstances a prerequisite of real progress, although the rise of other powerful entities such as China, India or a European Political Community may cause this condition to be modified.

Besides the existence of a strong desire for union and of a suitable balance between the strength of the prospective members, there were a number of background conditions in the case of the EEC that were favourable to the establishment of supranational institutions. It cannot be supposed that these conditions must necessarily apply in each case where supranational institutions are established. But it seems unlikely that the European Community would have been created in their absence; and it may reasonably be suggested that no supranational union is likely to be effected unless a majority of them are present.

First, the idea of the union of Europe had long been planted in men's minds. There was the powerful example of the Roman Empire; over three centuries ago Sully put forward a project for European union and Penn did the same at the end of the seventeenth century; and by the nineteen-twenties Briand was promoting the concept in the League of Nations. The idea of European union had, then, a respectable history, and to this was added the prestige of the federal principle that had been applied with such remarkable success in the United States and Switzerland.

Secondly, there was a consciousness of cultural unity: an awareness of the heritage of Greece, Israel and Rome and of shared historical experiences such as the rise of Christianity, feudalism, the renaissance, the enlightenment, the industrial revolution, imperialism, the two world wars and the retreat from empire.

Thirdly, there was a similarity of economic and social institutions and of economic levels. The economies of the Six are all based predominantly on privately owned enterprises; all are pluralist societies with a diversity of freely-functioning economic, social and cultural institutions; all are welfare states with highly developed full employment and social policies. There is, moreover, a fair degree of equivalence in the economic and technological levels of the Six, if southern Italy is excepted. This is important where economic union is concerned, for the direct impact of a higher technological level on a lower one can be disastrous, as the experience of southern Italy after the unification of Italy had demonstrated.

Fourthly, there was at the time when the Communities were negotiated (1950-51 and 1955-57) a similarity between the political institutions of the Six. Germany and Italy had emerged from fascism into parliamentary democracy, and France had not yet entered its phase of plebiscitary democracy. Not only were the formal institutions similar, however; the political parties that formed the governments of the Six during those years also had much in common. They could be classed preponderantly as either Christian Democrat, Socialist or Liberal, and their members found no difficulty in sitting together under such labels in the European Parliament. In these circumstances it was possible for the governments and political parties of the Six to remain sufficiently in harmony on basic issues to permit the establishment and satisfactory operation of the communities.

Fifthly, quite apart from formal politics there was an intense traffic of people and ideas between the countries concerned. Individual tourism was complemented by countless conferences and meetings of professional or other voluntary associations, which the cheapness of travel between these neighbouring countries made possible. Such traffic has its bearing on formal politics; for if a sufficient number of those whose attitudes influence formal politics had not had a minimal understanding of the points of view and needs of the partner countries, the national political institutions would hardly have been able to hold to policies that were sufficiently acceptable to the other members to enable the union to go ahead.

Sixthly, the desire for union was represented by statesmen (five of whom have been named earlier) who had the stature and the political ability required to make it effective. This was shown in the selection of the coal and steel industries as the first sector to be dealt with by a supranational organization. There was, as has already been explained, a widespread feeling among the Six by 1950 that a federal system was required; yet it would probably have been impossible to secure agreement on so bold a step. At that time, however, a major political problem had arisen in relation to the German steel industry. It was believed by the former Allies to be essential to keep the German steel industry, which had been the basis of the armaments industry, under some form of control. But the post-war limitation of the industry's production to a small tonnage was proving impracticable: Germany had to export to live and it needed steel as the basis for its exports. The creation of a supranational authority that would be responsible for the control of both the German and other European basic industries was seen as the only way of securing such control without subjecting Germany to a permanently inferior status, which democratic countries would have found it hard to do. The establishment of the European Coal and Steel Community was, therefore, both the best solution to an urgent and specific problem, and a decisive advance towards a system of supranational institutions that was widely accepted by the Six as the longer-term and more general aim. Following this break-through on a narrow front, the EEC was established without the pressure of an immediate specific problem of equivalent urgency; the success of the first venture, and the problems of integrating one sector of the economy without also integrating the others, were enough to carry the Six forward into extending the supranational principle from the coal and steel industries to the whole of their economic life.

It is not easy to prove that the conditions outlined above were necessary to the establishment of the European Community. It may be contended that an economic union with supranational institutions would be possible without the cultural, economic, political and social similarities that the countries of Western Europe have. This can hardly be more than a matter of judgement, but it seems unlikely that political institutions can work unless the people who operate them share a basic similarity of outlook; unless, in a democracy, this similarity of outlook to some extent permeates the electorates; and, again in democracies, it is hard to envisage an economic union being realized if fundamentally divergent economic and social conditions cause excessively disruptive effects on people's jobs or standards of living.

The experience of the European Community may usefully be compared with that of previous federations and other forms of union, which have been analysed by K. C. Wheare in his book on Federal Government.[10] The factors selected by Wheare as favouring a desire to unite or the capacity to work a federal union include a sense of military insecurity, a desire for independence, a hope of economic advantages, geographical neighbourhood, prior political association, some similarity of political and social institutions, statesmanship at the right time, and a balance of strength among the uniting states. The similarity between these factors and those to which attention has been drawn in the above analysis of the

European Community will be noticed. It is not coincidental: the writer wishes to acknowledge his debt to Professor Wheare's thinking on the subject. The relevance of Wheare's ideas to the case of the European Community indeed appears very real, although the circumstances of the industrial mass democracies of modern Europe differ from those of Wheare's 'classical' federations (Australia, Canada, Switzerland and the United States) at the time of their creation, and there are accordingly some differences in the conditions under which the European Community was set up, and some additional conditions have emerged.

Once the ECOSOC and, later, the EEC were established certain forces were set in motion that helped to consolidate their development. The political parties and economic pressure groups, realizing that there was a new source of decisions that affected their interests, set to work to influence the Community institutions.[11] They tended as a consequence to reflect the supranational character of the Community's own organs, and thus to acquire a vested interest in its perpetuation.

Probably more important, large numbers of producers and consumers have benefited from the new trade that the Common Market has opened up, and would conversely suffer if the channels were blocked again. Producers whose livelihood depends on the freedom of trade have a particularly strong interest in its continuance.

Less tangible, but nonetheless significant, is the prestige that the Community institutions have gained, both by their existence over a number of years as a major element in political life, and by a number of striking successes in solving difficult problems. The political initiative and skill of the European Commission has played its part here, as has the will to agree of the member governments represented in the Council of Ministers. Most of these successes have taken the form of 'package deals', balancing concessions and advantages on various issues for the various member countries, and often centring around a combination of agricultural gains (of interest to the French) and industrial gains (of interest to the Germans).

Many supporters of the community method believe that it generates not only forces that help to consolidate the supranational institutions, but also tensions that compel the member states to extend the method to new fields of a ctivity. Thus, it is argued, the common market in coal and steel could not operate fairly in the face of divergent national markets for the other fuels that compete with coal, or of strict price controls in one country in the transforming industries to which steel is sold: integration in one important sector of the economy led inevitably to integration in all economic sectors. Likewise a customs union brings with it the need for common economic, social and financial policies, without which full employment, social justice and the stable development of the economy would not be possible; the common external commercial policy that a customs union implies would conflict with other aspects of national foreign policies and this creates the demand for a common foreign policy; a common foreign policy will be found to be inconsistent with separate defence policies, and there will therefore have to be a common defence policy. Thus a common market in one sector is thought to lead logically on to a general common market, which leads in turn to common economic, foreign and defence policies, with the supranational institutions required to formulate and put them into effect: in short, to a federal system to deal with economics, foreign affairs and defence.

This line of argument seems valid, and was born out by the experience of the European Community, so long as the conditions favourable to the community system obtained. With the installation of de Gaulle as President of France, however, and the emergence of his policies based on a clear conviction that the national governments, not a supranational government, should be the supreme authority on all political issues, these conditions have ceased to apply. The political institutions in France are now markedly different from those of the other members of the Community, and the desire for a supranational form of union has been replaced in the French government by a rooted abhorrence of it. In these circumstances, the interdependence of the different sectors of economic and political life can lead not to the 'spillover' of the supranational principle from one sector to the next, but to a form of 'blowback' whereby the possible effects of Community policies on sectors still under national control causes a hostile member government to hinder the operation of the Community process in sectors where it has already begun to apply.

The crisis that arose in the Community in 1965 illustrates this point. The European Commission proposed that the supranational principle be applied fully in the field of agricultural policy. De Gaulle clearly resented this proposal, and used the failure of the Council of Ministers to agree on certain questions of agricultural policy within the allotted time (which was undoubtedly a fault on the part of the Council, but of a sort that in the past had been overcome by the device of 'stopping the clock' while negotiations were completed) as an occasion to force a trial of strength with the Community in general and the Commission in particular. Whatever the outcome, the incident is a reminder that while physical power remains with the member governments, any one of them, and particularly a powerful one, can hinder or reverse the process of integration as soon as that government's desire for union turns into a desire to prevent it.

It is not advisable to press analogies too far in history or political science. An attempt to apply lessons of the Community's experience to the problems of world organizations is therefore necessarily tentative. It may nevertheless be of interest to summarize some of the points that have emerged:

1. Supranational powers are not likely to be ceded to international

institutions without specific constitutional acts such as treaties or amendments to the UN Charter.

2. Those states desiring supranational union might have to proceed without waiting for the others, although this would not lead towards universal supranational union unless the states taking the initiative were widely enough representative of the world's main regions and political alignments.

3. Supranational union is not likely to occur unless there is a widespread loss of faith in the ability of national institutions to solve major problems; a corresponding hope of greater security and/or economic gain as a result of the supranational union; and an expectation among the main political forces in prospective member states that the union will be a vehicle through which they can increase their power to achieve these or other ends.

4. Supranational union is not likely to occur if there is a danger of its being dominated by one large member. If there were two predominant members of equivalent strength, the union could be established and function so long as they were in alliance. But it is more likely to work well if there are three or more members of the largest size and greatest strength.

5. A certain sense of cultural identity, and a degree of similarity of political and economic institutions, seem to be a prior condition of supranational union. Experience in international organizations at world level indicates that these conditions do not at present apply, but the universal progress of technology in general and the improvement of transport and communications in particular may well alter this situation in respect of at least a majority of states, representative of the main regions of the world, during the course of the next few decades.

6. Statesmen deeply committed to the principle of supranational union are needed to bring it about, in addition to a widespread

acceptance by those who wield significant political influence in the prospective member states.

7. Supranational organization in a key sector of economic or political activity tends to lead on to supranational organization in other sectors, unless the desire for union in an important member state or group of states turns into hostility, in which case the existing supranational institutions become endangered. This condition would apply at least until the use of armed force was under supranational control.

TEXT REFERENCES

1. Treaty establishing the European Economic Community, Article 157.

2. Article 7 of the UN Charter states that the Secretariat is one of the 'principal organs of the United Nations'; Article 100 that those who work in it are not to 'seek or receive instructions from any government or from any other authority external to the Organization'.

3. Treaty establishing the European Economic Community, Article 155.

4. Such proposals are contained in both the Western and Soviet plans laid before the Geneva Disarmament Conference.

5. See for example R. Triffin, *Gold and the Dollar Crisis*, Yale University Press, 1961.

6. Motion put by M. Cassimatis to the first session of the Assembly of the Council of Europe in 1949.

7. Statement made by M. Robert Schuman, French Foreign Minister, on 9 May 1950.

8. Ibid.

9. J. S. Mill, *Considerations on Representative Government*, London, 1947, p. 368.

10. K. C. Wheare, *Federal Government*, London, 1951, pp. 35-54.

11. The process has been studied in E. B. Haas, *The Uniting of Europe*, London, 1958.

BIBLIOGRAPHY

Camps, M., *Britain and the European Community, 1955–63*, London, 1964.

Camps, M., *What Kind of Europe?*, London, 1965.

Deutsch, K. W., *et al.*, *Political Community and the North Atlantic Area*, Princeton, 1957.

Gasser, A., *L'Autonomie Communale et la Réconstruction de l'Europe*, Editions de la Baconnière Neuchatel, 1946.

Haas, E. B., *The Uniting of Europe*, London, 1958.

Lindberg, L. N., *The Political Dynamics of European Economic Integration*, Stanford, 1963.

Pinder, J., *Europe against de Gaulle*, London and New York, 1963.

Pryce, R., *The Political Future of the European Community*, Federal Trust and Marshbank, 1962.

Treaty establishing the European Economic Community.

Wheare, K. C., *Federal Government*, London, 1951.

CONCLUSIONS

Evan Luard

The preceding chapters have considered a wide range of different international organizations and the type of development that has taken place within them. Are there any general conclusions about the factors influencing change in international organizations that may be drawn as a result?

In considering the nature of changes in institutions, it is necessary to distinguish between long-term *causes* of change; the short-term *instruments* by which changes are effected; and, finally, the *types* of change that are brought about.

Let us consider, first, the main causes of change in international organizations. The most obvious cause, which is brought out in a number of these studies, is that arising from an alteration in the political composition of the membership. The studies of the General Assembly, the ILO, and the economic organizations of the UN, all bring out in different degrees the effect of this factor. Just as the movement of political power to new classes may be the cause of widespread political change within states, so the rise of a new class of nations (such as the large numbers of newly independent states over the past twenty years) may initiate widespread political change in international organizations, by bringing about the adoption of new policies there. In this case the effect is the result of a change in the number of members. But a similar effect might take place through the accession to power of new governments of a different political complexion from their predecessors.

In both cases the effect is a long-term rather than an immediate one. Within international organizations, particularly, because constitutions are relatively rigid, because there is little direct legislation, and because what there is is usually only marginal in effect, changes in membership do not usually bring about immediate, or large-scale, changes in policy, structure and organization. Rather they bring about constant pressures, through resolutions and other means, for small-scale changes in policy. Even where little ultimate power can be exerted by the new entrants, they may still exert a significant *influence* as a result of competition for their support among the others. Changes as a result of this process can be seen in the proliferation and development of economic agencies in the UN, starting with the technical assistance programme, through the Special Fund, the IFC and the IDA, to the new Development Programme and the Trade and Development Conference. The same factor has been responsible for the increase in the membership of the Security Council and ECOSOC, the establishment of the Committee of Twenty-Four, and the increasing attention devoted to human rights questions. The effect inside such organizations as the ILO and the World Bank has been traced in the chapters on these subjects. Though none of these changes is revolutionary in itself, taken together they represent perhaps the most important development in the world's international organizations over the past twenty years. And they demonstrate the importance of persistent verbal pressures, even without the ultimate sanction of military power, in inducing changes in organizations of this kind.

Secondly, several of the studies show how change frequently occurs, even if only after a certain time-lag, as a response to changes in the needs to be confronted. Even some of the developments just described could be interpreted as a response to the emergence of new needs, rather than as the effect of political pressures from a particular section within these organizations. In some cases, it is true, the voting record, showing the wealthier and larger nations normally voting on opposite sides to the others, suggests that political pressure has been the more important factor. In other cases both influences have been at work: the expression of political demands within an organization may awaken wealthier nations not only to a realization of their political interest, but to a sense of the needs to be met and of their own responsibilities. But there are certainly some cases where changes in the situation prevailing, and the needs to be confronted, alone give rise to a general search for new policies. Mr Scammell's account of the adaptations to the IMF made already, and of the search for new solutions to the international liquidity problem for the future, is an example of this process at work. The changes in the policies of the World Bank, in which the wealthier powers possess a built-in majority, described by Mr Shonfield, are another example of the same type. The abandonment of the security system envisaged in Chapter VII of the Charter, and the increasing emphasis on more modest methods of peace-keeping, reflect a general acknowledgement of the need for adaptation from an imagined world of great-power unanimity and five-power supremacy to a real one of divided councils and many small states; from a world of big wars and external aggressions to one of small wars and internal conflicts. The development of the assistance rather than the research role of the specialized agencies equally reflects the increasing concern everywhere with disparities in the standard of living and the rate of growth between the developed and developing world.

New needs, however, are not necessarily alone enough to bring about the changes necessary. The needs for more effective international commodity arrangements, for a better international liquidity system, for more effective co-ordination of air transport, for better co-ordination of aid policies, though generally recognized, have not so far been successful in inducing the necessary changes within international organizations. Often it is only acute crisis situations that create a sufficient sense of urgency for important changes to become acceptable. On peace-keeping forces, as the article on this subject shows, long discussion at normal times has proved totally barren of results. Only urgent crisis situations were able to bring about the establishment of a UN force. Only the acute crisis over financing was sufficient to bring about a fundamental review of the Charter provisions concerning security and the existing division of labour between Assembly and Security Council: without that crisis it is most unlikely that the problem would have been confronted at all. Urgent emergency situations, such as those relating to the Arab and other refugees, have served to bring about the establishment of new agencies to meet their needs. But no international body was established for at least as many refugees from China to Hongkong, because, their arrival being extended over a ten-year period, the emergency never appeared so acute.

A third influence on change, brought out in a number of these studies, is the personality and actions of the chief officials. Both Mr Bailey and Mr Shonfield show the importance of this factor in relation to the organizations with which they deal. There are numerous ways in which the influence of officials may be brought to bear. They may influence or even sponsor the drafting of resolutions.[1] They may take initiatives of their own that have an important influence. They may make public statements on important questions under discussion. They may, in their annual reports, both in the UN and the Specialized Agencies, put forward proposals that are sometimes afterwards adopted by the representative bodies of the organization. Sometimes they are deliberately given a considerable degree of independent authority when the representative body is not meeting in order to provide leadership between sessions: Mr Jacobsson and M. Schweitzer in the IMF, Mr Sen in the FAO, Mr Black and Mr Woods in the World Bank, have all exerted authority of this sort.

Next, changes may in some cases be effected, or at least strongly influenced, by the action of individual governments. In the

League of Nations the promise of US support for an increase in economic functions did much to assure the acceptance of the Bruce Report recommending this. The leadership of the US in launching the Korean operation and initiating the Uniting for Peace Resolution, the initiatives of Canada and the Scandinavian countries in proposing peace-keeping forces and earmarking and training troops for this purpose, the demand of the US government for merging the Technical Assistance and Special Fund programmes, are all examples of actions of this kind during the UN period. Because, however, many important changes will require a two-thirds majority, and even the passage of resolution will require the support of over fifty governments in most organizations, initiatives of this kind are only likely to be effective if preceded by a considerable degree of lobbying, or if they express what is in any case a widely felt requirement.

Often, of course, the initiative is that of a group of countries. In these cases purely political factors, loyalty to ideological or regional groups, may be important in influencing the institution of changes, as in every other decision of international organizations. This was certainly one factor (though not the only one) in bringing about the effective revision of the UN Charter through the Uniting for Peace resolution; and in the creation of a special agency for reconstruction in South Korea alone among those suffering from the ravages of war. But because in general there is no clear unanimity, even within any group, about the types of change desirable within the principal organizations, factors of this kind have been less significant than might otherwise have been expected. In the discussions in the Special Committee on Peace-keeping, which were likely to result in the most important revision of the Charter system yet accomplished, there was no evidence of attempts to concert the positions within the major groups, except perhaps among the communist powers. Even on political matters, though there exist formal caucus-groups, these do not produce any great consistency of voting-pattern.[2] The only exception is on economic subjects where common material interests may bring about (as over SUNFED or UNCTAD) a fairly consistent and organized group activity.

Fifth, and perhaps ultimately more important than any other in influencing changes in international organizations, is the attitude of governments generally, irrespective of blocs, about the purposes such organizations may procure for them. Because of the need for substantial majorities, or even universal consent, for any important changes, even significant alterations in the balance of political power may be of little effect unless they are accompanied by a general shift in governments' attitudes. Public attitudes depend on a number of factors: the tradition of national sovereignty, conceptions of the material benefits international organizations may bring, the publicity and image the organizations receive in the country concerned, the degree to which they appear dominated by political enemies, and others. Attitudes to change in international organizations may bear little relation to attitudes towards change within states: communist powers today are highly conservative powers so far as international organizations are concerned, while the most revolutionary in attitude are those whose internal policies are relatively mild and neutral (such as Canada and the Scandinavian governments). The powers that are most ready to support change in international organizations seem to be usually relatively small powers (who will not suffer the same diminution of national power through loss of sovereignty as larger ones), of liberal, but not extreme, political persuasions. New states, though generally expressing vague sentiments of approval for the UN and its agencies, are not always more ready to undertake expenditure or sacrifice of national sovereignty for their sake than the great powers themselves.

The most important factor affecting such attitudes is of course the tradition of national patriotism and pride. These encourage among many an attitude of hostility and resentment to international organizations and their activities, at least in matters affecting their own state's freedom of action. Understanding of the value that international institutions may procure depends not only on a sense of their purpose, but on a clear understanding of the extent to which national independence is in any case limited by the actions of other states. Such understanding may appear first among national officials closely concerned with international affairs: those serving together within an organization often begin to feel the purposes of the organization their own purposes as much as they do those of their nation. Next, a similar sense of common involvement may become spread among the most politically conscious in all states, including many members of governments. Only last of all does this sense of common interest come to be shared by the bulk of the ordinary citizens, as they too become more conscious of the inevitable limits to national independence or capacities. But because the actions of governments are often finally conditioned by the attitudes and opinions of their publics, it may only be when such a sense becomes widespread that governments themselves feel ready to give active support to increases in the powers of international organizations.

If these seem to be the main *causes* of change in international organizations, do the preceding chapters give us a closer idea of the main *instruments* by which change is brought about?

The basic structure of most international organizations today is remarkably uniform. Nearly all have three basic institutions: an Assembly, representing all Governments which are members, meeting usually once a year, but sometimes once every two, three or even five years; a Council, sometimes weighted in favour of the chief money-givers (as in the IMF and the World Bank), or those most directly interested (as in IMCO), meeting more frequently; and a Secretariat, serving both these, in continuous operation, and subject to the authority of the other two. While nominally important decisions must ultimately be made or ratified in the Assembly, usually effective power resides in fact in the Council more continuously active, or even in the Secretariat, which always wields a powerful influence behind the scenes. Changes may be finally confirmed by the Assembly; but they are often initiated by one of the other two. (Cf. Mr McMahon above.)

It was suggested in the first chapter of this book that the most elementary types of change in institutions are those that occur in a centralized or hierarchical system, where the central authority determines the change and imposes it on all subordinate systems.

Owing to the lack of a firm basis of centralized authority in international organizations this was clearly less likely to be a common procedure of change within them. A number of the histories recounted here tend to confirm this hypothesis. In the League of Nations, although the dominant position of the council was no doubt designed to provide an element of centralized authority, in fact (as Mr Walters' chapter shows), the structure was so loose, national loyalties so powerful in relation to those to the organization, and its authority so weakened by the lack of comprehensive membership and particular failures, that no worthwhile degree of authority was enjoyed either by the Council or the Assembly. And the unanimity rule had the effect that even if decisions could be agreed at all, they were often anodyne in content. Within the UN system, the degree of authority necessary for centralized decision-making is rather greater, at least in matters where vital national interests are not at stake. Although the attempt to provide the Security Council with an instrument for direct authority in its own force broke down, authority may be exerted by it by less direct means: Security Council resolutions, such as that on the India–Pakistan War, possess a considerable authority even when they lack the force of 'decisions' under Article 25. The Assembly resolutions passed on genocide and on the orbiting of weapons of mass destruction, and the Declaration on the granting of independence to colonial countries and peoples, though technically they had the force only of recommendations, represented collective decisions having a fairly high degree of authority. So far as decisions for change *within* organizations are concerned, such moves as the creation of the Interim Assembly and the Uniting for Peace Resolution, as well as the formal amendments of the Charter to enlarge the Security and Economic and Social Councils, represent types of constitutional change effected through direct decisions at the centre: that is, formal resolutions in the main representative bodies. New activities, such as the Technical Assistance Programme, and new organizations, such as the Special Fund and the Trade and Development Conference, have received ultimate authorization by the same procedures. But in general, the studies assembled here provide comparatively few examples of change brought about by this means.

More frequent as an instrument of change has been *bureaucratic* decision-making. Though the scope of each individual change may here be smaller, the total number is very much larger. Sometimes these decisions themselves take the form of a direct and centralized authority from the secretariat on member states. Secretary-Generals may make requests to members which, though entirely without binding force, exert a significant pressure on the government concerned: the pressure of IMF officials on individual governments, the influence of international officials on development plans, Mr Hammerskjöld's demand and final attainment of a visit to South Africa, represent forms of pressure of this kind. Sometimes Secretariats undertake direct negotiations with governments: Mr Hammerskjöld's flight to China in 1955, his attempted visit to Hungary, and his dealings with the Congolese government in 1960, are examples of this sort. More frequently officials may bring about changes within the organizations themselves: the changes introduced by Mr Hammerskjöld in the structure of the Secretariat in 1954, the personal decisions of U Thant to give a representative political balance to the political under-secretaries, and to seek peace-keeping finance by the issue of bonds, are all examples of this kind. Bureaucratic decisions may take the form of creating new organs or appointments: Mr Hammerskjöld's establishment of UN presences in Jordan in 1958 and Laos in 1959, U Thant's expansion of the military staff in New York and of a research organization within the headquarters, are examples of these.

Still more important, perhaps, in securing changes in international organizations has been *indirect* decision-making, a series of small decisions which, taken together, bring about a significant alteration in the structure or powers of the organization concerned. Sometimes there is a gradual evolution in the *practice* of an organization that leads to a permanent evolution. The series of votes concerning the competence of the General Assembly to consider colonial questions and apartheid, notwithstanding the provisions of Article 2 (7), had the effect of changing the general nature of the Assembly's functions and effectively amending the interpretation of an essential element in its Charter. Even governments which had previously refused to accept the organization's competence to consider apartheid, like Britain have, through the persistent adoption of the practice, been brought formally to renounce their opposition. Each time a new peace force is established it alters the general conception of the organization's powers and nature that is held outside, and makes it easier to establish them on subsequent occasions. The practice that grew up in the Security Council of not counting abstentions as vetoes, and the more recent practice of adopting the chairman's summary of the proceedings as a 'consensus' of the Council, so by-passing the veto, have brought about a significant alteration in the original conception of the 'principle of unanimity', and increased its effective powers. Sometimes changes take place through certain provisions falling into disuse; for example the obsolescence of Articles 41-50 of the Charter, the effective abandonment of Article 25, the increasing readiness to hear complaints in the Security Council without ensuring that the parties have first exhausted preliminary procedures, the failure to apply Chapter XVIII on 'transitional security arrangements', and other matters.

Because of the resistances of governments to *explicit* changes in the powers of international organizations, change is often more likely to occur through a gradual series of decisions of this sort that may pass almost unnoticed. Perhaps commonest of all have been decisions to undertake activities in new directions, or to expand particular existing activities. For example, the series of decisions to extend the UN's own activities in the field of technical assistance and economic aid (as recounted by Mr Townley) has not only altered the balance between the economic and political functions of the UN proper; but also has significantly changed the relationship between the UN and the Specialized Agencies. The progressive decisions by UNESCO and ILO (described by Mr McMahon) to devote a greater part of their activities to helping the developing countries in educational and development assistance have drastically modified the purpose and function of those organizations. The increasing emphasis in all the Specialized Agencies on field programmes rather than on research and administrative work has brought about a considerable modification of their original nature.

Another type of small-scale decision by which changes are quite often brought about in international organizations is the appointment of *ad hoc* committees to consider particular topics. This quite often serves to produce a report with specific recommendations for change that is comparable in effect with the recommendations of a Royal Commission within states. These reports in turn may produce some impact on public opinion generally and governmental opinion in particular, and so lead to specific changes. Examples of this kind were the changes in GATT policy resulting from the Haberler Committee, the modification in the UN's public relations activities as a result of the committee set up on that subject, and the discussions of international compensation for fluctuations in commodity trade which have resulted from the recommendations of the expert committee which considered it.

Sometimes more permanent committees are established that may serve to keep the attention of an organization, and governments, permanently on a particular subject or form of activity. These may serve as a source of ideas, or may mobilize opinion to support a policy already adopted, or adduce reasons for a particular course of action already adopted in principle.[3] The terms of reference of committees of this kind may thus be crucial in determining the influence they play in bringing about change. The innumerable committees concerned with commodities, the Special Committee on Information from non-self-governing territories, or the Committee for Industrial Development set up by ECOSOC, are different examples of this type of committee. The establishment, through the action of the last, of the Industrial Development Centre within the UN headquarters in New York, is an example of the kind of institutional change that may be effected by this instrument. Committees of this kind may function, like a senate committee or a back-bench committee in the House of Commons, as a kind of permanent pressure group exerting influence on officials and assemblies for future action in their own field. The recommendations of such committees, however, are only influential in bringing about change if not too far removed from what governments will already accept: the fate of the Kaldor Committee's recommendations on trade measures to counteract deflation, and of these of other committees set up in the early years of the Organization, are examples of what happens where recommendations are too far beyond existing political realities.

A fourth instrument of change in international organizations are legal judgements. Just as the judgements of the Supreme Court in the US may bring about an effective alteration in the US Constitution without the political complexities of an explicit amendment, so judgements or advisory opinions of the International Court of Justice may have a similar effect in the UN. It is arguable that the Court's advisory opinion concerning peace-keeping costs, and the Assembly's resolution accepting this, served to bring about an effective amendment of this kind. Similarly, the judgement of the Court in the Corfu Channel case altered the interpretation to be given to the 'use of force' in interpreting the Charter. In other cases (for example, that concerning the constitution of IMCO), the Court has given interpretative opinions leading to the general adoption of a new practice (in this case the acceptance of nations issuing flags of convenience as maritime nations).

Finally, an effective change in the powers of an organization may come about merely through an increase in the respect accorded to it by governments, so that without any change in constitutional structure there nonetheless comes about an effective alteration in the force of resolutions and thus in the balance of influence and power. In the League, that respect, for a variety of reasons, progressively declined until the situation was reached in 1938 when many members explicitly renounced the obligations they had subscribed to under the Covenant. The authority the UN can wield has probably always been larger than that of the League even at its highest. There are today virtually no powers, even among non-members, who explicitly repudiate its aims and authority in the way that some nations openly did that of the League. China may attack US domination of the UN, but she does not attack the organization in itself, in the way that Mussolini and Hitler attacked the League. In most member countries, there exists a measure of sacrilege in outright attack on the organization today.

Factors of this kind are not easily influenced by international organizations themselves. But they do sometimes take deliberate steps to increase their influence. The UN training programme for the diplomats of new states in New York, by increasing their respect and goodwill for the organization, may do more in the long run to increase its authority than many constitutional amendments, unaccompanied by changes in attitude, could do. The effect of sustained and carefully directed pressure by an organization even without any ultimate sanctions in inducing conformity by governments is described in Mr McMahon's chapter on the ILO. Sustained use of publicity and public relations techniques, for example through television films on UN activities, or inviting visits from politicians, and others, might be similar in effect. Ultimately most important are probably educational measures affecting children's knowledge and conceptions of international institutions.

Such measures cannot ensure that UN resolutions are always obeyed, especially in cases where vital national interests appear at stake (as over Hungary or South Africa). But to say that the organization's impotence in such cases reveals its general uselessness is to judge it by wholly inappropriate standards. For few ever expected that in situations of that type the UN could exert authority effectively, unless entrusted with coercive power. Though it may be true that these are the most important types of incident occurring in international relations today, it is precisely over the most important incidents that international organizations are for long likely to be least effective. The fact that the UN is powerless in such cases does not mean that it may not exert considerable influence on less vital occasions. And even in these cases there may be an indirect effect. The pressure of opinion that has been manifested in overwhelming majorities in the UN (for example on apartheid) may not bring about immediate submission; but it may sometimes help to bring about long-term modifications of policy (for example in the establishment of Bantu states). Persistent votes in favour of SUNFED may not have resulted in action to establish it but have certainly exerted influence in other directions: the Special Fund, the IDA and the new Development Programme are all, directly or indirectly, the effect of those votes. Often the most important changes are those that take place by such imperceptible degrees that it is impossible to say when they occurred.

Finally, these studies may help us to consider what are the main *kinds* of change effected from these various causes and through these instruments.

The simplest kind of institutional change that can be effected is that which takes the form of a direct increase or decrease in the *subordination* of peripheral bodies to centralized agencies. Within states this has come about through the consolidation of power at the centre, including political and financial as well as military power; the functional advantages of centralized over local control, bringing the progressive removal of powers from lower to higher authorities; and the convergence of loyalties from local leaders and regions to national states. But factors having the reverse effect, the power of authorities already existing and entrenched at the periphery, local loyalties and resistances to centralized control, diseconomies of scale from excessive centralization, and the conscious desire to preserve diversity and a sense of community at the lowest level, have limited this process. It is the balance between these various factors that will determine the degree of subordination that exists within institutions at any one time. Within international organizations all four of the factors that inhibit subordination are powerful, whereas only functional considerations, among those favourable to it, can be considered strong. Here therefore the balance of factors remains, for the moment, strongly unfavourable to any large increase in subordination. As a result, as the preceding chapters demonstrate, a direct increase in subordination has not normally been a common type of change in international organizations.

Limited centralization has occurred, in some at least of the organizations here considered. There has been a persistent process for example, by which the Specialized Agencies have been brought under an increasing measure of UN control, from the

319

conclusion of the UN's special agreements with the Specialized Agencies, through the creation of the ACC, the establishment of the Technical Assistance Programmes and the appointment of resident representatives for this, to the creation of the new UN Development Programme. The successive operations of peace-forces have shown, as the article on this subject indicates, a constantly reduced deference to the national sovereignty of the host country. The system by which regulations of the WHO and ICAO on various subjects are automatically binding on members, unless they explicitly repudiate them, represents a type of encroachment on sovereignty that is new within the past twenty years. The perpetually rising proportion of the budgets voted for international organizations to those for national governments reflects a growth in the functions performed by the former, even without any direct increase in their power over national authorities.[4] Within individual Specialized Agencies there has been a tendency to reduce the power of the Assembly or conference, for example by extending the period between meetings to two years (UNESCO), three (ICAO) or even five (as in IMO and UPU), and increasing the role of the executive council (as in ICAO or UNESCO). Sometimes the process of centralization is confused, or even temporarily reversed. This may be seen in the complex competition for co-ordination of the Specialized Agencies between ECOSOC, the General Assembly and the ACC, described by Mr Hill. Sometimes there is deliberate decentralization: for example in the recent increase in the economic functions granted to the regional economic commissions, or the proliferation of sub-committees around the ACC. And in any case where national sovereignty is felt to be at stake, because ultimate powers remain still in the hands of nations, the increase in subordination can only be slow and marginal.

A more common type of institutional change consists in alterations in the *distribution* of power and authority among different organizations. Within states, the cabinet may increase its authority in relation to the legislature, or pressure-groups in relation to both; certain ministries, or local authority committees, may decline in authority or disappear altogether, while new ones grow more important; existing enterprises or organizations, because of their leadership or financial resources, may build empires that spread out their power in many new directions. This type of change may occur frequently within international organizations too. It may be seen both in changes affecting the distribution of powers between different international organizations; and in changes affecting the relation between international organizations and national states.

The internecine disputes between the Specialized Agencies, for example over the application of the technical assistance programmes, reflect the attempts of each to extend the area of their own authority in relation to that of others, and even more of the UN itself. As the articles of Professors Goodwin and Claude show, there has been a continued alternation in the balance of power between the General Assembly, the Security Council and the Secretariat, with a shift from the Security Council to the General Assembly during the late forties and early fifties, from General Assembly to Secretariat in the late fifties, and from Secretariat back to Security Council in the early sixties. Similarly, the Special Fund gradually gained in power in relation to Technical Assistance, and both in relation to the agencies. In some cases the balance has been altered by the appearance of non-UN organs. The creation and development of OECD has reduced the functions the UN economic agencies would otherwise have had as co-ordinators of multilateral aid. The existence of the Paris Club has reduced the authority and powers of the IMF.

In other cases organs that have played a significant role for a time have later declined or fallen out of use altogether. The Interim Assembly, the Collective Measures Committee, the Peace Observation Commission, the Transit and Communications Commission of ECOSOC, the Military Staffs Committee, have all passed, completely or effectively, into oblivion for one reason or another. Sometimes organs may retain a considerable measure of authority, but experience an alteration in functions: as Professor Claude shows, the functions of the Security Council have in practice been diplomatic rather than executive, as at first conceived, so that any executive functions required had to be devolved on to the Secretary-General or other bodies.

Another kind of institutional change consists in institutional *innovation*, the creation of wholly new bodies to confront new needs. Within states, the rise of new planning bodies (such as NEDC in Britain) and of regional economic authorities over recent years, or proliferation of unofficial research institutes (such as Chatham House and the Institute for Strategic Studies), are examples of institutional change by these means. The establishment of the ACC as a sort of cabinet among UN agencies is one example in the international field of a shift in the balance of power occurring through this means. The establishment by the Secretary-General of advisory committees to supervise the activities of peace forces was specifically designed to counterbalance the power accorded to himself, but also served to protect him from day-to-day supervision by the Security Council or the Assembly. The creation of new bodies does not necessarily, however, lead to any effective alteration in powers, for even when established, they may not be used. The fate of the Collective Measures Committee and the Peace Observation Commission are examples of this kind. In other cases, new bodies may act as effective forces for bringing pressure on governments. The Special Committee on Information for Non-self-governing Territories, the Committee on Colonialism and the Trade and Development Conference, though possessing few formal powers, have been able to exert considerable influence as the focus of political pressure in this way. Sometimes institutions are set up on a temporary basis, or existing organs acquire temporary powers, that in fact prove to be permanent and continually expand. *Il n'y a rien que le provisoire qui dure* is a maxim that has wide application in the field of international organizations (for example in the case of the UN expeditionary force in Sinai, or the Trade and Development Conference).

Finally, there is the kind of institutional change that occurs through a simple *extension* of the activity and functions of an already existing organization. This occurs in national states where a particular ministry, for example that of defence or trade or education, gradually increases its activities, budget and staff, without necessarily any corresponding reduction in that of other organizations; through the rise in the power of the press, as an influential organ; or the development of trades unions as a fifth estate in the political field. In the international sphere, similar developments sometimes take place. The growth of the power of the Secretariat in the UN itself; the gradual growth in the functions of the World Bank; the continuing increase in the budgets and activities of many of the Specialized Agencies; are all examples of this kind of development.

Significant changes in the institutional structures may take place through quite small moves. The merger of the Technical Assistance Programme and the Special Fund, though justified largely in terms of administrative efficiency, may be ultimately more significant in increasing the powers of the UN in relation to that of the Specialized Agencies. The establishment of a Co-ordinating Committee for the Development Decade, justified on the same grounds, may be similar in its effect. Decisions concerning appointments within the UN Secretariat, the form in which statistics of economic aid are published, the subject for the UN's annual economic survey, these have effects that are ultimately political. They may shift the balance of attention in new directions; or alter the balance of activity in new ways. In either case a significant development within the organization may come about.

Are there any more general conclusions concerning the process of change in international organizations that may be drawn?

First, the growth of the authority wielded by international organizations is an intangible factor that can never be clearly assessed. It might be possible to devise certain measures, for example, of the proportion of national income going to national budgets and to international organizations respectively, the relative speed of growth of national and international budgets, the changes in the number of employees of national and international authorities, and variations in the areas of competence of each. More important, however, are the degrees of compliance that may be expected from resolutions on particular subjects, and this cannot easily be measured. The most important factors ultimately may be the type of sanctions available to each type of institution. These sanctions are not necessarily, or even mainly, the sanctions of armed power. More essential are the relative psychological costs, in terms of disapproval and loss of good name, that are incurred by defying authority.

Secondly, as we have seen, it is not always the most obvious changes that are the most important in their long-term effects on organizations. A long series of small-scale decisions (of the sort we have called 'indirect decision-making') may bring about a more significant alteration in the powers and activity of the organization than an apparently sweeping constitutional amendment. For example, the gradual rise in the budgets of the Specialized Agencies over the past twenty years may be more significant than all the much more publicized developments in the economic activity of the UN proper. Similarly, small-scale and little-known changes in structure, like the growing authority of the resident representatives over the Specialized Agencies, may be far more significant than the high-powered struggle over co-ordination between the UN (represented by ECOSOC) and the agencies (represented in the ACC). Sometimes quite small actions can have long-term results that are incalculable. The decision to call the 1964 conference on trade and development may have been instrumental in establishing one of the most important international organizations yet to come into existence.

Third, certain kinds of change are much more easily instituted than others. In the Foreword a distinction was made between changes in international organizations that are essentially internal and changes that affect their relations with individual member states. It would seem that changes of the latter kind are considerably less easily effected than those of the former. Governments tend to resist anything in the nature of a direct instruction. The recommendations of international organizations to states may be ignored or even resisted. Those that affect the organization's own programme or method of work may seem to be of less direct importance and so more acceptable.[4] In practice a change in the nature or balance of an organization's work must always indirectly affect its relations to member states. But changes of this sort will be harder to resist. And because governments become committed to an organization or to a particular programme, they may not even wish always to resist in the way they will resist a direct assault on sovereignty.

Fourthly, these studies tend to confirm the assumption, often made in the past, that a development in power is more easily brought about in organizations concerned with functional and economic activities than in those that are concerned over the ultimate questions of peace and war. The chapters on the economic agencies of the UN, the World Bank and the IMF record a considerable development of activity and power; those in the political organs some change but little growth. Because demands for independence of action are centred above all in the field of defence and security, encroachments on national power here are those most strenuously resisted. While nations have important national interests on purely economic matters (for example over tariff questions, the volume of aid they may be asked to provide, the independence of their shipping and airlines), these are not usually thought of such overriding national concern as those that concern national security. Nations may therefore in these fields, if subject to sufficient political pressures, be more ready to make concessions and to concede marginal areas of sovereignty than they will if they may be imperilling their nation's capacity to defend itself. The comparison is in any case not an exact one. The authority wielded by a functional organization is usually specific and limited, so that nations are less concerned to oppose particular programmes. An increase in the authority of a political organization (such as the UN itself) is general, however, and may permanently influence the balance of authority between international and national organizations. Nations which wish to avoid an alteration in that balance (such as France today) will thus be especially stubborn in resisting changes affecting the authority of political organizations. Moves of this kind, therefore, may, as Mr Pinder suggests, require a considerable degree of consensus before they can become practicable at a world level.

Fifth, it appears that often there are important impediments to change within the structure of the organizations themselves. Frequently the tradition within an international body is so powerful that it cannot easily be resisted. As Mr Shonfield shows in his contribution, this tradition may change fairly rapidly according to the personalities of the moment. But there is little doubt that large international organizations, like most other bureaucratic structures, are essentially conservative in their traditions. The forces of bureaucratic inertia, the strength of established procedures, the reluctance to take responsibility for large-scale initiatives, habituation to the *status quo*, all these serve to inhibit adaptability. Only if some new force arises to disturb these, a crisis situation to be met, a new reforming Secretary-General, the rise of new political forces in the controlling Assembly, are such traditional factors normally overcome.

The resistance to change inherent in the bureaucratic structure is an element that is common to all large-scale administrative organizations, and does not differ in kind from similar resistances within national bureaucracies. But some of the difficulties of change in international organizations derive from their special nature. Their structure is specific, directed often more towards discussing than doing (though this applies more to the UN itself than to the Specialized Agencies). There is no decision-making cabinet. If they are to adjust more effectively there may be need therefore for changes in the existing structure.

There may be need for the establishment of some procedure, for examining and suggesting specific measures or changes in structure. At the lowest level, business efficiency consultants might do something to improve administrative methods. On policy matters a committee, meeting privately, might prove useful. This need not necessarily be a body similar to a cabinet within states: it may be a body of officials like the ACC or a committee comparable to the EEC's commission (the latter is a body that has precisely the role here suggested). The same effect might result from the development of improved facilities within the Assembly. The development of more homogeneous interest-blocs among the members might promote the political capacity for introducing specific changes there. In any case there may be need for more private discussion of such matters, whether in secret session or in the corridors, to develop corporate spirit.

So far, because of the very real political difficulties about formal amendment of constitutions, members have tended to shy away even from more limited discussions of the types of adjustment that might improve efficiency. The General Assembly set up a committee that recommended marginal changes in the procedure for the general debate, but the UN has only been stimulated to consider more drastic changes as a result of the crisis over financing. Only the establishment of some regular procedure, or a specialized committee, for discussing alterations in organization or activities is likely to encourage a greater capacity for adjustment than exists at present.

This leads to the final, and still more fundamental question:

how far is change in international organizations desirable in itself? To discuss the capacity of organizations for adjustment begs the question whether adjustment is always required. Not all will accept the assumption that change is necessary, implicit in much of this book. But it is at least undeniable that the environment which they confront is a perpetually changing one. Developments in communications and technology perpetually increase the area in which only international action can be effective. Only a highly developed capacity for change within international organizations could ensure their ability to meet the changing needs that they confront. More detailed study of the processes of change within them – far more detailed than this introductory volume could supply – may be required if their existing capacities for adjustment are to be effectively increased.

TEXT REFERENCES

1. Cf. J. G. Hadwen and J. Kaufmann, *How United Nations Decisions are Made*, Leyden, 1960, pp. 21-37.

2. See T. Hovet, *Bloc Politics in the United Nations*, Harvard, 1959.

3. See A. Loveday, *Reflections on International Administration*, Oxford, 1956, pp. 154, 159.

4. Cf. Hadwen and Kaufmann, op. cit., p. 41: 'Resolutions concerning specific UN programmes have had useful and constructive results; the resolutions involving policy recommendations to governments have been much less effective.'

BIOGRAPHICAL NOTES

F. P. WALTERS was a member of the Secretariat of the League of Nations from 1919-40. He is the author of *A History of the League of Nations* (1951).

GEOFFREY L. GOODWIN is Montague Burton Professor of International Relations in the University of London. After serving in the Foreign Office, 1945-48, he joined the staff of the London School of Economics. He is the author of *Britain and the United Nations* (Oxford, 1958) and of numerous articles on the United Nations in *International Affairs* and *International Organization*.

INIS L. CLAUDE, JR. is Professor of Political Science in the University of Michigan. Member of boards of editors, *International Organization* and *Journal of Conflict Resolution*; Chairman, Committee on International Organization, Social Science Research Council, New York. He is the author of *National Minorities: An International Problem* (1955); *Swords Into Ploughshares* (1956, 1959, 1964); *Power and International Relations* (1962); and of numerous articles and reviews.

SYDNEY D. BAILEY represented Friends World Committee at United Nations headquarters 1954-58. With Carnegie Endowment for International Peace, New York 1958-60. Secretary of Hansard Society for Parliamentary Government and editor of *Parliamentary Affairs*, 1948-54. He is the author of *A Short Political Guide to the United Nations* (1963); *The General Assembly of the United Nations* (second edition, 1964); *The Secretariat of the United Nations* (second edition, 1964).

MARTIN HILL is Deputy Under-Secretary for Economic and Social Affairs and Personal Representative of the Secretary-General to the Specialized Agencies. Member of the League of Nations Secretariat from 1927. With the United Nations Secretariat since 1946. Rapporteur of the Administrative Committee on Co-ordination and Chairman of its Preparatory Committee since 1948. He is the author of *The Economic and Financial Organization of the League of Nations* (1946); *Commercial Policy in the Inter-War Period* (1944); *Privileges and Immunities of International Officials* (1945).

JOHN F. MCMAHON is a Lecturer and Fellow in Law, Hertford College, Oxford, LL.B. (Cambridge) and LL.M. (Harvard). He is at present engaged in completing a book on the legislative techniques and control machinery of the United Nations Specialized Agencies.

W. M. SCAMMELL, was for ten years in business before becoming a university teacher. Was in Economic Section of the Treasury, 1956-58. Senior Lecturer in Monetary Economics at University College of North Wales, Bangor, until June 1965. He is now Professor of International Economics at Simon Fraser University, Vancouver.

ANDREW SHONFIELD is Director of Studies at the Royal Institute of International Affairs in London. He was formerly Economic Editor of *The Observer*, and before that (from 1949-57) Foreign Editor of the *Financial Times*. He is the author of a survey of the post-war British economy, *British Economic Policy since the War* (1959); *The Attack on World Poverty* (1960), a study of the problems of the under-developed countries; and of *Modern Capitalism: The Changing Balance of Public and Private Power* (1965).

RALPH TOWNLEY. Senior Deputy Chief of the Research Division in the United Nations Development Programme. Joined the United Nations Secretariat in 1951 as Special Assistant to the Assistant Secretary-General for Economic Affairs, Seconded to the United Nations Special Fund at its inception in 1959. Author of a textbook on developing international institutions to appear shortly.

JOHN PINDER was formerly a Director of the Economist Intelligence Unit, specializing in international problems, and is now the Director of Political and Economic Planning. He has taken a particular interest in problems of the European Community; is a trustee of the Federal Trust; and is the author of *Britain and the Common Market* (1961) and *Europe against de Gaulle* (1963).

Biographical Notes

EVAN LUARD was formerly a member of H.M. Foreign Service, and is at present a Supernumerary Fellow at St. Antony's College, Oxford, working in the field of international relations and M.P. for Oxford. He is the author of *Peace and Opinion* (1962) and *Nationality and Wealth* (1964), studies of international government in the political and economic fields respectively.

ABBREVIATIONS

ACABQ	Advisory Committee on Administrative and Budgetary Questions
ACC	Advisory Committee on Co-ordination
CCAQ	Consultative Committee on Administrative Questions
ECAFE	Economic Commission for Asia and the Far East
ECE	Economic Commission for Europe
ECOSOC	Economic and Social Council of the United Nations
EEC	European Economic Community
EFTA	European Free Trade Association
EPTA	Expanded Programme of Technical Assistance
FAO	Food and Agriculture Organization
GATT	General Agreement on Tariffs and Trade
IAEA	International Atomic Energy Agency
IBRD	International Bank of Reconstruction and Development
ICAO	International Civil Aviation Organization
ICSAB	International Civil Service Advisory Board
IDA	International Development Association
IFC	International Finance Corporation
ILO	International Labour Organization
IMCO	Intergovernmental Maritime Consultative Organization
IMF	International Monetary Fund
IRO	International Refugee Organization
ITU	International Telecommunication Union
NATO	North Atlantic Treaty Organization
OEEC	Organization for European Economic Co-operation
OECD	Organization of Economic Co-operation and Development

ONUC   United Nations Operation in the Congo
OPEX   Operational Administrative and Executive Personnel
SEATO   South East Asia Treaty Organization
SUNFED   Special United Nations Fund for Economic Development
TAB   Technical Assistance Board
UNCTAD   United Nations Conference on Trade and Development
UNDP   United Nations Development Programme
UNEF   United Nations Emergency Force
UNESCO   United Nations Educational, Scientific and Cultural Organization
UNHCR   United Nations High Commissioner for Refugees
UNICEF   United Nations International Children's Emergency Fund
UNKRA   United Nations Korean Reconstruction Agency
UNRWA   United Nations Relief and Works Agency
UNTSO   United Nations Truce Supervision Organization
UPU   Universal Postal Union
WHO   World Health Organization
WMO   World Meteorological Organization

INDEX

Index

Expanded Programme of Technical Assistance (EPTA), 281; established, 261; areas of support, 261; contributions pledged, 262; administration, 263; contingency fund, 264; OPEX, 264

Federation, EEC and, 286, 293, 299-300
Finland, 166
Flood control, 254
Food and Agriculture Organization (FAO), 105, 107, 113, 119, 129, 187, 239, 278, 279-80, 282
Food surpluses, 278-80
Forced Labour Convention (1930), 189
France, and Uniting for Peace resolution, 48; and Afro-Asian countries, 49; and Security Council, 51; and UNEF, 82; proposals for international force, 139, 169; and international force under UN, 140-141; and Suez crisis, 147, 148, 149, 150, 151, 152, 153; and Cyprus operation, 164, 166, 167; IMF and, 215, 220, 227; and EEC, 287, 291, 293, 294, 295, 296, 301
Franks Plan, 222
Freedom from Hunger Campaign, 127
Freedom of Association Committee, ILO, 191
Functional Commissions, of UN, 252-3

Gandhi, M. K., 93
Gaza Strip, 148, 149, 153
General Agreement on Tariffs and Trade (GATT), 19, 105, 275-6, 315
General Assembly, UN: 17, 21; membership, 42, 49; powers of, 42, 43-51; basic duality, 42, 51-4; status of, 42, 54-7; as mirror of diplomatic world, 42-3, 58-61; relations with Security Council, 42-51, 322; as instrument of 'power politics,' 43, 61-3; Interim Committee established, 47-8; factors influencing evolution, 61-5, 306; preference of smaller states for, 89; and ACC, 125-6; and threats to peace, 144,

145, 151; and Suez crisis, 149; calls for Special Fund, 267-9; and colonial question, 315
Genocide Convention, 46
Germany, League of Nations and, 31-2, 34. *See also* West Germany
Ghana, 189
Gizenga, A., 160
Goodrich, L. M., 80
Granting of Independence to Colonial Countries, Declaration (1960), 55
Greece, 146, 165, 166, 167, 168
Grotius, Hugo, 264

Haberler Committee, 315
Hammarskjöld, Dag, 19, 42, 51, 53, 80, 92, 93, 94, 95, 97, 101, 116, 117, 149, 152, 153, 154, 156, 159, 168, 171, 172, 286, 314, 315
Havana Charter, 273-6, 282
Hitler, Adolf, 34, 317
Hoffman, Paul, 240
Human rights, 252, 307
Hungary, 145, 149, 313, 318

India, 160, 183, 242, 243, 260, 280; World Bank and, 238, 242-3
Indian Iron and Steel Company, 233
Indian-Pakistan war, 312
Indigenous peoples, General Assembly resolution on (1961), 55
Indonesia, 58, 143, 156
Inter-Agency Consultative Board, 272
Inter-Allied Labour and Socialist Congress (1918), 179
Intergovernmental Maritime Consultative Organization (IMCO), 105, 129, 253, 317
Interim Co-ordinating Committee for International Commodity Arrangements, 276
International Association for Labour Legislation, 179
International Atomic Energy Agency (IAEA), 105, 118, 128
International Bank of Reconstruction and Development (IBRD), 105, 128, 250, 265, 266, 271

337

Index

341